AMERICAN WICKER

The Wicker Lady

AMERICAN WICKER

WOVEN FURNITURE FROM 1850 TO 1930

JEREMY ADAMSON

PRINCIPAL PHOTOGRAPHY BY KIT LATHAM

THE RENWICK GALLERY
OF THE
NATIONAL MUSEUM OF AMERICAN ART
SMITHSONIAN INSTITUTION

RIZZOLI
NEW YORK

FOR INGRID

Published on the occasion of the exhibition "American Wicker" at the Renwick Gallery of the National Museum of American Art, Washington, D.C., April 2–August 1, 1993

First published in the United States of America in 1993 by the National Museum of American Art, Smithsonian Institution, Washington, D.C. 20560 in association with Rizzoli International Publications, Inc. 300 Park Avenue South, New York, NY 10010

Library of Congress Cataloging-In-Publication Data

Adamson, Jeremy.
American Wicker : woven furniture from 1850 to 1930 / Jeremy Adamson ;
principal photography by Kit Latham.
p.   cm.
Includes bibliographical references and index.
ISBN 0–8478–1670–2 (HC)
ISBN 0–8478-1703–2 (PBK)
1. Wicker furniture—United States—History—19th century. 2. Wicker
furniture—United States—History—20th century. I. Latham, Kit. II. Title.
NK2712.7.A32   1993
749.213'09'034—dc20   92–27817
                                                                                          CIP

NMAA editor: Richard Carter
Designed by Pamela Fogg

Endpaper: "Wicker" fabric pattern. Courtesy of Ralph Lauren Home Collection.
Frontispiece: Reed rocking chairs and sofa, with motif backrests made by various manufacturers, ca. 1885–95. Courtesy of A Summer Place. Photograph by Kit Latham.

Front cover: Rocking chair with American flag motif attributed to Wakefield Rattan Company, ca. 1876. Courtesy of A Summer Place.
Back cover: Armchairs manufactured by Heywood Brothers and Wakefield Company, ca. 1898–1920. Courtesy of Charlie Wagner, The Wicker Lady, Inc.
Photographs by Kit Latham.

Printed in Hong Kong

Contents

A history of American wicker would be impossible to reconstruct without the dedication of individuals who, over decades, have assembled outstanding collections of woven furniture. They are to be honored for preserving an American heritage. It has been my pleasure and privilege to have encountered numerous collectors and aficionados of wicker whose kindness and generosity has made the compilation of this book a particular delight. They selflessly opened their homes, lent rare scholarly resources, and helped in the search for objects and information. I am especially thankful to the following: Mary Jean McLaughlin of A Summer Place, Guilford, Connecticut; Mr. and Mrs. Norman Bernstein; Mrs. Richard Mellon; Mrs. Prosser Gifford; Richard Moulton; Ms. Charlie Wagner of The Wicker Lady, Needham, Massachusetts; Mrs. Pamela Scurry of The Wicker Garden, New York; Frog Alley Antiques/Merry P. Gilbert, New York; Tom and Kathleen Tetro of The Corner House Antiques, Sheffield, Massachusetts; Robert and Carol Schoellkopf; Steve Poole and Robert Evans; and Marla Segal of Wicker Unlimited, Marblehead, Massachusetts.

I benefited greatly from the assistance of Frank McNamee of The Wicker Porch Antiques, Marion, Massachusetts, who consistently—and quite literally—went the extra mile in providing me with important introductions within the wicker world and later facilitating photography. I am particularly grateful, too, for the kindness and generosity of Richard Saunders, whose efforts over the past twenty years in researching and recording the history of American wicker have helped define the field and encourage its growth.

Individuals at numerous institutions offered valuable research assistance at various points over the past two years. I am indebted to Katherine Martinez, Robert F. Trent, and Bert Denker of the Henry Francis DuPont Winterthur Museum; Rodris Roth, Division of Domestic Life, National Museum of American History, Smithsonian Institution; Ford Peatross, Prints and Photographs Division, and Frank Evina, Copyright Division, Library of Congress; William Hosley, Wadsworth Atheneum; Robert Goler, Decorative and Industrial Arts Collection, Chicago Historical Society; Kenneth Ames, New York State Museum; Patricia Tice, Strong Museum; and Lorna Condon, Society for the Preservation of New England Antiquities. I am also grateful to archivists, librarians, and research assistants at the Archives, Chicago Historical Society; Library, Cooper-Hewitt Museum; Print Department, Metropolitan Museum of Art; Archives, New-York Historical Society; Library, Peabody Museum and Essex Institute; Warshaw Collection of Business Americana, Archives Center, National Museum of American History, Smithsonian Institution; Library, National Museum of American Art, Smithsonian Institution; and the Beinecke Rare Book Library, Yale University.

I am also grateful to Elizabeth Broun, director, National Museum of American Art, and Michael Monroe, curator-in-charge, Renwick Gallery, for their support and encouragement. Renwick Gallery museum technician Gary Wright provided invaluable research assistance and intern Sue Ann Griffin ably organized the campaign to secure outside photographs. Kimberly Cody of the NMAA's Registrar's Office and photographer Eugene Young expeditiously filled my many in-house photography orders. Richard Carter of the Publications Office deftly and swiftly edited the completed manuscript. At Rizzoli, many thanks are due to senior editor Robert Janjigian for his able supervision of all aspects of the design and production of the book. Assistant editor Jennifer Condon and the book's designer, Pamela Fogg, were also instrumental in seeing the book to completion. Photographer Kit Latham had an intuitive understanding of his subject matter, and it was a pleasure to work with him. Finally, I wish to thank my wife, Ingrid Maar-Adamson, not only for her insightful reading of the initial draft but for the constancy of her support throughout the project. This book is dedicated to her.

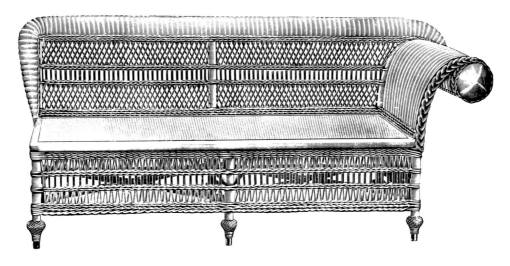

Heywood Brothers and Wakefield Company, Lounge from the 1898–99 Catalogue of Reed and Rattan Furniture. *Courtesy of the National Museum of American Art, Smithsonian Institution.*

For millennia, woven wicker objects and furniture were so common a fact of life around the world that they were rarely noted with more than passing interest. A wide variety of reeds, willows, canes, and bamboo were serviceable for their manufacture, so there was no special mystique about materials. Basic skills for weaving wicker were easily learned. It could be adapted to almost any form to make innumerable useful objects that comfortably fit the needs of people from diverse backgrounds and cultures. Like plain earthen pottery, it was used by almost everyone, but unlike pottery, it was perishable and seldom survived even in fragments to remind us of its importance. It was a quintessentially vernacular phenomenon—humble, cheap, ubiquitous, easily disregarded, serviceable, unexceptional—a small part of the "background hum" of daily routine.

Then, in the second half of the nineteenth century, a confluence of forces—economic, social, aesthetic—suddenly made wicker furniture a vehicle for the emerging ambitions of a rising middle class in America. For almost a century after Cyrus Wakefield first bought cast-off rattan packing from the wharfs of Boston in 1840, it assumed amazing prominence in the decorative art and design movements that swept the country. Wicker focused the passions of a people intent on a new kind of self-definition and proved capable of expressing a wealth of new ideas about life and ways of living it. With wicker, not only upper-class homeowners but middle-class Americans who had never before aspired to fashion could embrace graceful design and historical style, reflecting the new reverence for the beautiful and marking the "progress" of civilization. Wicker encouraged them to "diversify and specialize" in their homes, so distinctions between parlor and piazza, smoking room and sewing room, boudoir and library would signal their refinement. It fit the airy, detached homes that sprang up in the suburbs as a healthy alternative to steamy town houses in burgeoning cities, and it was just right for the verandas of resort hotels catering to the new vacationing middle classes. The lightness and adaptability of wicker reflected the quickened pace of people's lives and showed that they were sensitive to both sincerity and sophistication. Through wicker, they could give free play to those long-neglected aspects of the American character, fancy and imagination. In short, wicker appealed to that new arrival on the American scene, Taste, and all for an affordable price.

In his engaging account of wicker in America, however, Jeremy Adamson tells the story not only from the consumer's point of view, fascinating though it is. He also traces the manufacture of wicker furnishings, showing how it reflects the larger currents of a developing nation. This is the story of Horatio Alger–like self-made men relying on their ingenuity as the nation expanded rapidly across the continent after the Jacksonian era. It is the story of the China Trade, the Industrial Revolution, immigration, advertising, the sanitation movement, economic boom and bust, labor strife, capitalist competition, imports and exports, the rise of women as arbiters of domestic life, mass production and the decline of hand-craftsmanship. After reading this account, we can never again see a wicker chair as merely a chair; it becomes an index to the interwoven aspects of a developing nation.

This book is accompanied by an exhibition of exceptional pieces of American wicker furniture assembled at the Renwick Gallery of the National Museum of American Art. While the collections of the Renwick focus on twentieth-century crafts, the Gallery often presents exhibitions that trace the history of crafts, design, and the decorative arts through our nation's history. Under the direction of curator-in-charge Michael Monroe, the Renwick addresses the interplay of function and form, technique and material, ornament and taste in a wide variety of objects. As revealed through these shows, they have much to tell us about ourselves and our past.

Today's revival of wicker as designer furniture could serve as the basis for a second study. It would include some constants from the past, such as the desire for an affordable stylishness. But it would also address the way the love of wicker today reflects a nostalgia for the past—our idealization of the days when "home" was a place of special comfort and support, our search for a now-diminished authenticity or sincerity in objects of everyday life, our growing reverence for natural materials from cotton dresses to carved wooden toys, our rediscovery of the joys of ornament after decades of streamlined manufactured goods, even a disillusionment with the promises of modernism. The story of wicker, then and now, and the story of all the objects that surround us as we go about the business of living, can be read as a reflection of our culture, shaping the material landscape of our lives.

Elizabeth Broun
Director, National Museum
of American Art

Heywood Brothers and Wakefield Company, Three-Piece Suite from the 1898–99 Catalogue of Reed and Rattan Furniture. *Courtesy of the National Museum of American Art, Smithsonian Institution.*

Wicker in History

On November 29, 1620, a three-masted ship, normally used to transport wine along the west coast of Europe, dropped anchor in a small bay at the tip of Cape Cod. Eight days later, on December 7, as the *Mayflower* rocked at her moorings in Provincetown harbor, one of her passengers, Susannah White, gave birth to a son, Peregrine. It was cold and wintry: in the ship's log, the captain reported that it "snowed and blowed all day." The first Pilgrim born in America was swaddled and placed in a cradle that his parents had brought with them. It must have had a salubrious effect. While half of the 101 settlers who disembarked at Plymouth died during the first year, Peregrine lived to the age of eighty-four, the last survivor of the original band of colonists. A tenacious family tradition declares that a fine willow cradle donated to The Pilgrim Society, Plymouth, Massachusetts, in 1877 is the very same one that rocked Peregrine White. But even if it didn't arrive on the *Mayflower*, the Society's cradle is the earliest surviving piece of wicker furniture in America. In design and construction, it is identical to examples depicted in seventeenth-century Dutch paintings. Most scholars assume that it was made in Holland and brought first to England before being transported by colonists to the New World. If Peregrine's parents had acquired it before the voyage, they would have done so in Leyden, Holland, the *Mayflower*'s first port of departure. However, studies of probate inventories of early Massachusetts craftsmen suggest that the cradle could have been fabricated in America. If so, it would be the first extant piece of New England wicker.

One possible maker of such a cradle is Nathaniel Adams, a successful wood turner active in Boston. At his death in 1675, his shop contained typical lathe-turned wooden objects, such as parts for chairs, bowls, platters, spoons, and shovels, as well as a variety of wicker items including "five doz. & three wicker fanns," three baskets, and two cradles.[1] Craftsmen known as turners not only fashioned the simple framing elements for baluster chairs, but wove their rush and splint seats, and were thus familiar with standard basket-weaving materials and techniques. The Pilgrim's cradle is fabricated much like a stake-frame basket: pliant osier rods are woven in and out of vertical willow spokes to create a durable, interlaced container. Thicker osiers provide rigidity in the floor while a bent wooden rod creates a stiff frame for the outline of the curved hood. Decoration is achieved by alternating and mixing weaves and using different diameters of rods. Such wickerwork methods had remained almost unchanged since the beginning of basketry—one of the most ancient of crafts—and the construction of the willow cradle could have been easily understood by a Neolithic basketmaker.

Wicker furniture other than cradles was to be found in seventeenth-century colonial homes. None survive, but individual pieces are cited in probate inventories. "One chair of wicker for a child" is listed in the 1639–40 will of Captain Adam Thoroughgood of Princess Anne County, Virginia. Massachusetts residents appear to have prized wicker more than other colonists. A Captain Scarlet of Boston left three wicker chairs at his death in 1675, and when Cape Cod minister John Mayo died the following year, the wicker chair he left behind was valued more than his wooden one. In 1666 an inden-

tured servant in Maryland record-ed how the ships of "New-England men" were filled not only with Madeira wines, sugar, and tin can-dlesticks, but also "Wicker-Chairs" to sell to the colonists on the East-ern Shore. Possibly these were Dutch imports, but they may have been Boston products. To a lesser degree, wicker is listed in estate inventories in the eighteenth cen-tury, though woven willow fur-nishings comprised only a very small proportion of colonists' domestic furniture. Joined oaken chests, benches, tables, and chairs predominated.[2]

We know what willow basket chairs must have looked like in the American colonies—both English and Dutch—through depictions in European paintings and from liter-ary records. Among the most common designs was a hooded wicker chair. It was typically used by the elderly, the sick, and nurs-ing mothers to avoid drafts and could be found next to the fireside or near beds. So closely was this kind of chair associated with child-birth that English writers called such canopied willow designs "groaneing chairs," or "Child-Bed Chaires."[3] A splendid example can be seen in Jacob Jordaen's *The Holy Family* of ca. 1615, in which the Madonna is portrayed in a wicker nursing chair. To the Christ Child's obvious delight, the infant St. John has just released a bird—

Relief Sculpture from a Roman tomb at Neumagen on the Mosel River, Germany, 235 A.D. *Photograph courtesy of the Landesmuseum, Trier.*
The origins of the tightly woven basket chair are obscure, but by the first century A.D., willow furniture was commonly used by the Roman elite in their suburban villas. This relief depicts a provincial Roman matron having her hair groomed by maidservants, while seated in a wicker chair.

symbol of the Holy Spirit—from a wicker cage. Known in France since the sixteenth century as a *guerite,* or "sentry-box," the hooded wickerwork chair would survive well into the twentieth century, adapted for use as a portable beach chair. It not only sheltered vaca-tioners from the sun and wind but afforded a degree of privacy.

Since Roman times, flexible willow was the standard material used in Europe for the construction of baskets and wicker furnishings. No doubt this practice was transmitted by the tribes the Romans had conquered. In his thirty-seven volume compendium, *Natural History* (77 A.D.), Pliny recorded in detail how various species of willow were cultivated outside Rome expressly for the manufacture of woven household and farm utensils. One light-colored and especially pliant type, he wrote, was particularly useful "in the construction of those articles of luxury, reclining chairs."[4] No willow lounges from suburban Roman villas have lasted two thousand years, but sculptural representations of tightly woven Roman willow chairs from ancient tombs survive to reveal the origins of the modern wicker easy chair. The design with a flat apron,

enclosed curved skirt, low arms, and a tall, rounded back was known as a *cathedra,* and was generally associated in antiquity with philosophers and teachers—

Willow Cradle, seventeenth century. Courtesy of the Pilgrim Society, Plymouth, Massachusetts. This cradle is said to have sheltered the first Pilgrim born in America.

hence the modern tradition of a faculty "chair." In contrast, rulers sat on thrones—rectangular seats of wood or stone. The resilient wicker *cathedra* survived the fall of the Roman Empire and appears in biblical illuminations of the Middle Ages. In this context, it is a chair fit for an evangelist or monastic scribe.

The wicker chair had been introduced into Britain after the Roman conquest in the first century A.D., and when the western Empire collapsed in 476 A.D., the practice of weaving basketlike chairs from willow rods continued as a vernacular tradition well into the nineteenth century. With the Norse invasions of England in the ninth century, the term "wicker" was introduced into the English language. The word derives from two old Scandinavian

Jacob Jordaens, Holy Family, *ca. 1615. Courtesy of the North Carolina Museum of Art. The canopied willow chair was a vernacular form of seating used throughout Europe in the 1600s. In this painting by a Flemish artist, the Virgin is portrayed as a young mother in a commonplace nursing chair. The infant St. John releases a songbird from a wicker cage.*

dialects—Swedish "vikker" and Danish "viger." Both words mean pliant willow rod, or osier, and contain the meaning "to bend"—from the Swedish verb, "wicka." A seventeenth-century English synonym, "twiggen," was descriptive of the materials used—twigs. Another common name, "basket chair," characterized its manner of fabrication.

Two elemental forms of basket weaving have been used throughout human history: interlacing flexible rods through upright spokes (wickerwork); and spirally coiling sewn ropes of straw or other fibrous plant materials—like rushes and water reeds—into cylindrical forms (lip-work). The latter was used for making simple round seats at least as early as the Sumerian civilization of the third millennium B.C. In England and Europe, lip-work was an age-old method of making baskets and, more especially, beehives. From sturdy, conical hives it was a short step to the peasant's primitive but comfortable straw "beehive" chair, probably the most common form of seating in the Middle Ages—not only in Britain but in western and northern Europe as well. The beehive chair, like its cousin the stake-frame willow chair, also had a canopied version, using vertical wooden poles to support the hood. This form likewise survived well into the nineteenth century, again most often used to shelter nursing mothers, old people, and the sick in the rural homes of the poor. In the nineteenth century, the farmer's old straw chair also made its way up the social ladder and into the country houses of the gentry. In his *Encyclopaedia of Domes-*

tic Economy (1844), Thomas Webster observed that "the beehive chair . . . has long been used in Wales, Scotland, and some parts of the north of England. But it is only of late that they have appeared among our fashionable furniture. They are, however, warm and cheap, and are admired by some persons for their simple, homely, and snug appearance."[5] American colonists who had come from farming communities in the Old World doubtless knew the comforts of straw chairs, but it is not known if they re-created them in the New World. Only willow basket chairs can be documented.

In the eighteenth century, the use of wickerwork chairs in the American colonies dropped precipitously. Life was no longer a simple matter of survival, as it had been in Peregrine White's day. An increasingly populous, urbane, and affluent society was eager to flaunt its wealth and sophistication. In the early eighteenth century, furniture making in the colonies evolved into a dynamic local craft, attracting skilled, professional cabinetmakers from abroad. Expanding prosperity and a growing awareness of the latest European fashions in the decorative arts fueled demand in Philadelphia, New York, and Boston for more up-to-date and sophisticated interior furnishings.

Johnston-Kurtz Company, Buffalo, New York, "Atlantic Sun Chair" from the 1911 Willow Furniture Catalogue. *Courtesy of the Warshaw Collection of Business Americana, Archives Center, National Museum of American History, Smithsonian Institution.*
From about 1890 to 1930, the hooded wicker chair was a popular piece of beach furniture in Europe and America. It usually contained a small side window so that the occupant could spy discreetly on other bathers.

Woven basket chairs were definitely not among them. Included with the new luxury goods imported from William and Mary's England at the turn of the eighteenth century were elaborately carved, high-backed chairs with surprisingly resilient seats and backs. These springy surfaces were composed of open mesh panels of interlaced strips of cane. Cane was a by-product of rattan, a tropical plant totally foreign to Europe and the Americas. Cane and rattan had been originally introduced to the

The Sumerian Official Ebih-Il Seated on a Wicker Stool, ca. 2500 B.C. Musée du Louvre. *Photograph copyright © Photo Réunion des Musées Nationaux.*
This votive statue from the Mari culture of Mesopotamia offers the earliest representation of a piece of woven furniture.

West by the Portuguese after they opened direct trade with the Far East in the sixteenth century. By 1850 the vinelike Oriental plant was the basis of the burgeoning wicker furniture industry.

The tale of the introduction of rattan into Europe forms a fascinating preamble to the history of American wicker. The roots of the wicker industry in the New World are entwined with the tendrils of European empires as they stretched eastward towards the fabled Indies. In 1497, in search of a sea route to Cathay, the Portuguese mariner Vasco da Gama sailed far out into the Atlantic Ocean to catch the prevailing westerly winds that swept his ships south around the tip of Africa. In

Zanzibar, da Gama found an Arab pilot, Ibn Majid, who taught him the art, lost to the West since the days of the Romans, of using the monsoon winds to cross the open sea to a landfall on the west coast of India. A sea route to the Far East had at last been found. By the 1540s the Portuguese had established a trading network that included their own settlement at Goa on the west coast of India as well as centers in Java, Sumatra, and the Moluccas. For the remainder of the century, they dominated the extraordinarily profitable trade in Oriental spices. Advancing into the South China Sea in the 1550s, they finally made contact with China, then called the Celestial Empire. The Portuguese were the first Europeans the Chinese encountered since the Ming dynasty had cut all communication with the West in 1368. In 1557 the emperor fatefully granted the *Fan Kuai,* or "foreign devils," a permanent settlement at Macao. With this decision, after more than eighteen hundred years of commercial dominance, the legendary Silk Road that snaked from Peking west across the Asian landmass to Constantinople was rendered obsolete. Silks and spices no longer had to make their way to Europe by camel caravan but were transported aboard three-masted carracks that sailed directly to Lisbon, the new center for Oriental trade goods in the West. In 1580 the Por-

tuguese throne was left vacant by the death of its cardinal-king. A year later, Spain, which had already established trading centers in Manila and the Moluccas by sailing west around Cape Horn, successfully annexed the throne of Portugal. Spain, burdened with foreign policy problems and fearful of the consequences of the Reformation, no longer welcomed any Protestant merchants in recently annexed Lisbon. As a result, the price of spices rose dramatically in Amsterdam and London. Acquiring a means of direct trade with the East was now the overriding ambition of the sea powers of the Protestant north. In 1595 the Dutch first set sail for the East Indies, and in 1600 Queen Elizabeth I gave royal assent to a trading monopoly organized as the London East India Company. English merchants sent out five ships in 1601 laden with £30,000 worth of gold and silver coins and refined metals. Two years later, they returned with a cargo of spices worth a million pounds sterling. With such extraordinary profits at stake, international competition for spices became intense and bitter.[6]

In 1662 Charles II, who had returned to England and was restored to the throne, married a wealthy Portuguese princess, Catherine of Braganza. The history of wicker took another important step. The princess's dowry included £500,000 in ready cash and the trading port established by her countrymen at Bombay, India. But the dark-eyed Catherine also brought with her some stylish Portuguese furniture to outfit her dank English quarters. Luxurystarved after eleven years of privation under Oliver Cromwell's Puritan Commonwealth, the Royalists enthusiastically embraced the most innovative of these exotic Portuguese fashions—cane chairs. For more than a century, Far Eastern design had influenced Lisbon craftsmen. Furniture carvers employed exotic, new motifs, and turners gave the uprights of chairs an exuberant, Indian-inspired spiral twist. More significantly, Portuguese apprentices wove Oriental-inspired panels of elastic caning into the seats and backs of the high-backed chairs. Portuguese mariners had first encountered lightweight cane chairs and lounges in the sweltering East. Recognizing the advantages of such well-ventilated, tropical seating for the hot Iberian summers, they enthusiastically had brought them home. In the seventeenth century the Dutch also discovered the virtues of cane on their voyages to the Indies and adapted it to their own needs for cool and easy-to-clean seating.[7]

The history of cane furniture in the East remains obscure, but its use was widespread throughout the tropics: India, Ceylon, Burma, the Malay Peninsula, the Moluccas, Indochina, the Philippines, southern China and the islands of Java, Sumatra, Borneo—wherever rattan palms, the sole source of cane, grew wild in the steaming jungles and rainforests. Rattan is the stem or trunk of a climbing palm that belongs to the genus *Calamus* (swamp plants). The name is derived from the Malay "rotan," meaning "walking stick," and came into general use around the time European ships first began trading

in Southeast Asia. There are more than two hundred species, but only about a dozen are suited for the production of high-quality cane. The single-stemmed, vinelike plant grows vertically for about three feet and then begins to climb an adjacent tree. Rattan can reach immense lengths, up to six hundred feet, but spans between one hundred fifty and three hundred feet are typical. Stalks are uniform in diameter and remain extremely flexible. The species used for chair caning and wicker furniture vary in thickness from just under half-an-inch to an inch-and-a-half. Like other palms, it has dense fronds that sprout at intervals from a rough, spiny bark. But the fanlike leaves of rattan have strong, downward-pointing thorns on the underside that allow it to climb relentlessly up and around tall jungle trees. When harvested by natives, the stem is simply cut with a knife, left to dry, and then hauled down from the treetops. In the jungle, the withered fronds and bark are stripped off and the ropelike stalk cut into sections from sixteen to twenty feet in length. Bent in half and tied into thick bundles, the raw rattan is rafted downstream to processing sites near the coast, where native workers remove the bark residue, a silicate coating, by a process known as "loontying"—forcefully pulling each long stalk around a

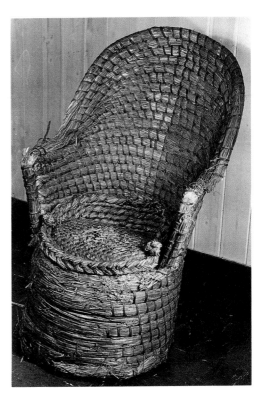

English Farm Laborer's Straw Chair, *ca. 1880.*
Norfolk Rural Life Museum, Gressenhall. Photograph courtesy of the Norfolk Museums.
This high-backed chair was made from rolls of unthreshed straw, coiled and sewn together with strips of bramble. This ancient form of construction is known as lip-work. During the Middle Ages, coiled straw chairs were the most popular form of seating in England and Europe.

tree or stake to chip off the brittle layer of silicon. The bumpy leaf nodes are then removed by scraping, and finally the rattan is sand-washed in a stream and sun-dried. At this point, the stalks have a hard, glossy surface, yellowish in color. This outer sheath is cane in its natural, uncut state. The harvesting, cleaning, and distribution of rattan was typically controlled by Chinese merchants who loaded bundles by the ton on *Tunkans*—heavy junklike vessels—and sailed for Singapore, the leading center for the rattan trade in the eighteenth and nineteenth centuries. When the Portuguese first arrived, the indigenous peoples used supple rattan as if it were rope. It was

Rattan Growing Wild in the Jungles of the Malay Peninsula *(top)*; Cleaned Stalks Being Sorted and Bundled for Export *(bottom)*. *Photographs from* A Completed Century, *1926, courtesy of the National Museum of American Art, Smithsonian Institution. Like other species of palm,* Calamus rotang *has broad leaf fronds. Native to jungles and forests along the coasts of Southeast Asia, it climbs through the tree tops, sometimes reaching lengths of six hundred feet. After being rafted down rivers to the coast, the rattan was sand-washed and sun-dried before being bundled for shipment to Western markets.*

hit, and a local industry soon emerged to satisfy an escalating demand for "cane bottoms." Throughout the seventeenth century, cane galvanized Europeans: they could not get enough of it. In 1666 the Great Fire of London consumed some 13,200 houses, and in the aftermath of the disaster, the demand for new furnishings skyrocketed. Among the most popular were cane chairs. They were easy to make and inexpensive, and were ordered by the thousands to outfit newly rebuilt dwellings. A new group of artisans soon formed, the Cane-Chair-Makers' Company of London. Their workshops sprang up along Old St. Paul's churchyard, near where the ships of the East India Company docked with eagerly anticipated cargoes of rattan. In the late seventeenth century, the trade in rattan—often called "India cane"—boomed. During a twelve-month period in 1697–98, the East India Company imported 894,205 (unidentified) units of "Rattans" and 116,695 of "Walking," or Malacca, cane. By contrast, only 3,220 units of bamboo were imported.[8] After bundles of raw rattan had been distributed to the workshops, chairmakers' apprentices first stripped off the cane with a knife, then interlaced pairs of the narrow strands vertically and horizontally inside seat frames and between the turned uprights of the backs. Single strips were then threaded diagonally across the square intersections to produce the distinctive pattern still common today. Initially the mesh was wide and the cane coarse, but as time progressed the strips became narrower and were woven more close-

used as rigging on small boats, for hauling and baling, as supports for suspension bridges, and for lashing the bamboo framework of thatched houses. When removed and cut into long, narrow strips, the hard outer coating had uses beyond chair caning—making baskets, hats, and matting. One nonclimbing Malayan species, *Calamus scipionum,* grew straight up, and its rigid stem was cut into lengths for walking sticks—hence the meaning of the original native name. Known as "Malacca canes," these brass-tipped sticks became extremely popular in eighteenth- and nineteenth-century Europe and America.

The cane chairs Catherine of Braganza introduced into Restoration England proved an immediate ly. The cane seats in early American wicker of the mid-nineteenth century followed the same evolution—from coarse to fine.

The ultimate utility furniture of its age, lightweight cane chairs were extremely popular and could be found in the homes of the rich and the poor. In fact, they had become so fashionable that it appeared that upholstered seating would go out of style altogether—and with it, much of the powerful woolen industry's market. Around 1680 English woolen manufacturers petitioned Parliament to suppress the manufacture of cane chairs. The petition was rejected, but two years later a clause to prohibit the production and sale of cane chairs was attached to a parliamentary bill. This quickly motivated the Cane-Chair-Makers to counter with a document of their own. In stating their case, they claimed that "about the Year 1664, Cane Chairs, & c. came into use in England" and gave "much Satisfaction to all the Nobility, Gentry, and Commonality." They were especially prized "for their Durableness, Lightness, and Cleanness from Dust, Worms and Moths which inseparably attend Turkeywork, Serge, and other Stuff [i.e., upholstered] Chairs and Couches, to the spoiling of them and all furniture near them."[9] In more modern language, American wicker manufacturers would proudly repeat the same claim during the nineteenth and early twentieth centuries. The Londoners also stated that they annually manufactured six thousand dozen "Cane-Chairs, Stools, Squobs [benches], Couches, Tables, and other Caned Work"—the wool lobby had given

the yearly output of upholstered furniture at twenty-five thousand dozen—while two thousand dozen cane chairs were "Transported into all the Hot Parts of the World," where the heat rendered upholstery "useless."[10] To its credit, the English Parliament refused to prohibit chair caning. If they had, American wicker as we know it simply would not exist.

The American colonies were among the "Hot Parts" to which the Cane-Chair-Makers exported their products. Like their counterparts in England, the colonists of late seventeenth and early eighteenth centuries loved the new chairs—and in large numbers. It was not uncommon to find a Boston or Philadelphia merchant's house furnished with thirty to fifty cane chairs and half as many stools. So numerous were they that estate inventories normally listed six as one item. But they were all imported; none were American-made. British law did not permit the colonists to import rattan directly. The East India Company retained its monopoly on all shipments from the Orient and, moreover, the Cane-Chair-Makers' Company did not want any competition from colonial craftsmen.

When William Penn returned from England in 1699, he brought a set of new cane chairs with him for his Pennsbury Manor. In May 1715, residents of Boston were notified by a local merchant advertising in the Boston News-Letter: "Lately arrived from England, Cain [sic] Chairs, and Couches." Other Bostonians were better connected. In 1720, when his daughter Judith married, Chief Justice Samuel

Seward ordered "a Duzen of good black Walnut Chairs, fine cane, with a Couch" direct from London for the bride, and, for good measure, threw in another "Duzen" for himself. By the 1730s the once ubiquitous cane chair began to disappear in English circles. Members of the Cane-Chair-Makers' Company now turned out leather-bottomed and wood seat chairs. Since there was no market to protect, Londoners now no longer wished to prevent colonists from making cane chairs. By 1734 a Philadelphia craftsman named Nicholas Gale could openly advertise in the Pennsylvania Gazette: "Cane Chairs of all Sorts made after the best & newest Fashion." But just in case sales of new cane chairs did not meet expectations, he wisely offered restoration services as well: "old Chairs caned or Holes mended (if not gone too far)."[11] But even in the colonies, the demand for cane chairs largely faded in the 1740s. High-backed chairs with flexible wooden back splats now offered a comfortable and more durable alternative. Caning revived briefly in the late eighteenth century when, under the stylistic influence of chinoiserie, the first fashion trend from China, so-called japanned chairs were "cane bottomed."

Before the American Revolution, teas, silks, porcelain, lacquered furniture, and other luxury goods from China had been shipped through London in sizable quantities to the colonies. Regular importation of tea — originally introduced to Europe by the Dutch in 1628—began in the 1720s, and by 1740 an English visitor could assert that the ladies of Boston "visit, drink tea and neglect their families with as good grace as the finest ladies in London."[12] During the 1760s Americans consumed 1.2 million pounds of tea annually. Only a quarter of the amount arrived as it should, aboard ships from the East India Company from London. The rest was smuggled in from Holland and the Dutch West Indies with the aid of such Massachusetts citizens as John Hancock and Samuel Adams. On the night of December 16, 1773, Adams was one of the principal hosts of the Boston Tea Party, an event that helped lead to the establishment of direct trade with China—one of the underlying goals of the political revolt in the colonies. After the American Revolution, the British briefly imposed trade sanctions that were lifted with the signing of the peace treaty in 1783, and American ships were free to sail the oceans in search of commerce. The war between England and France and political turmoil on the Continent, however, virtually closed the European market to American traders. The newest nation on earth now turned to the most ancient in its first independent and much-needed economic venture.

On the morning of February 22, 1784, the aptly named *Empress of China* sailed out of New York harbor on the first leg of a voyage that would circle half the globe. The journey was to prove another milestone toward the founding of the American wicker industry. The ship crossed the Atlantic to Africa, rounded the Cape of Good Hope, then followed the old Portuguese sea route across the Indian Ocean and into the South China Sea. The China Trade had begun, and with it the dawn of a new chapter in American cultural and economic history. Aboard were North American trade goods: furs, cotton, lead, and the root of a plant that grew wild in the forests of New England (the Chinese called it ginseng and prized it as a medicinal drug and aphrodisiac). The *Empress of China* reached Portuguese Macao, at the mouth of the Pearl River, on August 24, 1784. A Chinese pilot came aboard and the ship sailed slowly upriver to the anchorage at Whampao, the loading port for Canton. As in earlier days, the Chinese authorities tightly controlled all trade and contact with the *Fan Kuai*. According to an imperial edict of 1756, Canton was the only port open to foreign shipping. European traders were restricted to a small strip of land bordering the Pearl River, where the various nations built open warehouses or "factories" known as *hongs*. All business transactions were strictly regulated by a group of Chinese merchants (the *co-hong*) appointed by the emperor. The sudden appearance of the Americans was a great surprise for them: the nation and its "flowery" flag was entirely unknown. The newcomers spoke the same language as the British but were better behaved and far less arrogant in their treatment of the Chinese. Until the China Trade virtually stopped in the late 1870s—except for the commerce in rattan and Oriental wicker—the Americans remained favored and, as a result, the United States benefited enormously, both economically and culturally. The *Empress of China* sailed for home in May 1785, freighted with chests of black and green tea, silks, cotton yard goods, and chinaware. Also aboard was a complete set of home furnishings crafted by Cantonese artisans for the financier Robert Morris—the first Chinese furniture and decorations imported directly into the United States. The voyage proved a tremendous financial success, and by 1790 twenty-eight American vessels had made the round trip to Canton. Soon, fleets were sailing annually out of Salem, Providence, Boston, Philadelphia, and New York, transforming local economies and tastes. On its second voyage in 1786–87, the *Empress* brought back not only teas, silks, porcelain, and other goods, but an unusual lot described in the account book as "6 jars of sweetmeats, rattans & matting," which had been acquired through a Chinese merchant named Akee for thirty-six dollars.[13] The quantity of rattan brought back was not recorded, but it was the first shipment to reach American shores directly. A century later, thousands of tons of rattan products were being transported yearly aboard huge clipper ships—expressly for the wicker furniture industry. Cantonese mats and matting made from straw or rattan proved a popular import. Vast numbers were used in American homes as summer floor coverings.

Goods from China were divided into two basic categories: custom-made items based on Western designs, and distinctive Oriental products. Export furniture fell into both categories. Although precise figures are not available, the amount shipped to the United States during the late eighteenth and nineteenth centuries was substantial. Most pieces

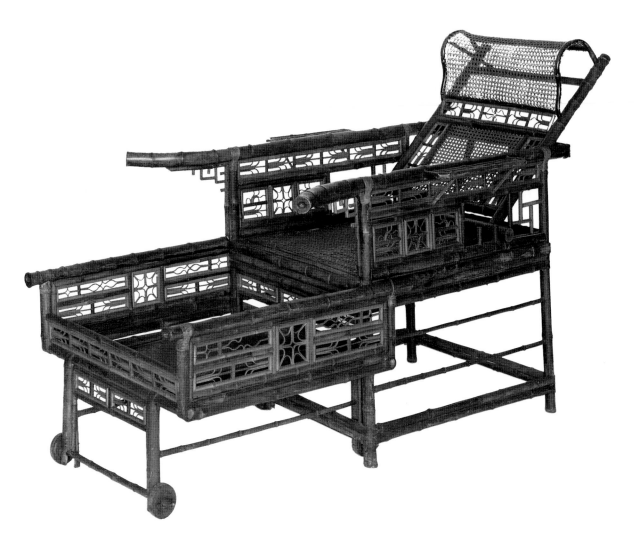

were shipped as commercial enterprises, but many were brought into the United States simply as personal belongings or souvenirs by those directly involved in the trade. In his richly detailed book, *The Canton Chinese* (1849), the American trader Osmond Tiffany described the essential types of Chinese export furniture: "The furniture of the Chinese is of two kinds, the bamboo and the rosewood. The first is exceedingly light, pretty, and adapted for a warm climate, withal very cheap. The stouter parts or framework is colored dark, and the ends of the stalks, tipped with ivory or horn. The young shoots of the plant are interwoven with those of stouter growth in pretty windings." The

other kind was far more costly, and was described as "very heavy and solid." It was made of "a kind of rosewood that is susceptible of high polish, and handsomely carved."[14] Although ornately carved and inlaid rosewood furniture proved a popular import for wealthy Americans, bamboo furnishings had a far wider appeal and helped create the vogue for American-made rattan furnishings.

Among the more popular souvenirs brought back to the United States by sea captains and traders was a type of Chinese reclining chair that had been used for centuries in the Far East. Constructed with a strong, yet lightweight frame of bamboo, it had broad, flat arms, and a mov-

Bamboo and Cane Chinese Export Expansion Chair, ca. 1810. Photograph courtesy of the Peabody and Essex Museum. Lounging chairs with retractable footrests were popular in the Orient long before American sailors and merchants first traveled to Canton and shipped them back to the United States. The ornate openwork sides and backrests of Chinese bamboo furniture helped influence the development of ornamental rattan-based, American wicker.

able back with an attached, caned headrest. For total comfort, there was an extension that could be pulled out from beneath the long seat so the occupant could stretch out at full length. The surfaces of these lounges were often fully caned. Southern planters adored them: they were cool and resilient—the perfect lounge for passing sweltering afternoons on

Chinese Export Rattan "Hourglass" Chair, 1913.
*Photograph from the Cooper-Hewitt Museum Picture
Collection, courtesy of the National Museum of
American Art, Smithsonian Institution.*
*The vernacular Chinese wicker chair had a distinctive,
hourglass-shaped base. First introduced during the China
Trade, it proved extremely popular. Between 1850 and
1930, untold thousands were imported into the United
States from Canton and Hong Kong.*

shaded verandas. Their wide, level armrests were exemplary supports for books, newspapers, and mint juleps. But New England traders enjoyed them just as much. In the late 1870s, when the taste for things Japanese and Far Eastern was all the rage, art critic and tastemaker Clarence Cook extolled not only the comfort, but the aesthetic qualities of the timeless bamboo and cane recliner. In his popular 1878 stylebook, *The House Beautiful*, he showed an example and declared the picturesque, comfortable, and versatile chairs "indispensible to a house in the country."[15]

Another Chinese chair was even more popular with Americans: the hourglass model made from rattan. From the late 1840s through the 1920s, these singular chairs were imported by the tens of thousands from Canton, Hong Kong, Shanghai, and other Far Eastern ports, and were used both indoors and out, on porches, patios, and garden lawns across the United States. Some American wicker furniture manufacturers even made their own versions. Its name comes from its distinctive shape, an open-weave rattan cylinder whose center, like an hourglass, is firmly cinched in. The top and bottom of the seat are formed by rings of rattan separated by strong vertical supports that take the place of legs. The latter were typically made of bamboo or wood. The uprights, circular rims, and the strip of bent rattan framing the backrest characteristically are tightly wrapped with strands of cane. Since no nails were used in its construction, the chair made in this peculiarly Chinese technique was strengthened by having its parts literally bound tightly together. But the technique also added an aesthetic dimension, ensuring that all the components, whether rattan or wood, had the same color, texture, and glossy surface. Wrapping with cane was to become one of the principal hallmarks of nineteenth- and twentieth-century American wicker. The origins of this unusual design are obscure, but American traders must first have encountered vernacular hourglass chairs in the houses and gardens of traders in Portuguese Macao, British Hong Kong, and Chinese merchants in Canton, and shipped examples home as souvenirs. American businessmen residing in the Far East regularly employed hourglass chairs as indoor furniture as well as cool porch seating. By the mid-nineteenth century, large commercial shipments of bamboo recliners and rattan hourglass chairs were being sold in San Francisco. The cargo aboard the ship *Rhone*, which docked in 1849, included "Cane Chairs of different sizes and patterns; bamboo Chairs; provision Baskets, large and small."[16] It can be argued that the Chinese hourglass chair wholly initiated the modern American vogue for wicker furniture, because the very first rattan chair made by the man who originated the American wicker industry was an hourglass model.

NOTES

1. Robert F. Trent, *New England Begins: The Seventeenth Century* (Boston: Museum of Fine Arts, 1982), 2:330.

2. Marion Day Iverson, "Wickerwork in the Seventeenth Century," *Antiques* 65 (March 1954): 206–07; see also, Abbott Lowell Cummings, ed., *Rural Homestead Inventories . . . 1675–1775* (Boston: Society for the Preservation of New England Antiquities, 1964).

3. Ralph Edwards, *The Shorter Dictionary of English Furniture* (London: Country Life, 1964), 170.

4. See Richard Saunders, *Collecting and Restoring Wicker Furniture* (New York: Crown Publishers, 1976), 11.

5. Quoted in Christopher Gilbert, *English Vernacular Furniture, 1750–1900* (New Haven and London: Yale University Press, 1991), 145.

6. John Vollmer, et al., *Silk Roads, China Ships* (Toronto: Royal Ontario Museum, 1983), 89ff.

7. Gertrude Z. Thomas, "Cane, A Tropical Transplant," *Antiques* 79 (January 1961): 92–93.

8. R. W. Symonds, "Cane Chairs of the 17th and 18th Centuries," *Connoisseur* 63 (March 1934): 180; Symonds, "English Cane Chairs," *Connoisseur* 127 (April 1951): 8ff, and (June 1951): 83ff; and Peter Thornton, *Seventeenth Century Interior Decoration in England, France, and Holland* (New Haven and London: Yale University Press, 1981), 202.

9. Symonds, "English Cane Chairs," (April 1951): 13–14.

10. Ibid., 14.

11. Ibid., 90.

12. *The China Trade: Romance and Reality* (Lincoln, Mass.: De Cordova Museum, 1979), 9.

13. Philip Chadwick Foster Smith, *The Empress of China* (Philadelphia: Philadelphia Maritime Museum, 1984), 265.

14. Osmond Tiffany, *The Canton Chinese, or the American's Sojourn in the Celestial Empire* (Boston: James Munroe, 1849), 83.

15. Clarence Cook, *The House Beautiful: Essays on Beds and Tables, Stools and Candlesticks* (New York: Scribner, Armstrong, 1878), 60.

16. Christina H. Nelson, *Directly from China: Export Goods for the American Market, 1784–1930* (Salem, Mass.: Peabody Museum, 1984), 13.

CHAPTER ONE

The Emergence of an American Industry, 1840–1873

Cyrus Wakefield, a New Hampshire-born farmboy turned Boston greengrocer, is rightfully acclaimed as the father of the modern American wicker industry. His story is a classic tale of Yankee ingenuity: the creation of an extraordinarily successful, nationwide enterprise based on a material at the time considered refuse fit only for burning. In its best-known account, the story of Wakefield Rattan's founding goes like this:

One morning in the year 1844 a young man stood on a wharf in Boston watching the unloading of a vessel just arrived in port. A stevedore threw a small bundle of rattan over the railing of the ship. The moment for which the youth was waiting had evidently arrived and he hastened up to the mate and asked what he intended to do with the discarded rattan. He was told it was of little value and chiefly served as ballast [sic] to prevent the cargo from shifting on its long voyage from the East. So he secured the rattan for a small sum, and, shouldering his burden, carried it back to the grocery-store on the waterfront which he and his brother

conducted. The purchaser was Cyrus Wakefield, founder of the rattan and reed industry in this country, and this transaction was the beginning of a business which later became that of the Wakefield Rattan Company.[1]

This somewhat fulsome narrative is from a corporate history published in 1926 for the Heywood-Wakefield Company. The firm was the successor to the original Wakefield Rattan Company and the largest manufacturer and retailer of wicker furniture in the world. The anecdote is authentic: Wakefield did purchase a single lot of cast-off rattan on the Boston docks one day, and with its profitable sale successfully launched an American industry. The date, however, is incorrect; the year was 1840.[2]

Cyrus Wakefield is a character straight out of a Horatio Alger story. He is an example of the nineteenth-century backwoods New Englander who rises from obscurity to eminence—and in the process has a town renamed in his honor. Born on a farm in Roxbury, New Hampshire, on February 14, 1811, Wakefield was clearly destined to become a businessman. According to one biographer, "the

executive and administrative qualities of his mind began to develop very early in life."[3] As a boy, he insisted that his father lay out long-term goals for farm chores that he then carefully planned and carried out with the help of his younger brother Enoch. Between school and work around the farm he found time to dig a charcoal burning pit on the family property and sell the product to local blacksmiths—an entrepreneurial pattern he would repeat. When relatives who had abandoned the New Hampshire hills for the cities of New England returned for family visits, they regaled him with tales of life in the city, and he grew increasingly restless with his lot on the farm. At first he obtained his parents' permission to let him strike out on his own and work as a picker in the harsh setting of a Peterboro, New Hampshire, cotton mill. It was not long before he was back in the warmth of the family homestead, this time dreaming of

Unidentified maker, Rattan Armchair, ca. 1850s. Photograph courtesy of Steve Poole. This rattan chair is the only known example of mid-nineteenth-century American wicker to survive. Like the Berrians' furniture, it echoes the looping, openwork designs favored by certain willow furniture manufacturers in Germany.

becoming a merchant prince in Boston. Although his father was strongly opposed to the idea, he finally consented, and the fifteen-year-old Cyrus left to seek his fortune in the city. He landed a job in a grocery store on Washington Street but soon found another, more agreeable one on India Street. With occasional time on his hands, he was permitted by his employers to buy and sell empty barrels and liquor casks in order to earn money for schooling. Soon, young Cyrus accumulated a thousand dollars in savings. However, his dreams of college vanished, replaced by the more alluring visions of wealth and property. But the teenager diligently attended evening classes, listened to public debates, sermons, and scientific lectures, soaking up as much knowledge as time and circumstance allowed.

In 1834 he started his own grocery business, Foster and Wakefield, on Commercial Street, across from Commercial Wharf, one of Boston's largest and busiest shipping piers. The partnership with Foster dissolved in 1836, and Cyrus sent for his brother Enoch, with whom he formed Wakefield and Company in 1838. Boston city directories of the late 1830s list the brothers' business address as 91 Commercial Street and their occupation as dealers in "West India Goods and Groceries"—spices as well as fruits and vegetables. For two years following the first purchase, Cyrus and Enoch sold rattan as a sideline. But in 1843 *Stimson's Boston Directory* reveals for the first time that Cyrus had his own business address and a new occupation. His office was located at 15 Com-

Cyrus Wakefield (1811–1873).
Photograph from Van Slyck, New England Manufacturers and Manufactories, *1879, courtesy of the National Museum of American Art, Smithsonian Institution.*

mercial Street, and his occupation is recorded as "Commission Merchant," or jobber. Enoch was cited as the sole operator of Wakefield and Company. Clearly, Cyrus had decided to go into the rattan business full time. The following year, he finally sold his share of the grocery firm to his brother. By 1848, Enoch, too, had switched trades: Wakefield and Company is described in the directory as selling "Wooden Ware, etc." Such goods not only included turned wood objects, such as bowls, but willow baskets, brooms, brushes, matches, mats, and matting of all kinds.

By 1840, when Cyrus casually acquired his first bundle, there was little market for raw rattan in the United States. Chairmakers who needed seat caning purchased their supplies already processed from European traders who picked it up in the Far East. So what did Cyrus Wakefield do with his first bundle of rattan? There are three conflicting reports. One states he sold the thin, flexible stalks to basketmakers; another declares he ped-

dled it to local chairmakers who found the cost of imported cane too high; a third alleges he experimented with the material himself, removing the cane in strips and wrapping it tightly around a conventional wooden chair to give it an Oriental look.[4]

Whatever the truth—and all three versions are probably correct—the first sale proved sufficiently profitable for Wakefield to buy and sell other lots he picked up from ships returning from the China Trade. In the 1840s, bundles of low-grade rattan were used as dunnage, or packing material, to cushion the tea chests and crates of porcelain stowed in the hold during the long return voyage from Canton. Rattan dunnage was readily available in the East and proved an effective and inexpensive means of keeping cargo safe from damage during storms at sea. Back in Boston, the rattan, having served its purpose, was simply junked. A fire hazard on the crowded docks, it was hauled off and burned as refuse. But in the early 1840s, the demand for comfortable cane-seat chairs suddenly picked up and Wakefield discovered that he was able to sell all the rattan he could obtain on the docks to Boston-area chairmakers eager for their own supplies. At this point he correctly calculated that dealing in rattan was likely to be far more profitable than selling foodstuffs—especially since he was the only local jobber in the material—and he decided to quit the grocery business. Stripping the valuable cane by hand with knives was labor intensive and costly in America, and it kept the price of Wakefield's rattan low. To increase his profits, he was determined to find a foreign source of ready-made cane to sell locally. He wrote to his brother-in-law who fortuitously worked for the American firm of Russell and Company in Canton, sending him samples of the sort of caning most in demand in the United States, and inquiring whether he could import processed supplies directly from China.

Wakefield was told he could, and by the late 1840s his imported "Canton Split Rattan" was widely retailed in New England. The supply, however, was not always steady. In 1850 a rebellion in southern China suddenly disrupted exports. This unexpected setback prompted Wakefield to increase his reserves of whole rattan by buying up as much as he could from stocks already in the United States in order to begin manufacture of his own chair caning. In 1851, the American Rattan Company, a small manufacturer in Fitchburg, Massachusetts, was the only New England firm using machinery to cut cane.[5] With a large supply of rattan bundles now on hand, Wakefield decided to compete with American Rattan directly and acquired two crude, hand-powered cutting machines. He installed these in a warehouse on Boston's Canal Street and began successfully to produce his own cane.

The warehouse proved too small for his burgeoning rattan business, and in 1855 Wakefield purchased land for a factory in the town of South Reading, just north of Boston. He had already acquired a home there in 1851, where he lived with his wife, Elizabeth, the daughter of a retired sea captain from Lynnfield, Massachusetts, whom he had married in 1841, just

as he was beginning to buy and sell cast-off rattan. The new industrial property, known locally as Green's Mill, included two mill ponds on either side of Water Street, an old homestead, a grist mill, and several small buildings previously used for manufacturing purposes. At this point, the future Wakefield Rattan Company began to germinate. At first Cyrus did not set up cane-cutting machines. Instead, using immigrant Irish labor, he produced a new and highly profitable rattan product— lightweight, flexible hoops for the hoopskirts popular in the mid-1850s. The Irishmen also manufactured a wide variety of baskets from rattan. At this point, the idea of manufacturing wicker furniture was the furthest thing from his mind.

During the early 1850s, however, stylish furniture made from rattan was one of the latest vogues in New York City. No one knows who precisely started the trend, but one of the earliest known makers was a man named Topf. He was one of 556 American manufacturers and craftsmen who exhibited at the "Great Exhibition of the Industry of All Nations" held in 1851 at the Crystal Palace in London. A garden chair "by Topf of New York" was reproduced in the lavishly illustrated catalogue published by the London *Art Journal*. It is among the first images of modern American wicker. Virtually nothing is known about its maker. He is mistakenly recorded in the official list of exhibitors as "Tuph, J. New York, Cane Chairs." A review of New York City directories for 1851 reveals yet another misspelling: "John Topp." But two out

Ornamental Rattan Chair Made by Michael Topf in New York and Exhibited at the 1851 Crystal Palace Exhibition in London. *Photograph from the* Art Journal Illustrated Catalogue, *1851, courtesy of the National Museum of American Art, Smithsonian Institution. An early depiction of American-made wicker, this garden chair design prefigures the ornate rattan and reed furniture made in the 1890s.*

of three directories agree: his name was Michael Topf and his trade "Chair Maker." Topf's home was at 84 Bedford Street, and his shop was located at 262 Bleecker Street. In all likelihood, he purchased his rattan from the only dealer listed in New York City directories—Ely Smith of 79 Fulton Street.

Topf's high-style garden chair remains a show-stopper. It is no wonder that the editors of the Great Exhibition's illustrated catalog selected it for reproduction from among the thousands of decorative objects on view at the Crystal Palace. In a suitably Victorian way, they praised it for "possess[ing] much novelty, and no little taste, in its ornamental design." How many or what types of "cane chairs" the New Yorker exhibit-

Cast-Iron Bench, ca. 1850. Photograph courtesy of The Metropolitan Museum of Art, Gift of Mr. and Mrs. James B. Tracy, 1966. (Inst. 66.4).

Benches with naturalistic patterns or more abstract Gothic-revival designs were popular forms of seating in mid-nineteenth-century American gardens. Decorative cast-iron benches helped stimulate the development of wicker garden and porch seating. Although they might not last as long as iron, chairs and settees made from rattan were far more comfortable—and much easier to move.

ed in London remains a mystery, but the model engraved clearly demonstrates that he had mastered the material capabilities of rattan. Topf's chair is the first known chair to be composed entirely of curvilinear elements. The seat frame and legs are made out of wood, but the arms and crest-rail are gracefully curved lengths of whole rattan which have been bound together with wrappings of cane. The decorative backrest and the area under the arms are filled with fancy C-scrolls, curls, and S-curves all joined to form a lacy, openwork screen. The 1851 chair is a remarkable harbinger of the ornate wicker styles of the 1890s.

There is little new about the shape of Topf's armchair. Like innumerable mid-century examples, its graceful design is rococo-inspired. The back, however, has

been heightened to support the head and neck—a Victorian concession to comfort. But in its insistent linear quality, it is extremely modern, reflecting the latest in innovative industrial design: European bentwood and metal garden

furniture. The influence of these novel forms on American wicker designs in the 1850s and 1860s cannot be overstated. Using flexible rattan instead of hardwood dowels, chair makers in New York could easily replicate the elegant curves and curls laboriously produced by the celebrated bentwood furniture manufacturer, Michael Thonet of Vienna—but in a fraction of the time and at minimal cost. There was no need to spend hours steaming lathe-turned beechwood rods, then forcibly bending and clamping them while still wet into cast-iron forms to dry for a day or more. The rattan was simply soaked for an hour or so and hand-bent to the desired shape, fixed in place with nails and binding cane, and left to dry. Once hardened, it retained its new shape.

Another contemporary form of garden seating similar in spirit to Topf's wicker chair—and a possible influence on its design—was twisted-wire garden furniture made in France. Taking advantage of recent advances in steel-making techniques, several overseas firms made

J. and C. Berrian and Company, New York, Gothic-Revival Rattan Sofa, Chairs, and Foot Stool, 1851. Photograph from Wheeler, Rural Homes, 1851, courtesy of the National Museum of American Art, Smithsonian Institution.

By 1850, New York was the center of a nascent wicker industry. The fashionable home furnishings store J. and C. Berrian sold a wide array of artistic summer furniture made from rattan.

durable, lightweight chairs out of thin, reinforced steel cable. Weather-resistant, this new material could easily be shaped into simple, yet elegantly curved designs. Available on the New York market by 1855, the new French chairs were described as "exceedingly light and unique in appearance" and "admirably suited for Lawns, Summer Houses, Cottages, Piazzas."[6] A type of metal garden seating made in the United States that also influenced both the design and use of early wicker was made of cast iron. Many of the heavy benches and chairs made after mid-century were ornately decorated with naturalistic fruit and flower motifs. But others, in rustic or Gothic-inspired openwork designs, were more emphatically linear and abstract in design.

At mid-century, Michael Topf was not the only manufacturer of ornamental rattan chairs in New York. Throughout the 1850s, the American wicker market was dominated by the firm of J. and C. Berrian, whose "ware-rooms" of fashionable home furnishings were located at 601 Broadway. The diversity of Berrian's household products made from rattan was quite astonishing, presaging the wide array of merchandise offered two decades later by the Wakefield Rattan Company. John M. and Cornelius A. Berrian not only retailed an assortment of artistic chairs for both children and adults, but cane-seated sofas, decorative fireplace screens, porch swings, arched cribs, tall sewing stands, wastepaper containers, and flower stands. The Berrians also sold high-backed Chinese hourglass chairs imported directly from China.

The Berrian's rattan and cane furniture was extolled as just the right sort for suburban, summertime living in architect Gervase Wheeler's popular 1851 style book, *Rural Homes; or Sketches of Houses Suited to American Country Life*. Richly carved and upholstered furniture in the latest styles was fine for city residences, he declared, but wholly out of place in the country, where simplicity, comfort, and convenience reigned. In the earliest extended discussion of cane and wicker manufacturing in the United States, Wheeler reveals just how great the popularity of cane and rattan furnishings was at mid-century:

A material now in very general use in this country, the rattan or cane of the East Indies, affords an immense variety of articles of furniture, so strong, light, and inexpensive, that it seems particularly adapted to general introduction in rural homes. Its manufacture is now becoming so important as to furnish employment to a very large number of persons. In the House of Refuge alone, there are between three and four hundred boys at work on cane seats, and at several places in Bloomingdale and in the suburbs of New York are a number of Germans who have in their employment at least two thousand girls occupied in this manufacture. The Messrs. Berrian, in Broadway, are the most extensive manufacturers of this article; they have, in fact, created the trade and with it a name for themselves.[7]

Interestingly, Wheeler states that

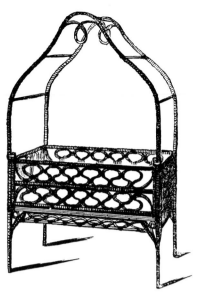

J. and C. Berrian and Company, New York, Rattan Crib, 1851. *Photograph from Wheeler,* Rural Homes, *1851, courtesy of the National Museum of American Art, Smithsonian Institution. This ornamental rattan crib was highly recommended because it was easy to clean and naturally hygienic. Rattan furniture was a popular feature in nurseries and children's rooms during the second half of the nineteenth century.*

New Yorkers purchased their cane supplies from Dutch traders who trans-shipped it from their Far Eastern colonies through Antwerp, Bremen, and Rotterdam. Wakefield's "Canton Split Rattan" had yet to make its mark beyond New England. To keep two thousand women at work in the New York area alone weaving seats, the quantity of cane bought from the Dutch must have been immense. As an entrepreneur, Cyrus Wakefield was clearly on the right track.

No documented examples of the Berrians' wicker have survived. But one early rattan chair—possibly the earliest extant piece of nineteenth-century American wicker—shares many similarities in design and construction with the furniture illustrated in Wheeler's book. One of the engravings in *Rural Homes* depicts an arrangement of

Advertisement, J. and C. Berrian's Home-Furnishing Ware-Rooms, ca. 1850s.
*Courtesy of the Warshaw Collection of Business Americana, Archives Center, National Museum
of American History, Smithsonian Institution.*
*As this engraved advertisement indicates, the Berrian brothers not only sold American-made,
bentwood-inspired rattan furniture, but Chinese hourglass chairs as well.*

the Berrians' wicker which includes a sofa, armchair, rocker, and footstool. According to Wheeler, the legs, seat frames, and vertical supports of the various pieces were made of carefully selected white oak or hickory, steamed and bent into their required shapes. The rest of the design, however, was composed of whole rattan, soaked and then manipulated into fluid, ornamental configurations and left to dry. The engraving clearly shows that the sections of bent rattan have been firmly tied together by bindings of cane where they intersect or abut. The elaborate backrests are decorative yet sturdy networks of bent rattan, providing, in Wheeler's words, "that greatest of all luxuries—a springy back." Like Topf's garden chair, the wooden legs and framework were wrapped tightly with strands of cane to conceal joints, provide extra strength, and give each piece a unified visual effect. The Berrians' rattan furniture was probably designed by,

and most likely fabricated by, recent German immigrants. The decorative openwork of the backrests is similar to engravings of willow furniture published in mid-century German trade catalogues.

Rattan was even more pliable than willow rods. Wheeler asserted that among "the principal excellencies of cane [rattan] as a material for chairs, sofas, baskets, etc.," was "its great facility of being turned and twisted into an almost endless variety of shapes."[8] The back support of the pictured sofa is a wonderful demonstration of rattan's flexibility. Like the stone tracery in a suite of Gothic windows, it is a complex of pointed arches enclosing loops and smaller round arches. Gothic-revival architecture was all the rage in the 1850s, and the sofa was just the piece to complement picturesque country homes built by Wheeler and his rival, Andrew Jackson Downing.

Among the American exhibitors at the Great Exhibition in London

was the Hartford, Connecticut, arms manufacturer, Samuel Colt. He must have seen Topf's garden chair, for his display of six-shooters in the Crystal Palace was one of the most acclaimed, and the judges personally awarded him a bronze medal. Colt, too, figures prominently in the early narrative of American wicker. It is an interesting story: a fruitful collision between Old World craftsmanship and American industrialism.[9] In the early 1850s, Colt's arms business was booming, and he needed more land on which to build new factories. He was able, through clever subterfuge, to acquire some two hundred acres of bottom land along the Connecticut River at Hartford known as South Meadows. It was a daring venture, for during spring thaw, the river regularly overflowed its banks. In order to hold back the floods, he followed the example of the Dutch and built an enormous dike nearly two miles long. It measured between ten and twenty feet high, was one hundred feet wide at the base, and stretched forty feet across at the top. As a means of erosion control, Colt planted deep-rooting willows all along this vast earthwork. It was the first significant cultivation of willows in America. The species was a European import, the gray, or brindled, *Salix viminalis,* commonly found along river banks in France and Germany.

One day, after Colt's dike had become well fringed with willow trees, a local basketmaker unexpectedly made him an offer to purchase the entire spring crop of osier shoots. He judged these willow rods superior to those he usually imported already cut and peeled from Holland, and expected to strike a better deal with a seemingly uninformed arms maker. But Colt, never one to miss a commercial opportunity, put the basketmaker off while he investigated the potential of the willow-ware business for himself. To his surprise, he discovered that, if properly organized, it could be a highly profitable venture—especially for someone who grew his own osiers. The local competition for skilled weavers, however, was great, and he would have to overpay to attract an American work force. This he refused to do. He decided it would be cheaper and more practical in the long run to import skilled willow weavers from Europe and charged his German business agent in Berlin, C. F. Wappenhans, to look into the possibility.

Wappenhans responded that basketweavers in Germany were not in the habit of leaving one employment for another. Instead, as members of a long-established trade guild, they lived and worked in tightly knit communities. Maintaining their village life and pre-industrial craft traditions was far more important to them than making money. In Wappenhans's opinion, the only way skilled weavers would be induced to leave was by inviting the entire group—along with all their relatives and belongings—to emigrate and work together as a unit. This, he thought, would put an end to Colt's scheme. But the American industrialist was undeterred. By now, he was firmly committed to the idea of adding a willow-ware plant to his factory complex and demanded to know every detail of the weavers' working and living conditions to see whether he could duplicate them in Hartford as an inducement.

Realizing that he would not be dissuaded, Wappenhans obligingly sent detailed descriptions of daily life in a small weavers' village near Potsdam, east of Berlin. He even included plans and elevations of their homes and workshops, as well as the local beer garden. The village was an unusual one—it had been established expressly for a band of Russian weavers recruited in earlier times by a previous Prussian monarch. Even more curious, its architecture was Swiss, because the monarch's queen had fallen in love with mountain farmhouses during a trip through the Alps. On a whim, she demanded that he build her one on the grounds of the Sans Souci palace. The king had obliged with an entire village. After careful consideration of all the facts, Colt communicated he could indeed reproduce a reasonable facsimile on his South Meadows estate, Armsmear. In turn, the Germans indicated strong interest, and so, behind a section of the willow-topped earthen wall along the Connecticut River, there arose a curious Swiss hamlet for Prussian basketweavers near the factories where Irish immigrants manufactured the famous six-shooters and repeating rifles. In 1859 the Germans began to arrive and quickly set up shop. The following year they were making willow furniture.

The compound had been called "Potsdam" by Colt's armorers after the city where Sans Souci is located, and the designation stuck. The new neighborhood in the southeastern part of the reclaimed land contained some seventeen buildings arrayed around three sides of a common. At the west end was the Willow-Ware Works, a three-story factory with a tall smokestack. It was the first of its kind in the United States. The dwellings were of various sizes: one was a tenement large enough to house eighteen families, but there were also a dozen more picturesque two-family units. The eaves of broadly sloping roofs extended well beyond brick walls laid between timbered frames and sheltered outside staircases leading to a second story. There was also, as promised, the beer garden for after-work socializing. But the German craftsmen could not have anticipated the new industrial techniques that were essential to Colt's manufacturing process, and to which they would have to adapt: the division and specialization of labor. Instead of one man producing a single object from start to finish—as had been the ancient practice—the new boss insisted that a sequence of workmen contribute to a rigid division of labor. Moreover, to speed up the process, he introduced novel machinery to peel and plane the willow rods. However grudgingly, the Old World craftsmen adjusted to the new factory system, and before long, production rose and costs fell dramatically. The wives and children of the Irish armorers supplied the elbow grease while the German craftsmen furnished the artistic talent.

By the close of the Civil War, there were about 120 persons employed in Colt's willow works. They produced some fifty items in

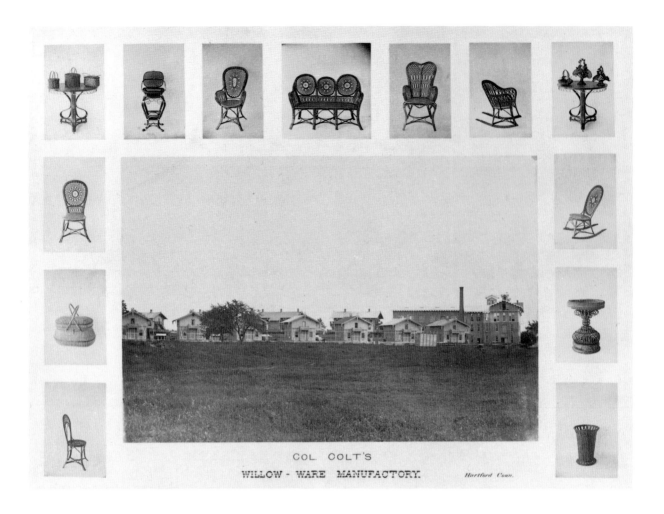

Above: Showcard With Photographs of Samuel Colt's Hartford, Connecticut, Willow-Ware Factory and Workers' Houses With Examples of Colt Willow-Ware, *ca. 1860s. Courtesy of the Wadsworth Atheneum, Hartford, The Elizabeth Hart Jarvis Colt Collection.*
In 1859 arms manufacturer Colt established a willow furniture works on the grounds of his new factory complex by the Connecticut River. He imported an entire village of German weavers who were settled into Swiss-style houses arranged next to the factory. From 1860 to 1873, when the plant burned, Colt's workers produced a wide array of intricately woven willow furniture.

Right: Colt Willow-Ware Manufactory, Hartford, Connecticut, Willow Settee, ca. 1860–73. Courtesy of the Wadsworth Atheneum, Hartford, The Elizabeth Hart Jarvis Colt Collection.
Colt's German-style willow furniture was of a more traditional sort than the rattan furniture retailed by the Berrians in New York. The craftsmen who braided and plaited the cobweb-like backrests belonged to a basketweavers guild established in the sixteenth century.

willow including sleigh bodies, wheeled invalid chairs, children's go-carts, doll furniture, sewing stands, baskets of every conceivable type, picture frames, flower vases—even whole arbors—as well as round and square tables, chairs and rockers, sofas and tête-à-têtes, étagères and bookcases. The weavers typically worked from patterns or drawings and, where possible, used lasts. For the more complicated pieces, upwards of a score of workers were involved in the entire production process. The quantity of furniture produced was considerable: an 1864 inventory records $8,593.97 worth of chairs in stock. If the average retail cost is estimated at ten dollars apiece, then the number on hand was significant. The total value of manufactured goods and supplies on hand that year was $23,000.39. By 1869 the figure had soared to $41,851.53.[10]

In design and construction, the chairs and settees produced by the Colt Willow-Ware Manufactory were distinctively German. High-style productions rather than vernacular basket seating, they reveal the revolutionary influence of contemporary bentwood. The frames of chairs and sofas were made up of gracefully curved clusters of three or more osiers of varying thickness and color. Typically, at least one of the thinner rods forming the arms and curving crest-rail was decorated with an ornamental spiral twist of cane, an Oriental stylism. Cane was also used as a means to bind various structural components together—stretchers to the legs, leg braces to the seat frame, arms to the vertical posts. Nails, squeezed through the osiers

with pliers, were also liberally used to affix the numerous constituent parts and create a flexible, yet stable structure. By toning, bleaching, and varnishing separate components as well as by mixing different types of peeled willow with cane and sometimes rattan, the craftsmen often created individual pieces with remarkably varied coloration.

The most characteristic feature of a Colt willow chair is the elaborately braided back support. The delicate, interlaced networks are woven with extremely fine skeins. The distinctive radiating pattern was known as an "esparto" weave, after the tough wire grass from southern Spain and North Africa originally used for such braided backs in willow furniture made in Germany. The thin willow fibers in Colt's backrests were first grouped in three parallel lines to achieve greater flatness and strength, tied to an inner ring, and then braided and plaited toward the outer rim of the panel where they were finally affixed. A wide strip of osier braidwork typically covered the joint where the back fitted into the chair frame. While the back supports appear to be as fragile as cobwebs, they were actually surprisingly strong, capable of tolerating considerable weight and pressure.

Although very few chairs or settees remain, Colt willow furniture occasionally can be seen in old photographs of summer homes in

Parlor of a Summer Cottage, Oak Bluffs, Martha's Vineyard, Massachusetts, ca. 1875. *Photograph courtesy of the National Museum of American History, Smithsonian Institution. Oak Bluffs was a summer residential development built on Martha's Vineyard in the 1860s. This parlor was furnished with Colt willow furniture.*

the post–Civil War era or as props in New England studio portrait photographs. It is known that the arms maker furnished the conservatory of his Italianate mansion with a pair of willow settees and that Joseph Henry, first Secretary of the Smithsonian Institution, kept a comfortable Colt chair in his quarters in the Smithsonian "Castle" on the Mall in Washington, D.C. Chairs were even shipped to Cuba, and, before his death in 1862, Colt reportedly planned to introduce them widely into South America. According to a later biographer, "furniture of such a make that it yields on pressure, and so is soft as a bed of down, while it is cool and self-ventilated at the same time, has an indescribable charm for dwellers in the tropics, and to the rest of men at such seasons as the tropics visit them."[11] Reputedly, Colt furniture was seen as far west as California, and it was known to be in use in the midwestern states where willow furniture of a similar sort was made by German immigrants in Chicago willow-ware workshops. Production ˙ceased abruptly in 1873. That year a disastrous fire completely destroyed the Willow-Ware Works. It was not rebuilt, and the weavers were forced to scatter in search of new employment. Many of them appear to have found work in the mid-1870s with the Wakefield Rattan Company and its rival, Heywood Brothers and Company of Gardner, Massachusetts, where they introduced the esparto pattern into the caned backrests of rattan chairs.

In 1856, one year after Wakefield set up his cane-splitting workshop in South Reading, a seemingly unrelated event half way around the globe put his business acumen to the test. The second Opium War had erupted in China, trade with the Far East was disrupted, and rattan imports dwindled. At this juncture, Wakefield chanced to learn that several large lots—the last remaining reserves of whole rattan on the East Coast—were for sale in New York. Recognizing a unique opportunity, he swiftly secured all the ready cash he could raise in Boston and rushed down to New York. Establishing himself quietly at the Astor House hotel, Wakefield, a later biographer wrote:

put his brokers at work to obtain the lowest price at which the entire stock could be purchased, enjoining upon them not to name the purchaser. Having obtained the desired information, he decided to take all the available lots, for which he paid

sufficient cash to make the material subject to his order. This gave him the whole control of the rattan stock of the country. Prices soon advanced, and he was enabled to sell, so he realized a handsome profit. This single operation not only put money and credit at his disposal, but also gave him a prestige in the business, which he ever after maintained.[12]

In one well-timed and daring act of speculation, Wakefield had cornered the rattan market and, in the process, transformed himself from a struggling businessman into a financial power. It was a long way from that fateful day on the Boston docks when he picked up his first bundle of rattan. The amount of money he made on the deal must have been substantial, since it allowed him to extend and overhaul his industrial operations in South Reading. The modernization was necessary, because in the years 1855 to 1856, when the nascent Wakefield Rattan Company had concentrated on the production of hoopskirts and baskets, the recent advances in steel wire-making, which had revolutionized the design and manufacture of contemporary metal furniture, also put an end to Wakefield's lucrative hoopskirt business. Thinner and more durable, the new lightweight steel strips suddenly supplanted rattan as the preferred material. The only alternative open to Wakefield, with his huge cache of rattan, was to turn seriously to the production of high-demand seat caning, but to do so profitably he would have to employ advanced machinery on a large scale.

The next decade and a half saw rapid industrialization in the South Reading plant. Working closely with his master machinist, Charles W. Trow, Wakefield introduced a stream of mechanized methods that revolutionized the rattan industry. By the early 1860s he had successfully introduced new rattan-splitting machines and was soon outproducing the rival American Rattan Company by several times its annual yield. With rising profits, he built more facilities and replaced water power with steam engines.

The cane-cutting procedures introduced by the Wakefield Rattan Company were later adopted throughout the industry. The machines were extraordinarily productive, increasing the amount and quality of caning cut from whole rattan in the United States exponentially. The first step was to sort and grade the bundled rattan by size and color. Next, the bent stalks were forcibly straightened by running them over a grooved wheel attached to an upright post. They were then washed and soaked in large, revolving metal boxes for a half-hour or more. The dampened stems were next put through a special scraping machine that removed the projecting leaf nodes and ensured a uniform thickness. In the following step, each smooth stalk was individually inserted in an aperture in the innovative splitting machine which automatically pulled it through the device. Inside, sharp blades could be set to cut the outer sheath into a series of five to eight separate strands, depending on the width of cane desired. These strips literally flew out of the machine and were quickly gathered up in large armfuls by boy attendants. The inner pith of the stalk, known as reed, was ejected at the opposite end. The rough strands of cane were then put through special shaving machines that trimmed off all remaining pith fibers from the underside and ensured uniform widths. Workers then collected the smooth strands into measured bundles of one thousand linear feet and stacked them in the factory's bleaching room, where they were treated overnight with fumes from burning sulphur. After whitening, the cane was sold in various widths to basket and chair-making firms in units of ten bundles containing ten thousand running feet.[13] If Wakefield's imported "Canton Split Rattan" had failed to dominate the East Coast market in the late 1840s, his machine-cut cane certainly did so a decade later. By 1873 it was in demand nationwide.

The by-products of split rattan—the shavings and the inner pith—typically were burned in the late 1850s as waste, but Wakefield, anxious to maximize all of his rattan, sought ways to use them. When wetted, thin lengths of reed became extremely flexible and were soon regularly employed by the Wakefield Rattan Company's basketweavers and were also sold commercially to others. The mountains of long, fibrous shavings were another matter. But in 1862 William Houston, an inventive Scots weaver in Wakefield's employ, invented a patented process to spin the shavings in a rough yarn from which to weave coarse matting and baling cloth on handlooms. Up to this point, the large American market for rattan matting used as summer floor cover-

RATTAN WORKS.

View of the Wakefield Rattan Company's Factory Complex, 1874. *Photograph from Eaton,* Genealogical History of the Town of Reading, Massachusetts, 1874, *courtesy of the National Museum of American Art, Smithsonian Institution.*
At the death of Cyrus Wakefield in 1873, the Wakefield Rattan Company was the largest of its kind in the world.

ings had been dominated by Oriental imports, but Wakefield's cool, moth-proof matting was soon prized by Victorian-era homemakers. Houston's inventiveness continued unabated through the Civil War years. In 1863 he added coir—the fibers of coconut shells imported from India—to his yarn materials and brought out two popular lines of floor matting, "Diamond A" and "Union Coir and Rattan." By this date, the Wakefield work force numbered two hundred employees. The same year, Houston, who spent forty years as the superintendent of the firm's profitable weaving activities, invented new looms and ingeniously wove the first brush mat from rattan shavings. By 1881 the Scotsman commanded a battery of more than one hundred steam-powered looms which produced a wide variety of rattan and coir mats and matting, as well as the Wakefield Rattan Company's popular Kurachee rugs, first introduced in 1876.

In 1865 Wakefield decided to import cargoes of high-grade rattan directly from the Far East and sent his nephew and namesake, Cyrus Wakefield II, to Singapore to oversee operations. Within a few years, some fifteen vessels were engaged by the Wakefields, carrying not only rattan, but coffee, pepper, tin, and spices to Boston.[14] With enormous amounts of the finest grades of rattan reaching the factory and the production of seat caning soaring, Houston invented his most remarkable device—a steam-powered loom which wove multiple strands of cane into sheets of dense webbing. Invented in 1870, it proved to be one of the most important advances in the rattan industry. The durable, easily cleaned, and cool cane fabric immediately became the favored covering for bench seats in trains and trolleys, and extended the company's business dramatically. The machine-made webbing eventually revolutionized seat caning, but it was the rival Heywood Brothers who invented the ingenious machines that could automatically insert the webbing into mass-produced wooden seat frames.

Rattan was not the only thing on Wakefield's mind. In the 1860s he had invested heavily in real estate in both South Reading and Boston's North End. In 1864 and 1865 he purchased several plots on Boston's Canal Street, where he soon established the company's headquarters. He also systematically assembled land and buildings on nearby streets and made several important acquisitions around Brattle Square, including the Brattle Square Church and the Quincy House. He was convinced that Washington Street would eventually be extended to Haymarket Square, so he purchased and developed numerous lots and properties in anticipation of future urban growth, becoming one of Boston's more important real estate developers during the Civil War and its aftermath.[15] In the town of South Reading, Wakefield had erected a magnificent Second Empire–style stone mansion on Main Street in 1861, and acquired as much property in the area of his factories and elsewhere in town as he could. He was active in the organization of the local Real Estate and Building Association that was formed to increase settlement in the town—no doubt to lure more employees for the rattan works. But Wakefield was more than a wealthy industrialist and real estate magnate; he was dedicated to both the spiritual and material prosperity of South Reading. Conscious of his own lack of formal education, he provided scholarships to deserving local youths to pursue their

studies, and funded a series of free lectures for the townspeople at large. In 1867 he offered land and thirty thousand dollars toward the construction of a new town hall that would be a suitable memorial to South Reading's Civil War dead. His fellow citizens were so overwhelmed by his generosity that they voted unanimously to rename the town in honor of its leading citizen. On July 4, 1868, South Reading, originally founded in 1644, became Wakefield, Massachusetts—which it remains to this day. On February 22, 1871, having finally spent close to 120 thousand dollars on the grandiose structure, Wakefield formally handed over the keys to the new Wakefield town hall. A year later, such a magnanimous gesture would have been impossible.

In 1872 the American economy went into recession. The Franco-Prussian War, enormous levels of personal and corporate debt, international trade imbalances, currency inflation, as well as excessive speculation and extravagant living on both sides of the Atlantic threatened financial stability worldwide. In the United States, four thousand businesses went bankrupt with a loss of some 121 million dollars. In the late spring of 1872, a mosquito-borne equine epidemic, which had a direct impact on Wakefield's business, broke out and by autumn had killed almost 25 percent of all the horses—many of them draft animals—in America. The sudden, drastic drop in the supply of horse power forced businesses to resort to teams of men to pull wagons in the cities or abandon deliveries altogether. The economic losses in Boston were com-

pounded by a devastating fire that, on November 9, 1872, razed sixty acres downtown from Washington Street to the harbor, causing an estimated sixty million dollars in damages. In the summer of 1873, doubtless in response to the worsening conditions, Wakefield decided to legally incorporate his rattan business. As the sole owner, he had no personal protection should the economic situation truly disintegrate. It was a wise decision. On Friday, September 19, 1873, the New York stock market, jolted by the sudden failure of several large securities, crashed. The resulting depression—known as the Panic of 1873—was the most severe the United States had experienced. A majority of American railroad companies declared bankruptcy, and more than two-thirds of the iron mills closed. From 1876 to 1877 more than eighteen thousand businesses failed. Hundreds of thousands lost their jobs. Hunger, crime, homelessness, and industrial violence became commonplace. In 1878, however, conditions improved markedly and the following year, the depression was simply a bitter memory.

In mid-October 1873 the Wakefield Rattan Company was formally chartered in the Commonwealth of Massachusetts. The value of the company's stock was set at a million dollars, and at the first stockholders' meeting held on October 14, 1873, Cyrus Wakefield—who owned virtually the entire stock issue—was elected president. At the outset of the depression, Wakefield was at the pinnacle of his business career. The rattan factory now employed a thousand workers—a five-fold increase since

1863—and covered four acres of land. The buildings contained ten acres of interior floor space and included a four-story brick machine shop and eight large workshops and storehouses. All the wooden structures were painted a distinctive yellowish hue, the color of raw rattan. Two large 250-horsepower steam engines powered the plant's extensive machinery, and the tall brick smokestack dominated the local landscape. The retail showrooms on Boston's Canal Street were filled with the company's popular rattan products: chair caning in different widths; a wide variety of floor mats and matting; baskets of all kinds; window shades; brooms and brushes; wall and fire screens; magazine racks and slipper holders; clothes and rug beaters; corset stays and whip handles; and a newly introduced line of rattan and cane furniture, including cradles and baby carriages.[16] By 1873, Wakefield's speculative investments in north Boston real estate had also paid off; the city had extended Washington Street. Planning to develop a rail terminus for freight trains near the docks, he had purchased large amounts of stock in three regional railroads: the Boston and Maine; the Fitchburg, Nashua, Acton, and Boston Railroads—and, fatefully, the Middlesex Horse Railroad. But with the sudden stock market crash, Wakefield's financial empire, like those of many others, began to unravel quickly. On Sunday, October 26, 1873, at 7:45 in the morning, Cyrus Wakefield, age sixty-two years and eight months, suffered a fatal heart attack while reading the newspaper. His funeral, attended by crowds of his former employees and fellow citizens, was held in his elegant Main Street mansion the following Wednesday. Later, the residents of Wakefield, Massachusetts, gathered at the town hall officially to commemorate their late, lamented benefactor: "The valuable citizen, the prosperous merchant, the progressive leader in ornamental and architectural improvements, the friend and helper of education, the chief promoter of our local industrial pursuits, our munificent namesake, whose numerous and generous benefactions will remain his enduring memorials."[17]

What the townspeople did not know was that Wakefield died bankrupt. The depression had wiped out his personal wealth and in all probability hastened his death. His wife, who had inherited a sizable estate from her father, made up the losses so that the local probate records would not list her husband's true financial status.[18] The Wakefield Rattan Company, chartered just eleven days before its founder's death, survived intact. Without heirs, Wakefield's stock passed to his estate. His executors now had the unenviable task of contending with the rattan business during a deepening national crisis. The economic future of the company—and the town itself—seemed bleak. The loss of Wakefield's "iron will and resolute purpose," his "energy, perseverance, and . . . indomitable courage"[19] seemed to be almost insurmountable.

NOTES
1. A Completed Century, 1826–1926: A History of the Heywood-Wakefield Company (Boston: Printed for the Company, 1926), 12.
2. J. D. Van Slyck, New England Manufacturers and Manufactories (Boston: Van Slyck, 1879), 2:624.
3. Lilley Eaton, Genealogical History of South Reading, Massachusetts . . . from 1639 to 1874 (Boston: Alfred Mudge and Son, 1874), 679.
4. See Richard Saunders, Collecting and Restoring Wicker Furniture (New York: Crown Publishers, 1976), 18; and Catherine Hoover Voorsanger, "Wakefield Rattan Company," in Doreen Bolger Burke, et al., In Pursuit of Beauty; Americans and the Aesthetic Movement (New York: Rizzoli, 1986), 478. Nineteenth-century accounts state his buyers were chairmakers. See D. Hamilton Hurd, History of Middlesex County, Massachusetts . . . (Philadelphia: J. W. Lewis, 1890), 2:744.
5. D. Hamilton Hurd, History of Worcester County, Massachusetts . . . (Philadelphia: J. W. Lewis, 1889), 1:831.
6. John B. Wickersham, A New Phase in Iron Manufacture (New York: J. B. Wickersham, 1855), 31.
7. Gervase Wheeler, Rural Homes; or Sketches of Houses Suited to American Country Life (New York: Charles Scribner, 1851), 199.
8. Ibid.
9. Henry Barnard, Armsmear. The Home, the Arms, and the Armory of Samuel Colt: A Memorial (New York: Alvord, 1866), 266ff.
10. Samuel Colt Papers, Connecticut State Library, Hartford, Conn.
11. Barnard, Armsmear, 271.
12. Eaton, Genealogical History of South Reading, 680.
13. Ibid., 486.
14. The non-rattan goods were shipped as "ballast." See Van Slyck, A History of New England Manufacturers, 2:265.
15. Eaton, Genealogical History of South Reading, 682.
16. Ibid., 487.
17. Ibid., 683.
18. Saunders, Collecting and Restoring Wicker Furniture, 21.
19. Eaton, Genealogical History of South Reading, 683.

CHAPTER TWO

The Great Rivals: Wakefield Rattan Company and Heywood Brothers and Company, 1874–1897

In 1855 Cyrus Wakefield had invited his twenty-one-year-old nephew and namesake, Cyrus Wakefield II, to come and work for him in Boston. Born in rural New York but raised on a Wisconsin farm, the younger Wakefield was delighted to move to the bustling city to work for his uncle, and soon became adept at grading and sorting raw rattan. In 1865, when the elder Wakefield decided to import his own supplies directly from the Far East, he sent his nephew to Singapore, the center of the Oriental rattan trade, to act as his resident agent to ensure that he received only the best qualities. Cyrus II exported not only rattan to Boston but, on his own account, coffee, pepper, tin, and spices. He was apparently content to remain in the Orient, returning only once, in 1870, to marry a young woman from Newburyport. But in 1873, soon after his uncle's untimely death, the anxious directors of the newly organized Wakefield Rattan Company, knowing next to nothing about the business, sent a distress call, requesting his immediate return to assist in running the corporation. He was elected president upon arrival.

The abbreviated minutes of the board of directors' meetings of the Wakefield Rattan Company from 1874 to 1897 provide fascinating glimpses into the corporation's financial history and business management.[1] On February 3, 1874, in response to the recent economic downturn and drop in sales, the directors voted to limit factory production by restricting the daily consumption of rattan for seat caning to eight thousand pounds and reducing the work week from sixty to forty hours. Yet the company's first-quarter profits were surprisingly strong—$59,691.00—and a dividend of five dollars a share was duly declared. In February 1875, with the economy still depressed, the directors authorized layoffs in the Boston showrooms and a further reduction in work hours at the Wakefield plant. Nonetheless, the treasurer confidently estimated sales of a million dollars for the coming year—minus fifty thousand dollars for discounts and losses. The projected expenses for 1875 were recorded as follows:

RATTAN (3 MILLION POUNDS)	$225,000
PAYROLL PER MONTH	$15,000
BOSTON EXPENSES	$75,000
AMERICAN RATTAN COMPANY	
FOR MERCHANDISE	$40,000
ADMINISTRATORS OF CYRUS WAKEFIELD'S ESTATE,	
FOR MERCHANDISE	$40,000
FOR RATTAN, TO SELL	$40,000
CHAIR SEATS, ROCKERS, AND DOWELS	$20,000
COIR WOOL	$35,000
COAL AND OTHER SUPPLIES	$25,000
NEW YORK EXPENSES	$20,000
INTEREST (INSURANCE)	$25,000
ROYALTY EXPENSES	$5,000
TAXES	$20,000
	$750,000
ESTIMATED PROFIT	$200,000
TOTAL	$950,000

This profit estimate proved far too optimistic. The company made only $27,098.62 above expenses during the first quarter—about half the figure for the same period of the previous year. But corporate earnings and credit were sufficient in 1875 for the Wakefield Rattan Company to buy its longtime rival in the cane-splitting business, the American Rattan Company of Fitchburg, Massachusetts. The sudden doubling of industrial facilities necessitated a restructuring of the

Wakefield Rattan Company. Lady's Reception Chair, 1896–97. Reed, wood, and cane. Courtesy of the McLaughlin Collection. Photograph by Kit Latham.

corporate management and the responsibility for daily operations. Cyrus Wakefield II stepped down as president to become the managing director of the Wakefield plant. The directors voted that he and his counterpart at Fitchburg receive an annual salary of five thousand dollars, while the company treasurer would earn ten thousand dollars per annum. Three years later, the directors closed the Fitchburg plant and moved its machinery to Wakefield. Once again, Cyrus Wakefield II changed roles and assumed the presidency.

In 1876, with sales improving, the Wakefield Rattan Company moved its offices and showrooms in Boston from Canal Street to more spacious quarters at 115 Washington Street. But far more important, the firm exhibited an extensive selection of its merchandise that year at the Centennial Exhibition at Philadelphia. The decision to participate at the international fair proved a turning point. Rattan furniture was rising

in popularity and, with its display, the Wakefield Rattan Company was immediately identified as the nation's leader in artistic wicker. The firm's wares were seen by an immense audience. Between May 10 and mid-November 1876, a figure equal to almost one-quarter of the population of the United States—9,789,392 people—made a pilgrimage to the "American Mecca" in Fairmont Park and gazed with awe at thirty-one thousand different exhibits from across the nation and around the globe. The exposition offered Americans a much-needed diversion from their domestic troubles. Patriotism and progress were the much-trumpeted themes. In the nineteenth-century mind, human progress was inexorably linked to the concept of material progress as accomplished through industrialization— the key to Cyrus Wakefield's success. The centerpiece and symbol of the vast show was the mighty Corliss engine, the largest machine in the world. Hailed as "an athlete

Cyrus Wakefield II (1833–1888). *Photograph from* A Completed Century, *1926, courtesy of the National Museum of American Art, Smithsonian Institution.*

in iron and steel," the towering, 680-ton steam engine demonstrated its awesome power by running all the mechanized exhibits in "Machinery Hall." In the exposition's main building—enclosing twenty-one acres of exhibition space—industrial and decorative arts displays from around the world were arranged hierarchically by nation and race. The British, Germans, French, and Americans anchored the exhibit. Other countries and peoples were arrayed outward, according to color of skin and degree of "civilization."

The 1876 exposition presented a vast material universe whose meticulous organization reflected the Victorian obsession with systems of classification and order. Originally, there were to have been ten exhibition departments, each with a hundred divisions. Eventually, they settled on seven basic categories. The Wakefield Rattan Company's display was included in group VII, "Furniture, Upholstery, Wooden-ware, Baskets, etc," and

Wakefield Rattan Company, Rattan Goods, 1878. *Courtesy of the Warshaw Collection of Business Americana, Archives Center, National Museum of American History, Smithsonian Institution.*
This engraving appeared on the cover of the Wakefield Rattan Company's 1878 price list.

located within the American section in the main building. The international awards jury praised all the goods in group VII as "strongly indicative of an increasing desire on the part of the public for something in the way of household furnishing beyond the demands of mere necessity and use." In its opinion, the various displays "mark[ed] an era in popular taste, healthy in its tone and elevating in its character."[2] The Wakefield Rattan Company received one of 326 prizes awarded within the division. It was commended for "original design and superior workmanship in furniture, chairs, and baskets, also for originality in the manufacture of mats and baskets of an otherwise waste material [i.e., cane shavings and pith]; and also for a new form of car seats, durable, clean, and economical."[3] What the firm presented is unrecorded, but the exhibit contained a wide variety of the company's consumer products. An advertisement in the January 1876 issue of *Scribner's Magazine* displays a selection of the firm's "Rattan Goods," while an engraving on the reverse of an 1878 price list records a broader range of merchandise of the sort doubtless viewed by streams of Centennial visitors. A correspondent for a Chicago furniture trade journal commented favorably on the company's display:

An extensive display is made by the Wakefield Rattan Co., Boston, Mass., of chairs, work baskets, boxes, and stands, music stands, centre tables, cribs, in fact every useful thing that rattan can be worked or contorted into. It is an excellent exhibit of thorough

Wakefield Rattan Company, Advertisement, *Scribner's Monthly, January 1876. Courtesy of the Warshaw Collection of Business Americana, Archives Center, National Museum of American History, Smithsonian Institution.*
This is the earliest known depiction of wicker furniture made by Wakefield Rattan. It includes a rocking chair with an esparto-pattern backrest, a footstool, sewing basket, firewood holder, and a large fireplace screen composed of decorative caning.

first-class workmanship, and a gratifying one of what can be done at home in such a line; for over there we have the English and French work, and up yonder at the west end the clumbsy [sic] handling of the Chinese and the Japs. With all this the firm can and do boldly come into competition in completeness and strength of work and in variety of uses to which they adapted the material. With the two latter they of course do not compete in their most delicate and fancy manipulations, but as to some of their patterns have boldly and successfully copied. This, however, seems to have been hardly necessary, for they have produced an abundance of finely worked and original designs.[4]

The correspondent's arrogant remarks notwithstanding, the Japanese exhibit proved tremendously influential on the development of new decorative arts ideals in America as well as sparking an enormous vogue for things Oriental. Mostly, it contained porcelain, metalwork of all kinds, carved ivory, and lacquer ware—but little furniture. On display in the Chinese Imperial Maritime Customs Collection, in the west wing of the great exhibition hall, were numerous examples of ornately carved, gilded, lacquered, and inlaid rosewood furniture. More importantly, there were bamboo recliners and rattan hourglass chairs. It was the first time that large numbers of Americans had an opportunity to take a good look at these indigenous, lightweight chairs from the Far East. The correspondent clearly recognized the strong family resemblance between the delicately caned Wakefield chairs with

Wakefield Rattan Company, Furniture and Basketware Designs, ca. 1875–78. Photograph courtesy of the National Museum of American History, Smithsonian Institution. This sheet of photographs is the earliest register of Wakefield Rattan's furniture designs. Some of the models are closely related to German-inspired rattan furniture made in America in the 1850s and 1860s.

their tightly wrapped legs and their Chinese counterparts and assumed the one had copied the other. At least in part, he was correct. The Wakefield Rattan Company's furniture had been influenced by the design and construction of bamboo and rattan chairs and lounges imported from the Far East. The delicate geometric patterns of caning were indeed Chinese in inspiration—as was the habit of binding the legs and frames with strips of cane. But Cyrus Wakefield, along with his engineers and his designers, had so firmly adapted the Oriental aesthetic to Western needs and industrial technologies that they had transformed Far Eastern rattan into a thoroughly New England material. From the beginning,

the elder Wakefield had known all about Cantonese chairs. After all, his very first—rather lopsided—rattan chair had been modeled on the distinctive hourglass design. He may also have seen examples offered for sale in Boston's East India goods stores. Possibly he had even bought one. Perhaps Wakefield's father-in-law, the retired sea captain, had been to Canton and brought home a souvenir hourglass chair that Wakefield subsequently may have seen.

It is difficult to determine precisely when the Wakefield Rattan Company began to produce furniture. While Cyrus Wakefield likely experimented by wrapping conventional wood chairs with cane before moving his operations to South Reading in 1855, it is improbable that he started manufacturing chairs, tables, and work stands before about 1870. Initially, he and his Irish workmen had concentrated on making rattan skirt hoops and baskets, and then, in the 1860s, on splitting cane and weaving cocoa mats and matting on

William Houston's inventive mechanical looms. But by 1873, the year of Wakefield's death, the factory was making a variety of artistic chairs, sofas, and sewing baskets. While few of the very earliest pieces have survived, there are records of what the first production models looked like. About 1875 to 1878, while still headquartered on Canal Street, the Wakefield Rattan Company published a sheet of diminutive, numbered photographs that served as a rudimentary trade catalogue. It is the earliest known register of their furniture designs.[5] Seat frames and legs were manufactured from hardwood, but the superstructures were composed of bent rattan while the resilient backrests were fashioned of decorative caning. All the structural components were tightly wrapped with thick strands of binding cane in the Chinese fashion. The broad back supports—certainly the most decorative features of the designs—were woven either in the intricate "star" pattern or in the radiating "esparto" weaves popularized by immigrant Germans. (Samuel Colt's workers or their German compatriots must have found employment in Wakefield. It is unlikely that the Irish basketweavers and cane splitters had the talent or experience to plait the delicate networks.) An alternate, nonwoven seat back employed rods of rattan, bent, twisted, and lashed to other vertical members to create a simple openwork design, the "double-back" pattern, that was essentially Gothic in inspiration and much like the Berrians' bentwood-inspired furniture. In all, the Wakefield Rattan Company's sheet reproduced forty-five chair designs for adults and fourteen for children, five reclining chairs, two lounges, and eleven sofas and tête-à-têtes. One of the sofas was convertible: its back could be lowered to create a broad sleeping surface. It was just the thing on which to stretch out and wile away a muggy New England summer's after-

noon. Other sofas have boldly arched crest-rails and dramatic, curvilinear backrests suitable for porch sitting or use indoors in a summer cottage or country parlor. There were also swinging cribs and cradles with wood rockers, a diversity of round and rectangular tables, magazine and firewood holders, so-called wall pockets for storing letters or newspapers, rug beaters, an assortment of baskets, both utilitarian and decorative, and all manner of sewing, music, and other useful stands. Some stands had sides composed of palisade-like arrangements of vertical reed sticks—the most distinctive and short-lived of the original Wakefield design motifs. The miniscule photographs reveal a diversity of artistic furnishings. By the time of the Centennial, the Wakefield Rattan Company was clearly the preeminent manufacturer of rattan furniture in America.

In 1876, however, a surprise

Wakefield Rattan Company, "Double-Back" Pattern Chair, 1881. Courtesy of Frog Alley Antiques/Merry P. Gilbert, New York City. With its looped rods of rattan bound by strips of cane, the "double-back" pattern was one of the Wakefield firm's earliest popular designs.

competitor appeared in the little town of Gardner, Massachusetts, fifty-eight miles northwest of Boston, by the name of Heywood Brothers and Company. After decades of building an enviable reputation as a leading maker of mass-produced Windsor, bentwood, and Hitchcock chairs, the firm had suddenly turned to fabricating chairs from rattan as well. The Heywoods had long purchased supplies of chair caning from the Wakefield plant and doubtless had enviously eyed its early success with rattan furniture. For the next twenty-one years, these two Massachusetts companies aggressively competed with one another. So intense was their rivalry, it shaped the course of nineteenth-century American wicker. No other firms matched their output, and their commercial competition stimulated new developments in design, production methods, and materials; they kept

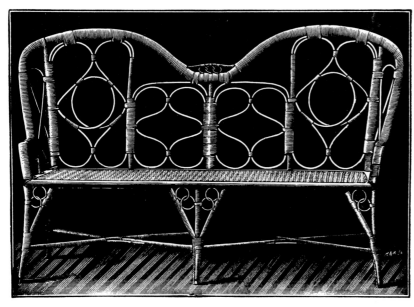

Wakefield Rattan Company, "Rustic High Back" Settee, 1881. Courtesy of Frog Alley Antiques/Merry P. Gilbert, New York City.
Although illustrated in the 1881 catalogue, this design originated in the early 1870s and is related to 1850s bentwood-inspired rattan furniture. By 1884 the "Rustic" pattern had been dropped from production, replaced by more up-to-date designs with decoratively caned backrests.

prices low, inspired imitators, and, more important, helped create a nationwide demand for artistic wicker furnishings.

The basic outline of the Heywood brothers' success story was similar to that of Wakefield: through hard work, perseverance, commitment to mechanization, and shrewd business management, obscure New England farmboys built an industrial enterprise with a worldwide reputation for excellence. Their story begins in 1826, when brothers Walter, Levi, and Benjamin Heywood started manufacturing simple wood chairs in a shed on their father's farm. Successful in their venture, they soon moved out of the shed and into a larger shop across the road, where fifteen to twenty workers were employed. They soon prospered and sent their entrepreneurial brother Levi to Boston to market their expanding line of wood chairs. In 1834 disaster struck. The shop caught fire and burned to the ground. Undaunted, the Heywoods immediately established a small factory at the outlet of nearby Crystal Lake, where a mill stream powered a whining circular saw and wood lathes. In 1835 Levi rejoined his brothers—who now included young William Heywood—and for the next forty-seven years he remained the single driving force behind the firm's constant growth. Levi Heywood clearly foresaw the future, and that future was mechanized. Utterly committed to industrialization, he insisted on buying every new piece of woodworking machinery he discovered. If he couldn't find what he wanted, he designed it. His obsession with machinery drove his sibling partners to distraction and, to escape what they presumed would be financial ruin, they dissolved the original company. One brother

Levi Heywood (1800–88). *Photograph from Van Slyck,* New England Manufacturers, *1879, courtesy of the National Museum of American Art, Smithsonian Institution.*

went on to Fitchburg, where he established the rival Walter Heywood Chair Company, later to be an important wicker manufacturer. But Levi was to be joined by a still younger brother, Seth, and then by sons and nephews, his own and his brothers' sons-in-law, and finally by members of a third generation of Heywoods.

For decades, Levi relentlessly pursued new systems and technologies of mass production, constantly adding or originating new circular, jig, and fret saws, lathes of all kinds, planes, sanders, drills, carving machines, and mortise and dovetail cutting devices. By the late 1870s, seventeen pieces of machinery were used to fashion the parts for a single chair. Among Levi's most successful engineering feats was the design and construction of powerful new machinery to bend steamed wood. After a trip to the Gardner factory, Franz Thonet, the son of the Austrian inventor of mass-produced bentwood furniture, wrote: "I must tell you candidly that you have the best machinery for bending wood that I

NEW PATTERNS OF RATTAN CHAIRS
FOR TRIMMING AND CUSHIONS.

MADE BY THE
Wakefield Rattan Company.
FULL DISPLAY AT THEIR SALESROOMS,

115 Washington Street, BOSTON. | 231 State Street, CHICAGO.
814 Broadway, NEW-YORK. | 38 Geary Street, SAN FRANCISCO.
Sold also by all leading furniture dealers. Complete catalogue sent upon application to above address.

Wakefield Rattan Company, Advertisement for Reed Chairs, Scribner's Monthly, *November 1879. Courtesy of the Library of Congress.*
In 1879, Wakefield Rattan was the first to introduce furniture woven from reed, the fibrous inner pith of rattan previously used for basket making or decorative details. Unlike cane, reed was absorbent and could be easily painted or stained. The Wakefield factory offered the new line in various wood tones and metallic colors, including gold, copper, and bronze.

ever saw."[6] This was high praise from the man who ran *Gebruder Thonet* in Vienna, then the world's largest chair company. But the single most important innovation at Gardner had to do not with bending wood but with caning seats.

In the 1860s and early 1870s Heywood Brothers and Company purchased its supplies of caning from the Wakefield and the American Rattan companies. Workers would routinely drop off bundles of cane and stacks of machine-made maple or hickory seats at workers' homes in Gardner, or at neighboring farms where women and children handwove the cane mesh strand by strand. But about 1875 this process of "farming out" piecework came to a halt as Levi finally mechanized all facets of his manufacturing process. With the able assistance of Gardner A. Watkins, a renowned Vermont inventor and mechanical genius who

came to work for him in 1870,[7] Levi first designed and installed his own rattan-splitting and cane-trimming machines. Importing bundles of raw rattan from Singapore through a New York agent, he not only processed his own cane but soon sold bulk supplies to local chairmakers. At their November 1875 meeting, the directors of the Wakefield Rattan Company learned to their surprise that Heywood Brothers and Company was not only producing its own cane but selling it, too, and voted to stop immediately the discount price they had been giving the Gardner, Massachusetts, firm. Heywood and Watkins next constructed their own updated power looms to weave strands of spliced cane into dense sheets of webbed fabric.[8] However, the firm's major engineering breakthrough, which placed it ahead in its competition with Wakefield Rattan had oc-

Wakefield Rattan Company, Reed Goods from the ca. 1880 Illustrated Catalogue and Price List of Rattan and Reed Furniture. *Courtesy of the Warshaw Collection of Business Americana, Archives Center, National Museum of American History, Smithsonian Institution. Wakefield Rattan's reed goods first appeared in an undated illustrated catalogue.*

curred when Watkins invented the revolutionary automatic channeling machine. The purpose of this ingenious device was to rout grooves in mass-produced wood seat frames so that webbed caning could be mechanically inserted. In four rapid revolutions, Watkins's new channeling machine cut clean, precise, half-inch grooves into each Heywood frame. Nearby on the assembly line, a worker using a steel press stamped out sections of webbing the size of chair seats then dipped them in a steam-heated water tank to loosen the weave. Another member of the assembly

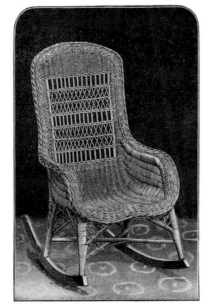

Above: Photograph of the Entrance Hall, James Wadsworth House, Geneseo, New York, ca. 1882. *Photograph from* Artistic Homes, *1882–83, courtesy of the National Museum of American Art, Smithsonian Institution. In the early 1880s, the opulent houses of the wealthy often contained willow basket chairs imported from England or Madeira. American-made reed furniture appealed more to middle-class householders.*

Right: Heywood Brothers and Company, Reed "Comfort" Rocker from the 1883 Illustrated Catalogue of Rattan and Reed Furniture, and Baby Carriages. *Courtesy of the National Museum of American History, Smithsonian Institution. The "comfort" rocker was introduced by Heywood Brothers in 1881. A soft basketweave roll ran around the outside of the chair, cushioning arms, head, and thighs. It was one of the most popular rocking chair designs, adopted by nearly all wicker manufacturers.*

team used a hose fitted with a valve-tipped, metal nozzle and swiftly filled the channel with a bead of hot glue. The wooden frame with its glue-filled groove and the piece of damp webbing were then passed to the operator of the crimping press, another of Watkins's patented inventions. He placed the section of cane—whose edges extended three-quarters of an inch beyond the channel—over the seat space and activated the machine. A sharp brass crimping ring was pressed down into the groove, forcibly inserting the rim of the caning into the circular channel. From here, the seat was immediately delivered to the work-man in charge of the spline and embossing press. This double-geared behemoth weighed 5,400 pounds and when operated, drove a triangular strip of wood deep into the groove, tightly wedging the damp webbing in place. The press also embossed the face of the seat around the outer edge of the spline, producing a perfect joint with an attractive bead. On the underside, it stamped the appropriate patent data.[9] The entire process, including the time needed to weave the webbing, took four minutes—a fraction of the time it took to plait the mesh by hand. The caned seat was then stored, to be used at the time of chair assembly. By then, the caning had dried out and shrunk, creating a durable, drum-tight surface. With the appearance of the automatic channeling machine and the related industrial presses, the hand-caning of seats for mass-produced chairs suddenly became an obsolete and increasingly costly process. Thereafter, the hand-caned seat was employed only by less industrialized workshops or by those who, for aesthetic reasons, preferred the traditional look of the open mesh. (In time, even this age-old pattern would be duplicated by machine.) The farm families around Gardner soon felt the loss of employment: understandably, they had come to rely on the piecework. It is difficult to determine when webbed chair seats came into widespread use, but by 1879 the Wakefield Rattan Company had started to set them into their own chairs.

In the late 1870s, just 467 workers were employed in the twenty-two buildings that comprised Heywood Brothers and Company's Gardner factory complex, far fewer than the one thousand at work in the more labor-intensive and diversified Wakefield operations. Many of the Gardner employees were recent Irish immigrants. Levi and his agents would often approach likely candidates as they disembarked from emigrant ships in Boston, offer them a job on the spot, buy them a train ticket, check their baggage through to Gardner, and tell the newcomers to report to the factory as soon as they were settled. In Gardner, they crowded into a neighborhood known locally as "The Patch"—as in "a patch of old Ireland"—and mixed warily at work with the French Canadians and Scandinavians, and later, the Italians, Poles, and Lithuanians who made up Heywood Brothers' increasingly multinational work force. Because of his extensive use of labor-saving machinery and mass production techniques—and his greater reliance on wood—Heywood needed fewer employees than Wakefield. With their steam-powered devices, Heywood's workers annually produced 450,000 chairs in the late 1870s—a truly astonishing number. The vast majority required minimal handwork, were inexpensive, and were often shipped out unassembled. The average price was $1.25, and in 1878 the firm sold seven hundred thousand dollars' worth of them.[10] It is no wonder that, along with several other resident chair-making companies, Gardner came to be known in the early 1900s as the "Chair Capital of the World."

Even though wooden chairs had been their sole enterprise since 1826, Heywood and his partners decided in 1876 to add a line of rattan chairs.[11] They correctly foresaw that wicker would be a money-maker: after all, the Wakefield Rattan Company's early success was proof enough. At first, these woven chairs constituted only a small proportion of their yearly output. However, by 1878, production and sales had risen to the point where Heywood Brothers proudly devoted a full page of its newspaper-sized trade catalogue to illustrations of rattan chairs.[12] Many items had elaborately braided "esparto" backs. It seems logical to assume that Levi had recruited immigrants from basket-weaving centers in Prussia or Bavaria, or employed some of Colt's wickerworkers. According to one observer in 1878, Heywood Brothers' wicker chairs were "tasteful and beautiful." Their "light and delicate" frames were made in the factory's wood shop and then carried to a large room above the paint shop, where, in the commentator's words, "men, women, and boys . . . cloth[ed] them, in the beautiful garb, with which they are adorned."[13] Like the Wakefield Rattan Company's chairs, Heywood Brothers' early models relied on intricate caning, architectonic cresting, and lines of looped rattan running up the sides and across the top of the rectilinear chair backs for decoration. Without a careful comparison of illustrations in trade literature, it is difficult to distinguish a Wakefield chair from a Heywood rattan chair. Wicker designs were neither copyrighted nor patented, and each firm's models differed only in minor details.

Little rattan furniture has survived from the 1870s. If the broad panels of intricate, ornamental caning in the backrests were damaged, it was difficult and expensive to have them repaired. Pets clawed or chewed the delicate webs of cane,

Chicago Rattan and Reed Company,
Advertisement, American Furniture
Gazette, *April 1885. Courtesy of the
Chicago Historical Society.*
*Chicago Rattan and Reed was the largest local
wicker manufacturer in the mid-1880s. Workers
produced 140 designs, including ornate chairs
with flower and fan motif backrests.*

the Wakefield firm began fabricating basketweave chairs and sofas out of reed, the inner core of rattan. These designs with their distinctive four-over-one, diagonal fitching weave first appeared in late 1879, and were described as "New Patterns" in a December advertisement placed in *Scribner's Magazine*. The long, thin strips of fibrous pith had already been used in the firm's line of basketware. Rods of pith had also been employed in the early Gothic-inspired "double back" designs or to create the ornate S-curves inserted in the center of "esparto" backs. The Wakefield Rattan Company's first full line of reed furniture was showcased in an undated, illustrated catalogue and price list entitled "Rattan and Reed Furniture," published around 1880. Previous price lists, dated 1878 and 1879, referred only to "Rattan Furniture." Inside the new sales catalogue the company printed, for the uninitiated, an explanatory statement: "The sign [R] against number in Price-List, or the words 'Extra in Colors,' indicates that these goods are made from Reeds or Pith, and may be finished in imitation of Ebony, Cherry, Mahogany, or Cocobola."[14]

Furniture made from unsplit rattan could not be easily colored: the smooth, glossy surface could

children stuck fingers or pointed objects through the mesh, and clumsy adults broke the strands one way or another. Once damaged, a chair's fate was sealed. Partly to provide a sturdier alternative to delicately caned rattan furniture,

Factory of Heywood Brothers and Company's Chicago
Subsidiary, Heywood and Morrill Rattan Company, *1895.
Courtesy of Steve Poole and Robert Evans.*

Factory Complex of Heywood Brothers and Company,
Gardner, Massachusetts, *1895. Courtesy of Steve Poole and
Robert Evans.*

neither absorb stain nor permanently hold a coating of enamel paint. Every time a painted chair knocked against a hard object, an enamel chip popped off, exposing the buff-colored cane underneath. With the sheath of cane removed, however, the absorbent reed could either be stained in popular hardwood tones, or painted in popular metallic hues. The catalogue listed these alternative colors: "These goods are also finished in three shades of Bronze, Light and Dark Copper and Rich Gold." It cost one dollar extra to have a chair factory stained, two dollars for a sofa or tête-à-tête. To order furniture bronzed, coppered, or gilded was much more expensive: ladies' chairs, two dollars extra; gent's three dollars; and sofas and tête-à-têtes, from six to ten dollars, depending on the style or size. Metallic shades, especially gold, would remain popular color options through the 1890s. In its unadorned state, reed furniture was the color of light straw. It was shellacked before it left the factory to provide a dirt-resistant, protective coating. But artistic homemakers in the 1880s generally added bright cushions and often trimmed both natural and painted reed chairs with colorful silk ribbons threaded through the spokes. One well-known tastemaker criticized the manner in which rattan furniture was "becushioned and bedizened into hopeless vulgarity." Wicker sofas and chairs, she declared, "are only admissible as naturel [sic] and should stand upon their own merits."[15] But the author voiced a minority opinion. Most buyers enjoyed trimming and painting their reed chairs.

Reed immediately caught on with other wicker manufacturers. Surprised by Wakefield's innovation, Heywood Brothers soon rushed their own line of basket-weave reed furniture into production. On September 1, 1881, they published a separate price list for the novelties to supplement their 1881–82 rattan furniture trade catalogue that was already in print.[16] The models were given names of fashionable resorts and Ivy League colleges—Nahant, Saratoga, Cape May, Harvard, Yale, and Princeton—to increase their appeal to middle-class consumers. When reed suddenly became useful, the children of Gardner were keenly disappointed. There were no more exciting bonfires. Up to that point, Heywood Brothers' workers had regularly burned mountains of cast-off reed and cane shavings in great roaring fires. Among other wicker manufacturers to shortly follow Heywood Brothers' example was a Chicago firm, C. W. H. Fred-

erick. It updated its own product line in 1883, publishing an extensive catalogue of "Rattan, Reed, and Willow-Ware" designed to capture the burgeoning western market for wicker. Throughout the 1880s, "rattan" almost always precedes

Heywood Brothers and Company, Baby Carriage from the 1883 Illustrated Catalogue. Courtesy of the National Museum of American History, Smithsonian Institution. Heywood Brothers and Company was among the first to produce extensive lines of fancy wicker baby carriages. Models introduced in 1883 included several shaped like canoes and rowboats. As the century progressed, they became increasingly ornate.

Child in a Reed Baby Carriage "Pulled" by a Goose, ca. 1890. Photograph courtesy of the Prints and Photographs Division, Library of Congress.

nacular willow basket chair fashionable in England during the second half of the century. The transatlantic models in all likelihood had influenced the Wakefield Rattan Company's initial decision to introduce their own versions. English willow chairs were stylish imports in the early 1880s. In photographs of lavishly decorated interiors of America's rich and famous published in a two-volume illustrated book, *Artistic Homes* (1883–84), there are many examples of rather crude willow basket chairs from England. But they may have come from the balmy island of Madeira, often visited by wealthy American invalids in search of salubrious climates and famous for vernacular chairs made from stiff willow rods. The examples in *Artistic Homes* are not American-made reed chairs; the latticework is too wide.

During the early 1880s, both the Wakefield Rattan Company and Heywood Brothers—and by extension, the fledgling wicker industry itself—underwent rapid growth and transformation. The economic depression sparked by the Panic

Heywood Brothers and Company, Carriage from the 1886 Illustrated Catalogue of Wood Chairs, Rattan and Reed Furniture, and Baby Carriages. *Courtesy of the Ohio Historical Society.*

"reed" in the titles of manufacturers' trade catalogues. Sometimes reed furniture was illustrated in a separate section at the back. But by the early 1890s, the roles were reversed: reed predominates, both in the title and in the manufacturing process.

When it first appeared, reed furniture was simpler in design and construction than rattan furniture. By comparison, it was austere and functional: there were no intricate panels of star caning in the back supports or interlocking decorative loops and rings between leg braces or running around the tops of chairs or sofas. Instead, the sides and backrests were simple, basketwork grids composed of bands of

widely separated, diagonally fitched spokes in a one-over-four pattern alternating with pairs of broadly spaced vertical spokes. The divisions were created by tight, horizontal pairing weaves that separated the spokes into their constituent bands and contributed to structural rigidity. In comparison to taut panels of decorative caning, the open-weave backs of reed chairs and sofas were more springy and comfortable. Aprons and skirts were gently arched to provide structural support, and edges were covered by strips of decorative braid. The furniture was also much more relaxed in appearance and feeling. The obvious inspiration for 1880s reed furniture was the verof 1873 had ended and demand for wicker skyrocketed. The Wakefield Rattan Company advertised in November 1879 that it had sold a cumulative value of two million dollars' worth of rattan furniture.[17] Prices were not low—a ladies' rocker with an "esparto" back cost sixteen dollars, while a fancy "Extra Ring Back" sofa cost forty dollars—but even so, the quantity sold was clearly immense. In 1878 Clarence Cook, the definitive tastemaker of the American Aesthetic movement, confidently declared: "It is well known . . . what a prosperity the Wakefield manufacture of rattan furniture is enjoying, and it deserves it too."[18]

With the popularity of rattan furniture steadily on the rise in the 1880s, the battle between the Wakefield Rattan Company and Heywood Brothers and Company now began in earnest. At the beginning of the decade, the Wakefield firm displayed its wares not only in its Boston salesrooms but in stores rented or purchased in New York, Chicago, and San Francisco. Hey-

Children Playing with a Wicker Go-Cart, or Stroller, *ca. 1900. Photograph courtesy of the Prints and Photographs Division, Library of Congress.*

American Rattan Works, St. Louis, Missouri, Baby Carriage from the 1897 Catalogue of Children's Carriages. *Photograph courtesy of A Summer Place.*

wood Brothers had established similar exclusive outlets in New York, Philadelphia, San Francisco, and Baltimore, where they sold wicker as well as wood furniture. Heywood Brothers' San Francisco warehouse received its first delivery of rattan furniture in 1882. In 1884, soon after the completion of the Northern Pacific Railroad, the Pacific coast store opened a branch in Portland, Oregon. A second California branch of Heywood Brothers was established two years later in Los Angeles, then a boomtown with a soaring population. Until 1886, when it opened its first store in Boston, Heywood Brothers and Company's rattan and reed furniture was sold exclusively in the commonwealth's capital by Paine's Furniture Company. Wholesale orders from New England retailers were otherwise easily filled from the firm's headquarters in

Gardner, Massachusetts, which was well served by railroads. Heywood Brothers' furnishings reached a surprisingly wide audience. From the late 1860s their wood chairs had been exported through New York to countries bordering the Mediterranean, to the West Indies, South America, and even far-off Australia. Simpler versions of their reed chairs were produced exclusively for the export market. They were shipped knocked-down and assembled overseas. By 1893 Heywood Brothers had opened a large store on Queen Victoria Street in London that showcased their fancy wicker in display windows. In cities where it had no established outlets of its own, the Wakefield Rattan Company also retailed its merchandise through "first-class" furniture dealers. Homeowners were also encouraged to write for free catalogues and price lists, and the

Wakefield Rattan Company, Wakefield, Massachusetts, Settee, Model 456, dated April 1880, rattan, wood, and caning. Courtesy of A Summer Place. Photograph by Kit Latham.

company even advertised that it would custom make furniture to clients' own designs. In 1882, production facilities were expanded at the Wakefield plant when a large, four-story brick factory was constructed to replace the original wooden main building which had burned the previous year. By 1885 there were twenty-four factories and storehouses on the premises. It would have been difficult for Cyrus Wakefield to have imagined such a large and sprawling complex when he first started out in South Reading thirty years before.

In 1882, rival Heywood Brothers and Company underwent major changes. After the deaths of Levi and his son Charles that year,

brother Seth retired. The firm's original generation of founders had gone, leaving one son and two sons-in-law to guide the family business. Like Cyrus Wakefield, Levi Heywood had been a model Victorian philanthropist, financing local schools and college students. His children continued his largess. In 1886 Levi's surviving son and daughter built and endowed a Romanesque-style library in his memory in downtown Gardner. It was constructed no more than a hundred yards from the original shed where the young Heywood brothers first made wood chairs. Public spiritedness proved a family trait. A nephew would later donate a hospital to the town, and a grandson would add a fancy public bathhouse. Levi Heywood had also been active in political affairs. In 1853 he had been a member of the Massachusetts constitutional

convention, and in 1871 was elected to the legislature. With the death of the firm's longtime chief executive, Seth's energetic son, Henry, was elected president, a decision that inaugurated a new

Heywood Brothers and Company, Gardner, Massachusetts, Music Stand, ca. 1883–86, rattan, wood, and caning. Private collection. Photograph by Kit Latham.

era. During his tenure, the manufacture and sale of rattan and reed furniture was steadily emphasized. Early on, Henry Heywood decided to extend his firm's operations westward and establish a strong presence in booming Chicago.

In the aftermath of the Civil War, numerous furniture-making companies moved to or were started in the city on Lake Michigan. Timber was plentiful, and the constant expansion of tracks from the Chicago railhead ensured that manufactured goods could be distributed easily to growing markets in the west. From the outset, Chicago's furniture factories employed the latest in steam-powered woodworking machinery. Quantity far surpassed quality as demand for home furnishings accelerated with increasing settlement throughout the Midwest. By 1919 Chicago was the leading furniture manufacturing center in North America; in 1925 it had become the world's largest. Germans formed an important segment of the early immigrant population. With their basket-weaving heritage, they founded willow-ware workshops in Chicago as early as the mid-1850s. Although willow was native to Illinois, Indiana, and Wisconsin, it was not cultivated by local farmers, and Chicago willow-ware manufacturers had to import most of their osier stock from Kentucky, a long-established American basketware center, or all the way from Germany, a major exporter of fine, processed willow rods. The customs duty on the imported material was exorbitant—thirty-five percent above cost. But with inadequate local stocks, the Chicago weavers simply had to pay the tax

Heywood Brothers and Company, Gardner, Massachusetts, Display Cabinet, 1890s, rattan, wood, caning, and pigment. Courtesy of A Summer Place. Photograph by Kit Latham.

to obtain the best grades of basket willow. Most of the early Chicago willow-ware factories were small, employing about five workers and turning out utilitarian and decorative baskets. The disastrous Chicago fire of 1871, however, wiped out the willow-ware industry. Not a

workshop survived. But an enormous demand for furnishings developed as Chicago was rapidly rebuilt from the ashes and soon the willow factories were re-established and expanded. In the mid-1870s, when western farmers did realize that osiers were a profitable cash

C. W. H. Frederick and Son, Chicago, Fancy Willow Work Stand from the 1883 Catalogue of Rattan, Reed, and Willow-Ware. *Courtesy of the Warshaw Collection of Business Americana, Archives Center, National Museum of American History, Smithsonian Institution.*

crop, they began to cultivate willow. As a result, the local production of willow furniture increased dramatically. Chicago chair designs were less elaborate than Colt's willow-ware, but in the time-honored German fashion, seat backs were braided nets of elastic osiers. A reporter noted in 1877 that the artistic quality of Chicago willow-ware was high, affording "a relief to the sameness in [wood] furniture which now prevails."[19]

In 1871 German-born Charles W. H. Frederick, who had joined Matthias Tillmann's early Chicago willow-ware company as a journeyman weaver six years before, became a full partner in the new firm of Tillmann and Frederick. An innovative designer, he is credited with making, in 1873, Chicago's first rattan chair. Soon Frederick was combining flexible rattan rods imported from the East Coast with locally grown willow branches.

Tillmann retired in 1880, and the new enterprise, C. W. H. Frederick and Company, began manufacturing separate lines of rattan and willow furniture. Three years later, it added reed chairs. In the 1880s Frederick imported large quantities of rattan from Singapore through brokers in New York who shipped boxcar loads west by rail. He not only used the material himself but established a lucrative wholesale trade, catering to the needs of western chair caners. By 1884 the company had thirty workers and was manufacturing a wide variety of functional items in willow, rattan, and reed. But active as he was, Frederick was not the city's largest manufacturer of rattan furnishings. The Chicago Rattan and Reed Company, formed in 1880 as the successor to an earlier willow-ware firm, was the leader. It, too, imported raw material directly from the Far East, and in 1882 went Frederick one better by installing cane-splitting machines in its plant. Business was so brisk that in 1886 the company moved to a larger factory where a hundred workers fabricated some 140 different chair designs for children and adults. Most of its rattan furnishings were sold to customers in the West who were able to save the cost of shipping goods by rail from eastern manufacturers. Other local firms active in the mid-1880s—before the leading Easterners set up production facilities in Chicago—included the

Western Rattan Company, known for its wide assortment of rattan and reed rocking chairs; George J. Schmidt and Brothers, manufacturers of colored willow furniture and rattan chairs; and the smaller Valley City Rattan Company.[20]

Cyrus Wakefield II recognized that he would be shut out of the lucrative western market unless he substantially increased the company's meager activities in Chicago. In 1883 he moved the Wakefield Rattan Company's Chicago store from its small State Street quarters to more spacious showrooms at 144–46 Wabash Avenue. For its part, Heywood Brothers and Company organized a whole new subsidiary enterprise, the Heywood and Morrill Rattan Company of Chicago in 1884. At first, it operated a small factory at Washington and Union Streets. Although they were fierce rivals in the East, in 1887 Heywood Brothers and Wake-

The Clipper Ship *Hoogly* Unloading a Cargo of Singapore Rattan on Boston's Constitution Wharf, ca. 1886. *Photograph courtesy of The Metropolitan Museum of Art, The Elisha Whittelsey Collection, the Elisha Whittelsey Fund, 1957. (57.573.7 p.3) Privately owned by Cyrus Wakefield II, the Hoogly regularly made the trip between Singapore Straits Settlement and Boston carrying huge cargoes of rattan to be made into chair caning, matting, and furniture at the Wakefield factory. It was only one of a small fleet of ships chartered by Wakefield Rattan to deliver raw materials.*

field Rattan Company decided to combine forces and set up a joint manufacturing venture in order to conquer the western market. Representatives from Wakefield and from Heywood-Morrill met in Chicago to look for available factory sites. According to a Heywood descendant, however, the rivalry between the two was just too strong to maintain an alliance:

The first day's search was fruitless, so it was decided to renew the quest the following day. The next morning, however, the Wakefield men left early, found a plant and informed the Heywood representatives that the building was so satisfactory that they would purchase it independently and operate it themselves. After the storm subsided, Henry Heywood and Amos Morrill of Heywood Brothers and Company found a plant to their liking. . . . Competition was keener than ever during the years following this Chicago episode.[21]

The Wakefield Rattan Company moved into its Robey Street factory late in 1887 and the following year bought out C. W. H. Frederick and Company, installing Charles Frederick as the experienced resident manager of the new plant. In 1888 Heywood and Morrill decided to build its own large brick factory at the muddy intersection of Taylor and Rockwell Streets, at the edge of town. During the following decade, their rattan works was to be the most industrious wicker factory in the United States, employing fifteen hundred workers. They produced more rattan and reed furnishings than those of the parent firm. The factory also manufactured wood chairs. One reason why the Heywood-Morrill plant was so productive was that its immediate pool of consumers exploded in size. Between 1870 and 1890 the population of Chicago soared from three hundred thousand to one million residents, and cities throughout the Midwest also experienced enormous growth.

In addition to rattan and reed furniture, Heywood and Morrill produced a line of fancy wicker baby carriages. In the mid-1880s the Gardner, Massachusetts, plant had been among the first to manufacture an extensive line of reed carriages. These decorative vehicles caught on so quickly that within years, virtually every large wicker factory was producing elaborately woven, upholstered prams with attached silk parasols. Their popularity was so great in the 1890s that some companies were formed to manufacture nothing but ornate baby carriages. In 1902 annual sales in California were reported to be ten thousand strong.[22] Another Heywood Brothers innovation that delighted consumers was the "comfort rocker." Introduced in about 1881, this reed easy chair was molded to the sitter's body: the seat and back were woven into a con-tinuous, supporting curve. A hollow basketweave roll ran right around the chair, cushioning the sitter's thighs, arms, and head. It was one of the most comfortable and popular of all wicker designs. It, too, was soon part of every manufacturer's line of rockers, and the distinctive design lasted into the 1920s. The story of its invention is plausible—and charming. One winter afternoon, two rattan workers on their way home from the

The Wakefield Rattan Company's Factory Complex at Wakefield, Massachusetts, 1896. *Photograph from* Proceedings of the 250th Anniversary of the Ancient Town of Redding, *1896, courtesy of the National Museum of American Art, Smithsonian Institution.*
By 1896, the eleven-acre industrial complex at Wakefield, Massachusetts, included thirty buildings. Five were large, four-story brick factories devoted to cane and reed splitting, furniture making, rug and mat weaving, and woodworking.

Wakefield Rattan Company, Settee from the Supplement to the Illustrated Catalogue of 1890. *Courtesy of Frog Alley Antiques/Merry P. Gilbert, New York City.*

Heywood Brothers and Company, Gardner, Massachusetts, White-Painted Fireplace Screen, Model 4428, ca. 1894–95, rattan, wood, and paint. Courtesy of A Summer Place. Photograph by Kit Latham.

Gardner factory began playfully to push each other into snowbanks. After picking himself up, one looked at the rounded imprint his backside left in the deep snow. In seeing his contour, the idea for the comfort rocker was born.[23]

In the 1880s the Wakefield Rattan Company had one distinct advantage over Heywood Brothers. Wakefield owned a huge clipper ship that could rapidly transport enormous cargoes of rattan directly from Singapore to Boston. The sleek, three-masted vessel, owned privately by Cyrus Wakefield II, was christened the *Hoogly*, after the estuary of the same name at the mouth of the Ganges River in

Bengal, India. A detailed engraving depicting the unloading of the *Hoogly*'s cargo on Boston's Constitution Wharf was published in a Wakefield trade catalogue about 1886. The caption accompanying the print describes the bustling scene: "The celebrated clipper ship 'Hoogly' owned by Cyrus Wakefield & Co. as she appears discharging a cargo of Rattans at Constitution Wharf, Boston, after a voyage of sixteen thousand miles from India via Cape of Good Hope. . . . She has landed the largest cargoes of Rattan ever brought to America; is noted for her quick passages, and the fine condition in which her cargoes are delivered."[24] Aside from the *Hoogly*, the Wakefield firm regularly chartered other vessels to deliver its supplies.

Since his days as a rattan trader in Singapore, Cyrus Wakefield II

had maintained a keen commercial interest in the Far East. After returning in 1873, he had continued to conduct an extensive trade in Oriental goods under the name of Wakefield and Company, with stores in Boston and New York. According to the minutes of the board of directors of the Wakefield Rattan Company, the corporation first contracted with Cyrus II and his business partner, D. G. Bacon, to deliver "first class rattans" at a

Heywood Brothers and Wakefield Company, Gardner, Massachusetts, Lady's Reception Chair, Model 6055, (full view and back detail), ca. 1898–1910, rattan, wood, and caning. Private collection. Photographs by Kit Latham.

Wakefield Rattan Company, Wakefield, Massachusetts, Tête-à-Tête, Model 3458, ca. 1895, rattan, wood, caning, and pigment. Courtesy of Richard Moulton. Photograph by Kit Latham.

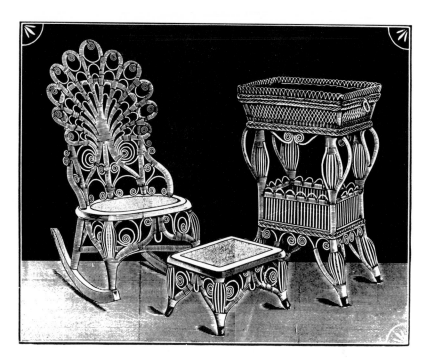

Gendron Iron Wheel Company, Toledo, Ohio, Sewing Set from the 1892 Catalogue of Reed Furniture and Bamboo Novelties. *Courtesy of the Warshaw Collection of Business Americana, Archives Center, National Museum of American History, Smithsonian Institution.*
In the early 1890s, wicker designs became increasingly ornate, and suites of furniture, such as this sewing set, were introduced. The Gendron Iron Wheel Company of Toledo displayed their fancy wicker at the World's Columbian Exhibition held in Chicago in 1893.

price of one-and-three-quarters cents a pound for a period of one year beginning July 1, 1882. The contract was renewed until Cyrus II's sudden death in January 1888, when Temple R. Fay of Boston offered to deliver to the Wakefield firm "what rattan you may need in your business, at 10 percent advance on actual rates of freight." Fay immediately became indispensable to the business and in late 1889 was made a company director. By that date, however, the major New England wicker manufacturers had decided that it was time to halt competition for supplies. They wished to control not only the acquisition and distribution of rattan to their mutual benefit, but also its price. Like many other American businesses of that era, they created a trust. The combine, named the Central Rattan Company, was

chartered in Illinois in October 1889 but headquartered in Wakefield. Among the original members were the Wakefield Rattan Company, Heywood Brothers and Company, the Union Rattan Company, E. Newton's Sons, and a group listed only as "the chair manufacturers." Each participant owned a percentage of the new combine and was able to contract for the delivery of set amounts of whole rattan and cane at predetermined prices. In late 1892 several new members joined the trust: the American Rattan Company of New York, Leominster Rattan Works, the James Hay Company, the New Haven Rattan Company, the New Haven Chair Company, the Columbia Chair Company, and from Illinois, the Joliet Reed and Rattan Company, and the Chicago Reed and Rattan Company. The

Central Rattan Company apparently had a monopoly over all rattan shipped to the United States from Singapore. Stocks were sent straight from the Boston docks to Wakefield where the rattan was "split, cut, and prepared for use for the leading manufacturers in Gardner, New York, Chicago, and other places in the United States." Those who refused to join the trust were forced to find alternate sources in the Far East. The bi-weekly *Wooden and Willow-Ware Trade Review,* which printed news about the rattan and wicker industry, trumpeted on June 10, 1892, that an "IMMENSE QUANTITY OF RATTAN, the largest lot ever stored in one place in the history of the business" was on the premises of the Wakefield Rattan Company: "over 3,500 tons of the raw material are stored in the [ware]houses and stacked outside, representing hundreds of thousands of dollars, and another cargo is expected soon. The full force of employees, upwards of one thousand, are at work, and Mr. Richard S. Stout, who has charge of the splitting department, has 'stacks' of work on hand."[25]

Cyrus Wakefield II's untimely death before the founding of the rattan trust had come as a complete shock to his associates. He had been inextricably linked with the firm since 1855, guiding it through the difficult years following the Panic of 1873 to its leading position in the following decade. On January 25, 1888, he had left the firm's Boston business offices and, as usual, had caught the 5:00 p.m. commuter train to Wakefield. His "dear friend and faithful coachman" had picked him up at the

station in a horse-drawn sleigh for the short trip home to the old Wakefield mansion erected on Main Street by his uncle. But just as they neared the Post Office, blocks away from the mansion, Wakefield suffered a heart attack, slumped against his driver, and died. Four days later, employees and townspeople crowded into the same family home to pay their respects to yet another Cyrus Wakefield. Once again, the firm and town mourned the loss of their leading spirit.

The death of Cyrus II did not affect the Wakefield Rattan Company as severely as had the passing of its founder. The business was mature, well organized, and financially sound. The capital stock was fully paid up and was still valued at

the original amount of one million dollars—even though the company's business had virtually doubled in size since incorporation. Its factories and warehouses were models of their kind. A plant established in San Francisco around 1886 employed about a hundred people; four hundred were at work in Chicago; one thousand in Wakefield. The complex at Wakefield— the largest rattanworks anywhere in the world—had recently been expanded. Thirty buildings were now arranged across eleven acres. Four were massive, four-story brick factories. In Building No. 1, cane was split, shaved, and trimmed, and sheets of cane webbing were mechanically woven; Building No. 2 contained the steam engines that powered the plants' machinery as

Wicker Workshop in the Joliet, Illinois, State Penitentiary, ca. 1895. Photograph courtesy of the Chicago Historical Society. In the economically depressed mid-1890s, numerous manufacturers, among them Joliet Reed and Rattan, fired their employees and contracted with state officials to set up wicker workshops in prisons. Cheap convict goods devastated the commercial industry, forcing many wicker firms to lay off workers or go out of business. This photograph is the only known interior view of a nineteenth-century wicker factory.

well as the woodworking department; rattan and reed furniture was made in Building No. 3; and in Building No. 4, rattan and coconut fiber rugs and mats were mechanically woven. There were separate brick structures for bleaching, dyeing, and painting, as well as several containing boilers, supplies, and offices for factory managers. Frame buildings housed lumber, bundled

Heywood Brothers and Wakefield Company,
Gardner, Massachusetts, Fancy Reception
Chair, Model 6337, *ca. 1898–1904, rattan,*
wood, and paint. Courtesy of A Summer Place.
Photograph by Kit Latham.

rattan, coir yarn, and coal.

The company's letterhead for the year 1890 lists an extraordinary range of supplies and rattan-based merchandise available to the trade: "rattans, coir yarns and fibre, reeds, umbrella ribs, carriage mouldings, chair cane, pith cane, corset cane, rattan and reed furniture, children's carriages, baskets, burial caskets, brooms, summer doors, mattings, mats, and rugs, railway car seats, and specialties in rattan generally." Chair cane could be purchased in eight different widths: carriage, superfine, fine fine, fine, narrow medium, medium, wide medium, and common. Binding cane, used for wrapping the legs, structural members, and decorative components of furniture was slightly thicker and came in five separate widths. Reed, or "pith," was offered in seven different diameters. An 1890 illustrated catalogue of "Reed and Rattan" furniture displayed 374 different patterns and revealed Wakefield designers moving increasingly in the direction of ornate and flam-

Unidentified Manufacturer, Armchair, ca. 1890s, rattan, wood, and pigment. Courtesy of A Summer Place. Photograph by Kit Latham.

Unidentified Manufacturer, Table, ca. 1890s, rattan, wood, and pigment. Courtesy of A Summer Place. Photograph by Kit Latham.

boyant patterns.[26] The company published a supplement to the 1890 catalogue, and another listing children's reed carriages was also available to the trade. In the early 1890s the Wakefield Rattan Company stood at its zenith. The treasurer reported in January 1893 that sales for 1892 were $125,000 above the previous record-setting year.

Despite the glowing financial report at the beginning of the year, 1893 proved to be a disaster. At the November 1893 board meeting, the company directors learned that sales had already dropped $115,000 below the previous year's level. The reason for this unexpected decline was the economic crisis precipitated by the Panic of 1893, a spectacular financial disaster, even more devastating than the Panic of 1873.

Its causes were the normal factors conditioning the boom and bust business cycles of the era, but they were also compounded by outside forces. During the 1880s capital investments had been excessive, precipitating a downward trend in prices. In 1890 hysteria in the British securities market virtually halted foreign investment in American companies, diminishing the amount of available capital. Nervous European investors soon began selling their American securities. The New York stock market collapsed and gold exports soared. As the U.S. Treasury's gold reserves declined rapidly, there were wide-

=1895=

WAKEFIELD RATTAN COMPANY.

COMPLETE

ILLUSTRATED CATALOGUE

OF

REED FURNITURE.

FACTORIES:

WAKEFIELD.   CHICAGO.   KANKAKEE, ILL.   SAN FRANCISCO.

Wakefield Rattan Company, Title Page from the 1895 Illustrated Catalogue of Reed Furniture. *Courtesy of A Summer Place.*

spread fears the United States would be forced off the gold standard. Falling federal revenues coupled with enormous expenditures legislated by the Sherman Silver Purchase Act of 1890 also contributed to deepening financial uncertainty. In April 1893, after two years of relative stability, gold reserves dropped below the generally accepted minimum of a hundred million dollars. Depositors be-

gan emptying their bank accounts and almost six hundred banks nationwide suspended activities. As a result, businesses also failed in record numbers, investors panicked, the stock market plunged, and by late summer, cash had almost dried up in New York City commercial banks. During the winter of 1893 and 1894, the nation slid into a worsening economic quagmire. Unemployment soared,

violent industrial strikes broke out, and large numbers of farmers lost their farms, contributing to a rising tide of human misery. In the spring of 1894 a force of fifteen hundred unemployed men formed "Coxey's Army" and marched on Washington to attempt to force the federal government to act on behalf of the nation's newly destitute.

There was, however, one bright note to 1893: the World's Columbian Exhibition, held in Chicago. It was an extravagant creation: a vast, 633-acre model city erected along the edge of Lake Michigan. Built in the grandiose, classical beaux arts style, it abounded in heroic statues and enormous fountains. Some twenty-five million visitors crushed onto the site to view the tens of thousands of displays in mammoth exhibition halls painted gleaming white or to gawk at the sideshow attractions on the mile-long midway. If the mighty Corliss steam engine had been the emblem of the Centennial Exposition, a new, revolutionary source of power, electricity, was the Chicago fair's rightful symbol. At night, the buildings and fountains were set ablaze with lights. One important American manufacturer that had participated in the Philadelphia Centennial nearly twenty years before was absent from the Columbian Exhibition: the Wakefield Rattan Company. Nor did Heywood Brothers show their products at the Chicago fair. The only wicker companies that took part were the Gendron Iron Wheel Company of Toledo, that made not only reed baby carriages but a full line of furniture, and the New Haven Chair Company, the largest manufacturer of wheeled reed and rattan

Wakefield Rattan Company, Conversation Chair from the 1895 Illustrated Catalogue. *Courtesy of A Summer Place.*

chairs in the United States. In the fall of 1892 the directors of the Wakefield Rattan Company had considered taking the concession for the "rolling chairs," the wheeled wicker vehicles that transported the public around the grounds, but decided against it. The commercial opportunity was decreed to be of "too small importance," perhaps a misjudgment given the crowds that poured into the exhibition. The Wakefield Rattan Company was also having labor problems. In July 1892 forty "winders"—the skilled workers who wrapped the chairs and settees with cane and reed binding—went on strike for higher pay. According to an alarming report in the *Wooden and Willow-Ware Trade Review*, the reed workers who created the fanciful designs would soon be idled: they could not continue without the winders. The situation, however, was temporarily resolved. The winders had their own union, but in October 1892 they joined with the reed workers at the Wakefield plant to form the "Reed and Rattan Furniture Workers Union." In February 1893 the winders struck again: "The men complained they could not earn their average pay on the twenty-six new styles which are being introduced," the *Wooden and Willow-Ware Trade Review* announced. Winders were paid on a piecework basis and the increasing ornateness of the chairs to be wrapped demanded a slower work pace and thus reduced the number of items a worker was able to finish in a day. Labor strife continued. In late 1895 striking women employees were reported to have attacked scabs brought in to fill their places. The atmosphere was poi-

Heywood Brothers and Company, Title Page from the 1895–96 Illustrated Catalogue of Reed and Rattan Furniture. *Courtesy of Steve Poole and Robert Evans.*

sonous: the attack took place right after a dance held as a benefit for the strikers.

During the depression of 1893 to 1898, many wicker manufacturers and their work forces experienced economic hardships. The *Wooden and Willow-Ware Trade Review* reported in November 1893 that the Hammond Reed Company of Worcester, Massachusetts, "has reduced its running time on account of the general depression, to practically about four days a week. The concern has been able to run till now on full time on orders, but a lack of orders at present necessitates a reduction in working time. The concern employs nearly 150 hands when running full." Employees were thrown out of work not only for lack of orders, but because of lockouts. In October 1895 seventy-five reed workers walked off the job at the Heywood-Morrill plant in

Chicago after management refused to recognize their union and demands for a 4.5 percent raise. Henry Heywood and Amos Morrill responded by throwing all workers out and closing the plant until the strikers reluctantly returned. Two years later, the company economized by reducing workers' wages twenty-five percent. Times were so hard that the workers could do no more than grumble. Nevertheless, there were a surprising number of new entrants into the industry

Heywood Brothers and Company's Warehouse and Retail Store in London, England, *1893.* *Photograph courtesy of The Metropolitan Museum of Art, Max G. Wildnaver Fund, 1958. (58.613.3 p.6) Beginning in the late 1880s, Heywood Brothers exported its rattan and reed furniture to England, where it was sold at the company's warehouse store in London.*

Unidentified Manufacturer, Lady's Reception Chair, With Initials "C. W.", ca. 1890s, rattan, wood, caning, and pigment. Courtesy of Richard Moulton. Photograph by Kit Latham.

during the depression, and a number of existing firms expanded their factory facilities. The lean years notwithstanding, wicker's popularity remained undiminished. In April 1894 the firm of St. Germain and Rheaume was established in Chicopee Center, Massachusetts, "for the manufacture of reed and cane goods of all kinds." Seven persons were employed, and the owners hoped to expand the work force to twenty-five. In July 1894 the Cliftondale Reed Chair Company of Lynn, Massachusetts, was formed. Five workers were employed and produced, according to the *Wooden and Willow-Ware Trade Review*, "in the vicinity of two dozen patent rockers each week." Their output was quite substantial: it took twenty-seven men at the rival Keystone Rattan Company in

Unidentified Manufacturer, Round Table, ca. 1890s, rattan and wood. Courtesy of Richard Moulton. Photograph by Kit Latham.

Huntington, Pennsylvania, to produce one hundred chairs per week. The quantity of furniture annually manufactured at the Wakefield or Heywood Brothers' factories is unfortunately not recorded.

In the economic climate of the 1890s a number of wicker manufacturers found plentiful supplies of cheap labor in state penitentiaries. The practice of contracting with officials to set up workshops inside prisons to make baskets, furnishings, and cocoa mats was widespread in New England and the midwestern states. Corruption in the awarding of lucrative contracts was commonplace. In Ohio, two prisons even purchased with taxpayers' dollars machinery that enabled one convict to do the work of five outside laborers. The firms, which had to compete using regularly paid, free workers, were

Heywood Brothers and Wakefield Company, Gardner, Massachusetts, Lady's Armchair, Model 6068A, ca. 1898–1910, rattan, wood, and caning. Private collection. Photograph by Kit Latham.

furious and lobbied state legislators to restrict the practice—or to have their rivals' contracts voided and given to them instead. One of the manufacturers who operated workshops in New Hampshire and Massachusetts prisons was the iniquitous H. A. Marston, a former Wakefield Rattan Company employee. In 1889, lured by local townspeople with the offer of a factory building, he established the Phoenix Rattan Company in Natick, Massachusetts, which employed sixty men. He refused to join the rattan trust, and as a result—or more likely because he was simply tightfisted—he used shoddy, second-rate materials. His

weavers bitterly complained about the poor quality stock he gave them, and in May 1893 thirty-five of them who had gone on strike once before went out on strike again. By December, Marston had fired them all, paid off state officials, and moved his operations into penitentiaries where the work force was cheaper and more docile. In 1897, his company insolvent and creditors closing in, Marston tried to evade the law by "selling" the firm to his wife. He did not succeed. He was taken to court and eventually lost his business.

Among the more successful companies using convict labor in the Chicago area was the Joliet Rattan and Reed Company, which during the 1890s maintained a prof-

Heywood Brothers and Company, Five-Piece Set from the 1895–96 Catalogue of Reed and Rattan Furniture. *Courtesy of Steve Poole and Robert Evans.*
In the mid-1890s, leading wicker manufacturers offered "suits" of three to five matching pieces. This particular set cost fifty-two dollars.

itable workshop in the Joliet, Illinois, state penitentiary. A photograph showing the Joliet prisoners at work making ornate wicker chairs survives and is a fascinating document. For one thing, it demonstrates that as a craft, weaving fancy wicker was easily taught to an unskilled labor force. For another, it is the only known photographic record of how a reed and rattan furniture factory was actually set up in the nineteenth century. The state government had actually invested half-a-million dollars on new machinery for the prison laborers.

In 1892, Illinois governor John Altgeld, a Democrat, had campaigned on a reform platform to outlaw the unfair prison competition, yet during his administration, the level of convict production increased four-fold. The economic impact of cheap, prison-made goods from Joliet was devastating. In the winter of 1895 and 1896, three thousand wickerworkers in

the Midwest went on strike to protest the "ruinous policy." The strike failed and the laborers blamed the governor for their defeat. In a November 1896 stump speech, the rival Republican candidate for the Illinois governorship excoriated his opponent for his support of prison labor:

All the terrible consequences of having the great State of Illinois, with its boundless resources, put into sharp competition with the manufacturing business of its citizens, is felt in many lines of trade. The Heywood-Morrill Rattan Company, which manufactured chairs on the west side in Chicago, giving employment to fifteen hundred men, I am told, has had to reduce the number of its employees about one-half, and those that remain get far less wages per day than they did before Governor Altgeld flung his cheap, prison-made chairs

ESTABLISHED 1826

1898-1899

INCORPORATED 1897

HEYWOOD BROTHERS AND WAKEFIELD COMPANY

MAKERS OF
REED AND RATTAN FURNITURE
CHAIRS, CHAIR CANE CHILDREN'S CARRIAGES

FACTORIES:
Gardner, Mass.
Chicago, Ill.
Wakefield, Mass.
San Francisco, Cal.

WAREHOUSES:

NEW YORK, 195-197 CANAL ST.,
NEW YORK, 297-303 CHERRY ST.,
BOSTON, 182 PORTLAND ST.,
PHILADELPHIA, 1010-1014 RACE ST.,
BALTIMORE, 536-542 W. PRATT ST.,
CHICAGO, 270-272 WABASH AVE.,
SAN FRANCISCO, 659-663 MISSION ST.,
PORTLAND, ORE., 80-86 FIFTH ST.,
LOS ANGELES, 355-361 UPPER MAIN ST.,
LONDON, ENG., LIVERPOOL, ENG.

upon the market. The Wakefield Rattan Company, of Chicago, has had, for the same reason, to shut down completely, throwing seven hundred men out of employment. [27]

The Republican challenger won the election, and in 1897 agreed to support a bill outlawing wicker factories in prisons.

The Wakefield Rattan Company was among the firms that had protested convict labor, supporting a 1897 bill in the Massachusetts senate that drastically limited the number of prisoners employed as contract workers. In fact, in 1896 the company's officers had been forced to reduce their dividend from five to four percent because of the unfair competition. Since the onset of the depression, the firm's fortunes had dipped. Sales

Heywood Brothers and Wakefield Company, Title Page from the 1898–99 Illustrated Catalogue of Reed and Rattan Furniture. Photograph courtesy of the National Museum of American Art, Smithsonian Institution.

After twenty years of fierce competition, Wakefield Rattan merged with Heywood Brothers and Company in 1897. After consolidating operations and selecting the best designs, the new enterprise issued its first catalogue for 1898–99. For the next thirty-five years, Heywood-Wakefield dominated the American wicker industry.

figures for 1894 were well below those of 1893—which had been disastrous. By May, sales were down $140,000 and the annual profit for 1894 was $66,899.64—virtually the same amount the company had earned for 1874. Sales rose during 1895, but only marginally, and the directors approved a companywide accounting study to determine how they

Wakefield Rattan Company, Wakefield,
Massachusetts, Tête-à-Tête, Model 3935,
ca. 1895–97, rattan, wood, and caning.
Courtesy of A Summer Place.
Photograph by Kit Latham.

might economize. The following year proved miserable. In June 1896 the *Wooden and Willow-Ware Trade Review* reported: "business is very slack at the Wakefield Rattan Company's works at Wakefield at present. The spinning room is shut down altogether and will remain so until August, and several other of the departments are running on short time with a possibility of a general shut-down."[28] With sales off sharply, the directors approved a plan at their August 1896 meeting to save money by moving the corporation's offices from Boston to the Wakefield factory whenever "the best interests of business" would be served. In the fall, losses were reported from Chicago as well as Boston and the move took place. The Gibbs Chair Company,

Above: Heywood Brothers and Company, Gardner, Massachusetts, Lady's Reception Chair, Model 2905A, *ca. 1895–96, rattan, wood, and caning. Courtesy of A Summer Place. Photograph by Kit Latham.*

Left: Unidentified Manufacturer, White-Painted Display Cabinet, *ca. 1895–1905, rattan, wood, and paint. Courtesy of A Summer Place. Photograph by Kit Latham*

a bankrupt wood chair factory in Kankakee, Illinois, which had been purchased incautiously by the company only the year before, was also closed. To tide the firm over, the directors borrowed ninety-five thousand dollars from the Central Rattan Company. Again, in November, they were forced to borrow another twenty thousand dollars from the Boston banking firm, Kidder, Peabody. It is difficult to know today whether to ascribe the company's problems to poor management or a hostile business climate. In all likelihood, it was the latter. *Wooden and Willow-Ware Trade Review* reported in April 1896 that "General business conditions at the present time are almost as unsatisfactory as they have been at any time since 1893. An unrest pervades the whole commercial world, and merchants and manufacturers are transacting business very timidly. They appear to be very much afraid of the future."[29] In the absence of specific information on Heywood Brothers' corporate earnings and performance during the depression, one must assume that they, too, experienced financial difficulties and were forced to adjust to the deteriorated economy. But wicker was only one part of their production: wood chairs for homes, schools, and theaters remained their mainstay and continued to sell well. Larger, well managed, and with diversified product lines, Heywood Brothers and Company apparently weathered the economic storms of the 1890s. Late in 1896 the less secure directors of the Wakefield Rattan Company began exploring radical ways to stay in business. Drastic action was needed if the firm was to survive into the twentieth century.

On February 17, 1897, *The New York Times* headlined a major business story: "Two Large Firms To Merge. An Important Consolidation to be Made in Boston." The front-page article gave further details on the report:

. . . the Wakefield Rattan Company will be merged with the firm of Heywood Brothers and Co., thus effecting one of the most important consolidations of capital thus made in New England. The Wakefield Company manufactures all sorts of rattan goods, including corset stock, and the Heywoods are the most extensive manufacturers of chairs in the United States. The new concern will be the Heywood Brothers and Wakefield Company and will have a capital of $4,000,000 in 6 percent cumulative stock, and $2,000,000 in common stock. The business of the combined firms will be prosecuted in all parts of the world.[30]

Apparently, the deal had "been in the air for some months." The day before the *Times* story appeared, the annual stockholders meeting of the Gardner firm had approved the merger; the Wakefield meeting took place in Boston the following evening. The late edition of the *Boston Globe* announced the result: of 7,622 shares voting, not one dissented. President Temple R. Fay was quoted as saying the merger would save the Wakefield firm one hundred thousand dollars a year. An anonymous source stated it would be closer to $160,000. The reporter noted that "the consolidation of these two companies places the rattan manufacturing business of the country under one head, with practically no competition." Fay was defensive about the idea of industrial domination; it was, after all, an era when progressive thinkers were increasingly critical of trusts and monopolies. "We have not a monopoly of the rattan business by any means," he retorted, "as there is a great quantity of inferior goods on the market. . . . The greatest competition at present is from prison labor."[31] But with factories and warehouses under its management across the United States, the new corporation had, in reality, little to fear from convict workers. Instead, it was beginning to be threatened by something more troublesome and demanding: revolutionary changes in public taste.

NOTES

1. The minutes of the board of directors of the Wakefield Rattan Company are in a private collection, Needham, Mass.

2. Reports of the U.S. Centennial Commission (Washington, D.C.: Government Printing Office, 1880), 4:728.

3. Ibid., 738.

4. "B.," "The Centennial," *Western Furniture Trade* (August 1876): 8. (Note: This source was located in the files of the Chicago Historical Society.)

5. *Wakefield Rattan Company, Boston, Mass.*, ca. 1875–77. (Note: this source was located in the files of the Division of Domestic Living, National Museum of American History, Smithsonian Institution, Washington, D.C. Another exists in the collection of the Beinecke Rare Book Library, Yale University. The company's Boston address is given as Nos. 82 to 98 Canal and 173 to 177 Friend Streets.

6. *A Completed Century, 1826–1926; A History of the Heywood-Wakefield Company* (Boston: Printed for the Company, 1926), 3.

7. See W. D. Herrick, *History of the Town of Gardner . . . Massachusetts* (Gardner, Mass.: Published by the Committee, 1879), 306–13 for a description of Watkins's inventions. For a discussion of the rattan industry in Gardner, Massachusetts, and inventions at the Heywood Brothers factory, see D. Hamilton Hurd, *History of Worcester County, Massachusetts* (Philadelphia: J. W. Lewis, 1889), 1:830–36.

8. See Hurd, *History of Worcester County*, 1:833.

9. Herrick, *History of the Town of Gardner*, 179–181.

10. Ibid., 174.

11. J. D. Van Slyck, *A History of New England Manufacturers and Manufactories* (Boston: Van Slyck, 1879), 1:331.

12. Heywood Brothers and Company, *Catalogue of Chairs, Rattan Furniture, and Chair Cane*, 1 October 1878. (Note: This source was located in the Winterthur Museum and Garden Library, Winterthur, Del.)

13. Van Slyck, *A History of New England Manufacturers*, 1:184.

14. Wakefield Rattan Company, *Illustrated Catalogue and Price List of Rattan and Reed Furniture*, ca. 1880, 9. (Note: This source was located in the Warshaw Business Americana Collection, Archives Center, National Museum of American History, Smithsonian Institution, Washington, D.C.)

15. Lady Barker [Mary Anne Barker Broome], *The Bedroom and the Boudoir* (London: Macmillan, 1878), 80.

16. Heywood Brothers and Company, *Price List of Reed Chairs and Furniture . . . Supplement . . . September 1, 1881*. (Note: Source found in Winterthur Museum and Garden Library, Winterthur, Del.)

17. "Wakefield Rattan Company," *Scribner's Monthly*, November 1879, 16.

18. Clarence Cook, *The House Beautiful: Essays on Beds and Tables, Stools and Candlesticks* (New York: Charles Scribner, 1878), 60.

19. Quoted in Sharon Darling, *Chicago Furniture: Art, Craft, and Industry, 1833–1983* (New York and London: Chicago Historical Society with W. W. Norton, 1984), 117, n. 26.

20. For a history of Chicago wicker manufacturers, see Darling, *Chicago Furniture*, 116–122.

21. Richard N. Greenwood, *The Five Heywood Brothers (1826–1951). A Brief History of the Heywood-Wakefield Company During 125 Years* (New York: Newcomen Society, 1951), 17–18.

22. "Pacific Coast Trade Topics," *Wooden and Willow-Ware Trade Review*, 14 August 1902, 88.

23. *A Completed Century*, 9.

24. Wakefield Rattan Company, *Complete Illustrated Catalogue of Reed and Rattan Furniture*, ca. 1886. (Note: This source was located in the Print Department, Metropolitan Museum of Art.) Van Slyck, 2:332, notes that in 1879 the Wakefield company had a fleet of fifteen ships engaged in the East India trade.

25. "Immense Quantity of Rattan," *Wooden and Willow-Ware Trade Review*, 10 June 1892, 1.

26. Wakefield Rattan Company, *Complete Illustrated Catalogue of Reed and Rattan Furniture*, 1890. The entire catalogue is reproduced in Richard Saunders, *The Official Price Guide to Wicker* (Orlando, Fla.: House of Collectibles, 1985), 59ff.

27. "Gov. Altgeld's Prison Policy and Rattan Goods," *Wooden and Willow-Ware Trade Review*, 25 November 1896, 29. See also "Editorial Notes," op. cit., 10 October 1896, 20–21.

28. "Wakefield Rattan Company's Business Slack," *Wooden and Willow-Ware Trade Review*, 25 June 1896, 61.

29. "Editorial Notes," *Wooden and Willow-Ware Trade Review*, 10 April 1896, 20.

30. "Two Large Firms to Merge," *New York Times*, 17 February 1897, 1.

31. *Boston Globe*, 17 February 1897, 7. (See story on corporate merger.)

CHAPTER THREE

Victorian Wicker and the American Home, 1876–1900

The prevalence of wicker in the daily lives of Americans increased dramatically after the 1876 Centennial Exhibition. The Wakefield Rattan Company's landmark display at the Philadelphia fair certainly helped boost consumer demand for its products: by late 1879, the company announced it had sold two million dollars' worth of furniture and advertised that "its popularity increases every day." That same year, Heywood Brothers' sales of rattan furniture had climbed to twenty-five percent of their aggregate business. What caused such a demand for furnishings fabricated from a tropical vine transported to America from halfway around the globe? Several interrelated reasons help account for wicker's surging popularity after the centennial: a mass migration of middle-class families from cities to new suburbs, where they could build large houses with expansive porches; a craving to ornament these houses with "morally uplifting" household art; and a dramatic increase in summer houses and resort hotels. Each of these factors directly affected the design, manufacture, use, and sales of rattan and reed furniture in

the last twenty-five years of the nineteenth century.

During the 1850s and 1860s, early wicker had been recommended as summer furniture for picturesque country houses and summer cottages. It was lightweight yet strong, well ventilated, and inexpensive. With their elegant linear configurations and esparto patterns, the early designs in willow and rattan admirably suited the Gothic-revival-style residences built at mid-century by progressive architects such as Gervase Wheeler and Andrew Jackson Downing. In Downing's view, "a country house . . . should always be furnished with more chasteness and simplicity than a town house." City parlors in the 1850s and 1860s were filled with elaborately carved rosewood furniture in the sculpturesque rococo-revival or the monumental Renaissance-revival styles. But in the country, the homeowner wanted much greater ease and convenience. Period photographs reveal that Colt's willow-ware was used to furnish Gothic-revival summer cottages on Martha's Vineyard and that the Berrians' rattan seating appeared on well-appointed porches in rural Massachusetts. Mid-century wick-

er was not intended for urban residences: it was informal furniture, easy to move from indoors to veranda, to garden, and back, even by children. It was most useful in summertime. In warm weather, the occupant of a willow or rattan chair was far less likely to perspire than someone on a wood or upholstered one—especially since the fashions of the day demanded so much clothing. A cast-iron bench might be equally cool and stylish, but without lots of cushions it was next to impossible to sit on for any length of time.

In the antebellum period, only the wealthy could really afford to move out of the city, build homes in the countryside, and relax on wicker sofas. They alone had the money and leisure to drive into the city whenever they wished in private horse-drawn carriages. Those who worked had to live close to their places of employment, usually within easy walking distance. Since mid-century public transportation systems were extremely limited in the areas

Various Manufacturers, Square Table, Basket, and Three Ladies' Reception Chairs, ca. 1895–97. Rattan, caning, and wood. Courtesy of A Summer Place. Photograph by Kit Latham.

FRONT ELEVATION.

NEW LONDON.

A SUBURBAN villa with picturesque exterior and adequate accommodation for a genteel family. The outlines are subdued, while the details of finish are ornate, expressive of domestic feeling and cultivated taste. The veranda and wide balcony above shown, on the front, are inviting and pleasing features, indicating

S. B. Reed, "New London" Model Suburban House, 1885. Photograph from Reed, Dwellings for Village and Country, 1885, courtesy of the National Museum of American Art, Smithsonian Institution.
In the 1870s, there was a mass exodus of middle-class families from the cities to the suburbs, where they built houses in the eclectic, Queen Anne style, often from mail-order plans. These picturesque dwellings, which featured large, breezy porches, proved the perfect setting for artistic wicker furniture, used indoors and out.

they served, commuting to factory or office from any distance was next to impossible. Horse-drawn omnibuses were neither roomy nor speedy enough. Even the updated horsecars that ran on steel rails and were introduced in the late 1850s traveled only at a rate of six miles an hour between stops. This was fine for traveling inside the city but not out to neighborhoods built on the periphery. But in the 1870s, as cities underwent explosive growth, urban transportation systems were expanded, and with the addition of steam power in the 1880s and electricity in the 1890s, they greatly increased their distance, speed, and efficiency. This allowed middle-class salaried employees to escape the increasing noise, dirt, and congestion of downtown neighborhoods filled with row housing, and enabled them to build detached, single-family homes in what came to be known as "streetcar suburbs." This growing migration was a notable fact of life in urban America. On April 19, 1877, the *New York Herald* commented: "New York is gradually becoming, year by year, the home of the very rich and very poor. The middle classes are surely, rapidly, and permanently removing to the neighboring localities; the ample railroad facilities to all places embracing a radius of twenty miles around the city, together . . . with pure air, and freedom from infectious diseases caused by dirty streets and other causes prevailing in large cities, tending to make residence in such places more and more sought for."

In the 1870s and 1880s the urban middle classes felt increasingly threatened by the deteriorating physical and social conditions around them. The fragile infrastructure of cities across America was crumbling under the pressure of swelling populations. Residential streets were narrow, muddy, and refuse-strewn; downtown housing was generally old, dilapidated, and unhealthy; sewage systems and supplies of clean water were woefully deficient. Epidemics were rampant and increasing poverty among the growing ranks of the urban poor resulted in rising rates of crime and social unrest. While the problems of urban Americans were exacerbated by the economic depression of the mid-1870s, they had originated earlier with population explosions that simply overwhelmed available housing and public services. During the thirty years before the Civil War, the urban population of the United States had grown more than 700 percent, from five hundred thousand to 3.8 million persons. After 1865 the increase was even more explosive. A post-war baby boom was coupled, in some centers, with a rising tide of migrants from the rural South, and in most others, with an increasing flood of immigrants from Mediterranean countries, Eastern Europe, and Russia. By 1900 eleven million immigrants had arrived, altering the very character and structure of the urban environment. The impoverished newcomers crowded into tenements and boarding houses in slums that expanded to fill the vacuum created by the constant departure of middle-class families. Some of the wealthy also relocated to the outskirts, others moved into the protection of new luxury apartment buildings, but still more remained isolated and protected in their exclusive neighborhoods. Compounding the problems of noise, dirt, and overcrowding was the fact that, with coal-fired steam engines, factories no longer had to be situated in small towns next to mill streams. Like the Chicago plants of the Wakefield Rattan Company and the Heywood-Morrill Company, they could be built inside city limits to take advantage of better systems of supply and distribution and a larger pool of workers. Factory laborers typically

Porch of the John Farson House, Oak Park, Illinois, ca. 1910. *Photograph courtesy of the Historical Society of Oak Park and River Forest.*
Wicker chairs were the most popular form of summertime seating on porches across America. The long veranda of this house, designed by Prairie School architect George W. Maher in suburban Oak Park, was furnished with Victorian-style reed rockers and more up-to-date Bar Harbor–style willow chairs.

lived in cramped frame dwellings often built one behind the other on narrow lots laid out in the immediate vicinity of their workplaces. In the economically bust mid-1870s, these new factories attracted more unemployed people to cities in search of work.

During the period from 1870 to 1900, America rapidly industrialized. This had an important impact not only on the manufacture of rattan and reed furniture, but more importantly on the creation of what would be its major source of consumers: an expanding class of white-collar workers that included managers, accountants, salespeople, office clerks, factory supervisors, and other salaried employees. In 1860 the U.S. Bureau of the Census had counted some

Last Photograph of President Ulysses S. Grant, *July 19, 1885. Photograph courtesy of the Prints and Photographs Division, Library of Congress.*
This photograph was taken at General Grant's summer home in the Adirondacks in upstate New York four days before he died. The former president is sitting in a Wakefield Rattan Company reed chair.

750,000 persons engaged in such "professional service." By 1890 that number had risen to 2.16 million, and in 1910 it mushroomed to 4.42 million.[1] During these years the purchasing power of white-collar workers' weekly paychecks increased more than twenty percent. This class was precisely the demographic group that was enthralled by the suburban ideal and built homes in new residential developments on the outskirts of cities and towns across America—

and bought all manner of rattan and reed furnishings with which to embellish their houses. By the hundreds of thousands, in crowded cities across the nation, they heeded the sort of advice printed by the *Chicago Tribune* on August 29, 1880: "Put your money where it will be safe and sure to increase, and buy yourself a residence where the pure air will prolong your lives and make your children strong."

Nothing made educated Victorians more anxious than the quality of their "lung food." Fresh air—or the lack of it—was one of the most compelling reasons to move to the suburbs. City air was foul and seemingly unfit to breathe. Full of smoke, coal dust, and other pollutants, it stank of "sewer gas" and industrial waste. When the wind changed, the stench of outlying stockyards and

tanneries was overpowering. But the air indoors was believed to be even more dangerous. With the windows and doors closed tight against the unhealthy outdoor air, the interior atmosphere was reputed to be literally poisonous. The presumed villain was "carbonic acid"—actually carbon dioxide. Exhaled from the lungs, it was widely considered to be the deadliest of toxins. As one public health authority bluntly put it: "Man's own breath is his worst enemy." Respired air was responsible, he said, for fully one half of all deaths.[2] Popular housekeeping manuals and medical treatment books of the last quarter of the nineteenth century are full of dire warnings about the dangers of suffocating in closed rooms that quickly filled up with gaseous carbonic acid. The novelist Harriet

Parlor of the Judge Augustus Macon House, Canon City, Colorado, ca. 1890.
Photograph courtesy of the Colorado Historical Society.
Ornate reed and rattan furniture was considered highly "artistic" and typically displayed in the front parlor where visitors could see it and recognize the homeowner's good taste. The elaborate reed rocker with esparto-pattern back in the Macon residence was further embellished with a fancy silk bow.

Beecher Stowe argued that children who slept in unventilated bedrooms suffered "moral insanity." It is no wonder that airy rattan cribs proved so popular; they were "so thoroughly adapted for ventilation that [they were] always sweet and cool."[3] Simply opening doors and windows was no solution to stuffy rooms: in came sickness-causing drafts, the deadly "night air," and dreaded "bacterial swarms" of airborne germs from decaying organic waste on the streets outside. In the words of a home economist writing in 1893, "ventilation, seemingly the simplest and easiest of things to be accomplished, has thus far apparently defied architects and engineers." She continued:

In capitols, churches, and public halls of every sort, the same story holds. Women faint, men . . . fall into apoplectic fits, or become victims of new and mysterious diseases, simply from the want of pure air. A constant slow murder goes on in nurseries and schoolrooms; and white-faced, nerveless children grow into white-faced and nerveless men and women.[4]

In the Edenic borderlands beyond the city, parents were told, lay salvation. In the wooded suburbs, vegetation naturally absorbed the deadly carbonic acid and revitalized the air with fresh supplies of oxygen. In such a paradise, the middle classes presumed they were safe from all the social, moral, and medical ills of the city. Their new suburban homes were their fortresses, sacred precincts in which to practice the Victorian cult of domesticity. By the hundreds of thousands, families sat on their porches in airy wicker chairs and watched their neighbors walk by.

In the last quarter of the nineteenth century, real estate developers, building and loan associations, architectural plan-books, and texts on artistic interior decoration offered middle-class families various means, ways, and ideas to build, decorate, and furnish their new homes. For as little as twenty-five cents, the potential home builder could purchase George Palliser's *Model Homes for the People, a Complete Guide to the Proper and Economical Erection of Buildings* (1876),

Sitting Room, General John B. Gordon House, Atlanta, Georgia, mid-1890s.
Photograph courtesy of the Atlanta Historical Society.
In the South, wicker was used indoors in greater abundance than it was in northern states. Summer heat and humidity demanded well-ventilated chairs. In this sitting room, the reed furniture has been arranged informally, with a wicker conversation chair placed in the center of the airy room.

which included a series of well-designed, moderately priced houses and advice on how to construct them. After selecting a model, the customer completed a questionnaire about his lot size, budget, and other details and mailed it back to Palliser's Bridgeport, Connecticut, office. He then received a set of lithographed drawings: fifty cents bought plans for a popular, three-thousand-dollar home; forty dollars purchased detailed blueprints for a larger, more complex, $7,500 house. Palliser and his brother Charles also custom designed buildings based on written answers to a series of questions. Plan-book authors such as the Pallisers—and in the last quarter of the century there were a host of others—offered a wide range of house designs, large and small; provided in-depth advice on a panoply of subjects including site selection, drainage, building materials, and construction methods; offered guidance on selecting suitable plumbing, heating, and ventilating systems; and advised readers on artistic home decoration. But more important, their detailed instructions and constant assurances made home construction seem so easy and thus greatly encouraged what one popular plan-book author described as "this most noble calling of life, 'Home Building.'"[5]

Mail-order architecture was extraordinarily popular in the last quarter of the century. Immense numbers of plan-books were sold nationwide, circumventing the need for local architects and thoroughly democratizing the home construction business. By 1887 the Pallisers had sold seventy-five

Front Parlor of the C. Milo Williams House, New Orleans, ca. 1890s.
Photograph courtesy of the Southeastern Architectural Archive, Tulane University Library.

thousand copies of plans for a single, eight-room model.[6] The popularity of plan-books and individual designs notwithstanding, the architecture of the new American suburb was anything but bland and repetitious: the books' authors exhorted their readers to be creative, selecting combinations of different features, materials, and ornament. Individual expression was a Victorian ideal, and home builders eagerly sought to distinguish the appearance of their houses from those of their neighbors—even though the basic plans and lot sizes were often similar.

After 1876 a new style of architecture flourished in the burgeoning suburbs. Eclectic and exuberant—and highly romantic—it proved the perfect environment for the flowering of Victorian wicker. In fact, without this ornamental style and the novel schemes of interior decoration it helped stimulate, the evolution of rattan and reed furniture designs likely would have taken a very different course. Known as Queen Anne, or "free classic," the new style of architecture had evolved from picturesque, Elizabethan-style manor houses designed in the 1860s by the English architect Richard Norman Shaw. The "Shavian" style was an explicit rejection of the historicism of the Gothic

Unidentified Manufacturer, Fireplace Screen, ca. 1890s, rattan and wood. Courtesy of A Summer Place. Photograph by Kit Latham.

revival and was a strong endorsement of a postmedieval, English vernacular architecture. It was transmitted to America first through illustrations in architectural and builders' magazines, and then by two ornamental Queen Anne buildings constructed by the British government for official use at the Philadelphia Centennial. Although it had originated in the English countryside, the Queen Anne dwelling was to find its true fulfillment in the American suburbs. Anglo-Americans found its historical associations irresistible, and in the last quarter of the century, the free-form, decorative

style was the most popular architectural mode for new homes built on the outskirts of cities and towns across America.

Architects, designers, and plan-book authors eagerly promoted the Queen Anne style but were unable to define it satisfactorily. One writer, echoing the consensus, simply declared "eclecticism is the rule."[7] The essential motivation behind the widespread adoption of the Queen Anne style by middle-class home builders was a fervent desire to create an expressive form of domestic architecture that eliminated all reference to the inartistic, boxlike house. Mail-order plan-books offered two basic sorts: a moderately scaled and priced "cottage," and a larger, more expensive "villa." In plan, circular,

octagonal, and irregular forms were joined to conventional squares and rectangles to create an asymmetrical arrangement. This asymmetry was readily apparent in elevation as well: no two sides were alike. To maximize picturesque effect, a single dwelling might combine different types of roofs and sport not only a turret, but towering chimneys, finials, and cast-iron cresting, as well as projecting gables and high-peaked dormer windows. Below the roof line were overhanging eaves and rafters, recessed and protruding balconies, bays, and porticoes—as well as roofed "piazzas," or wraparound porches furnished with wicker. The exterior was covered with combinations of assorted ornament: fish-scale or rough-

New Haven Rattan Company, New Haven, Connecticut (attributed to), Baby Carriage, ca. 1890, rattan, wood, and metal. Private collection. Photograph by Kit Latham.

cut shingles, false half-timbering, intricate gable treatments, terra-cotta tiles, fretwork moldings, and stucco panels. There were also numerous decorative brackets, and palisades of elaborate, lathe-turned posts, balusters, and spindles supporting porch and balcony roofs and railings. Typically, the inexpensive plan-book "cottages" were clapboard-sided, decorated with attached stickwork. The exteriors of the "villas," on the other hand, were often composed of masonry and brick as well as shingles. The Queen Anne style was strongly pictorial. Not only was there a

Living Hall, "Clonniel," Dr. T. G. Morton House, Strafford, Pennsylvania, 1895.
Photograph courtesy of the Historical Society of Pennsylvania, Philadelphia.
In this comfortable sitting area, an ornamental, sea-shell motif American rocker shares space
in front of the fireplace with an ornate wicker table and an Oriental hourglass chair.

dramatic play of light and shadow across broken and textured surfaces, but different zones, areas, and decorative components were painted in harmonious colors to achieve a picturesque effect. In the East and Midwest, the hues were mostly earth tones and soft blues and grays heightened with dark reds, but in San Francisco, the often fog-shrouded houses were brightly painted.

The British-inspired Queen Anne style was not the only architecture popularized in the aftermath of the Centennial exhibition. The Philadelphia fair provoked a new interest in and nostalgia for America's colonial era. Stunned by the effects of rapid urbanization and industrialization, and disenchanted with the corruption of President Grant's administration, Americans in 1876 viewed the pre-Revolutionary period as the "good old days" when life was simpler, healthier, and certainly more honest. In the late 1860s and early 1870s, when city dwellers had begun to vacation by the sea in increasing numbers, they encountered delightful shoreline towns and villages off the beaten track that had changed little since the eighteenth century. They were treasure troves of colonial building styles. More progressive architects, delighting in the weathered gray shingles that covered the sloping roofs and plain walls of many of the old Puritan-era houses, created a new, less ornamented style rich in historical associations. By the early 1880s features of the vernacular colonial style had merged with the irregular massing of Queen Anne to produce the planar "Shingle style" that, although it found its purest expression in examples built in New England, was popularized coast to coast through architectural plan-books. But whether shingled or embellished with ornamental detail, or constructed in Iowa, Connecticut, Louisiana, or California, the eclectic Victorian house of the period 1876 to 1900 shared one common

Smoking Room, J. A. St. John House, Boston, Massachusetts, ca. 1890s. *Photograph by Charles H. Currier, courtesy of the Prints and Photographs Division, Library of Congress.*
A special feature of the multiroomed Queen Anne–style dwelling was a smoking room set aside for the man of the house. In this Boston room, two rather feminine-looking reed chairs flank the fireplace. An upholstered wicker lounge stands against a wall covered with a William Morris wallpaper.

feature: the porch. It was an essential component. On its broad, shaded surface, shielded from neighbors' view by bamboo or rattan shades, family members and friends gathered together during warm weather, reading, gossiping, or just relaxing on comfortable wicker chairs—the definitive porch furniture.

Described alternatively as a veranda or piazza in the literature of the late nineteenth century, the porch was the informal, outdoor living room. Simultaneously open yet enclosed, it mediated between the indoor world and nature. Although it had been a regular feature in domestic architecture since the late 1700s, the porch developed into a truly American phenomenon in the last quarter of the nineteenth century. Virtually every new home either had a front, side, back, or an expansive, wraparound veranda—especially if it was a suburban Queen Anne or Shingle-style dwelling. Part of its extraordinary popularity was its obvious healthfulness. The breezy piazza was the single most ventilated part of the house, and with the ground floor windows open yet sheltered, it facilitated the circulation of fresh air indoors. In 1884 architect A. W. Brunner argued "we need broad verandas, large windows, and doors so arranged that we can get a current of air through the rooms. . . . The veranda . . . should be encouraged, not only because it is American, but because it is a great comfort and sensible contrivance. Let it be broad and low, to keep out the sun's rays; let it be large enough for plenty of chairs . . . and during the long summer months it

Bedroom, Livingston Griggs House, St. Paul, Minnesota, 1884. *Photograph courtesy of the Minnesota Historical Society.*
This feminine room is filled with definitive late-Victorian art-decoration, including wall-mounted feathers and fans, swathed and swagged dressing and tea tables, family photos, pictures, mirrors, and ceramic figurines. A plain-style wicker chair—possibly English—is pulled up in front of the fire and a wicker lounge is placed at the foot of the bed.

will be a most delightful retreat."[8]

An illustrated 1894 article, "Furnishing the Piazza," extolled the virtues of the summer porch along with its "dainty" wicker furniture:

In our almost tropical summer climate, true comfort dictates that we shall spend a great portion of our time out of doors; or at least those of us that are fortunate enough to possess a cottage in the country. The summer cottage without a piazza would be almost worse than useless, and it should be no mere narrow-covered balcony . . . but a broad room projecting from one corner of the building, roofed over and provided with a railing to prevent the little tots from tumbling off. Such a piazza may be comfortably, even artistically furnished and form a veritable paradise, where the summer days may be spent in a *dolce far niente* existence, and the daily round of life's duties may be undertaken mid the softly blowing zephyrs that bring perfumes of roses and of woodbine, and the trumpet creeper and clematis can climb round the posts, more beautiful than any new-painted decoration, or embroidered tapestry. . . . But the furniture! Can anything be more artistic or delightful than those dainty creations in rattan and reed. . . . There is the large comfortable rocker in which madam can lie back and loaf at her ease, and while away the fleeting hours with the last fashionable novel. A number of smaller rockers should also be scattered about. Then there are comfortable couches made of rattan, half lounge, half bed, on which a couple of denim covered cushions . . . tempt one to lie and half doze away the sultry summer afternoon. Charming

Above and below: Heywood Brothers and Company, Lady's Armchair and Lady's Rocker from the 1895–96 Illustrated Catalogue of Reed and Rattan Furniture. *Courtesy of Steve Poole and Robert Evans.*

In the 1890s, embellishing painted reed furniture with colorful silk bows and bright upholstery was fashionable. Major manufacturers capitalized on the fad by offering factory-upholstered and beribboned wicker.

low wicker tables may also be secured, and one of these should stand in one corner, bearing the tea-kettle and the dainty paraphernalia of that sacred mystery that women celebrate as the sun begins to crawl down the western horizon. For what more fitting place can there be for an afternoon tea than sitting on the broad piazza and gazing upon the distant landscape of hill and valley, or looking out over the white capped breakers as they roll in upon the sandy beach.[9]

Wicker was suitable not just for verandas during hot weather but more important, for year-round use indoors. Actually, the vast majority of Victorian wicker was designed for service inside the home. Increasingly ornate in design, rattan and reed furniture played a vital role in the Victorian housewife's campaign to decorate artfully the rooms of her residence. In the last quarter of the century, the home was specified as the "woman's sphere," the domain where she educated her children and displayed her artistic skills through aesthetic schemes of interior decoration or "household art." The masculine world remained outside the home in the cutthroat realms of commerce and industry. For better or worse, the feminine milieu was defined by the walls of the family home. In the Victorian era, women were believed to have special gifts—the powers of revelation and creation—and they were expected to

use them in the refinement of civilization. One of the best ways to ensure such improvement was for women to employ their innate aptitude for beauty by enhancing home environments through household art. In the 1870s, 1880s, and 1890s, there was an extraordinary emphasis on creativity and artistic self-expression in the home. The ideal late-Victorian house was to be an instrument for exhibiting, both privately and publicly, the civilized nature of its inhabitants. Filled with objects of all sorts, from sea shells to Japanese porcelain, plaster statuary to Dresden china, Oriental carpets to peacock feathers, it was to be a minimuseum of world culture and natural history in which children were schooled in the enduring principles of beauty and morality. It was also to be a complex vehicle for impressing upon visitors the sophistication, taste, and social standing of its owners. As the visitor walked through the ground-floor rooms studying the art-decoration, he or she could judge the family's level of culture and social status by decoding the symbolism inherent in the innumerable things on display—including ornamental wicker. As the visitor moved from room to room, he literally was exposed to a carefully staged aesthetic drama peopled with objects filled with significance.

The first area a guest entered in one of the larger Queen Anne- or Shingle-style houses was a large central living hall. This was the first chapter in the domestic mystery story, the initial statement of the essential themes expressed throughout the house through its decoration. The hall contained a prominent fireplace with a dominant mantel and cozy inglenook. It was a place where wicker chairs and a table were often situated. Even though advances in central heating had rendered it obsolete, the fireplace was invested, in the 1870s and 1880s, with a mystical, quasi-religious significance. It was the "domestic altar, the true rallying point of the household" and its presence in the living hall was a declarative statement of the householder's strong family values. A piece of comfortable Oriental wicker expressed his sophistication and ease with foreign cultures. A book or two on the table was a clue to his intellectual interests. The adjacent parlor was the important display area in the house and contained a less ancestral-looking fireplace. In fact, the fireplace was the principal focus of the room, and over it was one of the most significant features of a suitably aesthetic Victorian house—an elaborate mantelpiece composed of numerous shelves on which were arrayed an assortment of carefully selected curios, portrait photographs, and objects. Clarence Cook described this mantel museum as "the spiritual and intellectual center of the family's life." Because these knickknacks most often had been acquired through inheritance, gift, or during travels, they contained strong personal associations and symbolic significance for the family. As a total environment, the late-Victorian parlor was literally bursting with objects whose relationship to people, places, or events outside the home gave important clues as to the family's social standing, friendships, and experience in the larger

Sitting Room and Parlor of a House in Roxbury, Massachusetts, *ca. 1890.*
Photograph courtesy of the Society for the Preservation of New England Antiquities.
In the last quarter of the nineteenth century, middle-class housewives were urged by tastemakers to fill their houses with morally uplifting "art decoration." Although organized in a seemingly casual fashion, the eclectic furnishings and symbolic ornament in this interior were thoughtfully arranged to strengthen the family's piety, cultural values, and aesthetics—and to impress visitors with the homeowner's sophistication and social standing. A piece of ornate or decorated wicker was an essential component.

world—as well as its knowledge of accepted aesthetic values. Aside from the mantel, other important pieces of specialized display furniture for the parlor included fancy "whatnot" shelves and corner étagères for curios and exotica, often made of rattan, fabric-draped round tables or piano tops suitable for framed photographs and

Veranda of the Original "Breakers," Newport, Rhode Island, *before 1892.*
Photograph courtesy of the Redwood Library and Athenaeum.
Before the original Newport summer home of the Vanderbilt family burned in 1892, its veranda was furnished with wicker ornamented with silk tassels, macramé, swagged fabrics, and bright cushions.

Various Manufacturers, Three White-Painted Armchairs, *ca. 1890s, rattan, wood, caning, and paint. Courtesy of A Summer Place. Photograph by Kit Latham.*

arrangements of dried flowers, and three-legged easels, often made of bamboo or rattan that might hold a family portrait or an engraving of a sentimental subject from art or literature. The parlor was the chief exhibit area for contemporary art furniture and, in the 1890s, antiques that clearly demonstrated the homemaker's level of all-important "taste." An overstuffed, rococo-revival parlor would reveal a chatelaine to be well behind the times, whereas a mix of unmatched furniture—including ornamented reed and rattan—would show her to be up-to-date. The selection of chairs, tables, sideboards, and shelves was of supreme significance in the "Aesthetic" home. The quality of the furniture gave the home its character—even more than the architecture. One instructive critic declared:

[a] hideous house may be made to seem home-like and attractive, to either an inhabitant or a visitor, by a skillful use of artistic furniture and decoration, while inartistic and ugly furniture will effectively destroy the charm of

the most correctly planned and built home. In both cases, the effect of the interior on the mind does away with that of the exterior.[10]

Wicker was an essential component not only in the parlor but elsewhere in the home. In fact, the late-Victorian house was full of specialized rooms in which occasional pieces of rattan and reed

were regularly introduced. The Queen Anne residence typically contained a library with a stylish wicker chair or two. It might also have a separate smoking room or "growlery"—a novel feature in Queen Anne houses—where a husband could withdraw into a private inner sanctum and relax on a wicker lounge or chair, to smoke his pipe or cigar in peace. Wicker was particularly suitable for

women's bedrooms or boudoirs upstairs. Tastemaker Ella Rodman Church advised her female readers to acquire a comfortable rattan chair for their private bedrooms, where they could "lounge in a wrapper and unbound hair before the fire, and think over the events of the day."[11] Seldom was a room outfitted entirely with rattan or reed furnishings—unless it was a domestic work space such as a sewing room, where aesthetics were secondary.

After the 1870s, artistic taste and how to acquire it was the suburban housewife's obsession—and dilemma. Up to that point, the middle-class American had not been trained in matters aesthetic. For the most part, Gothic-revival- and Italianate-style houses of the mid-century had been furnished with wallpapers, carpets, and furniture mostly on the basis of gaudy colors, overstuffed vulgarity, and extravagant carving, all purchased at different stores. To furnish the parlor, the homeowner went to the upholsterer and acquired a cumbersome set of site-specific, rococo- or Renaissance-revival furniture along with heavy drapery treatments for the windows. The chairs and sofas, covered with the same fabric, were arranged formally around the room, parallel to the walls. Carpets with strong, illusionistic flower patterns in brilliant shades were purchased elsewhere, along with the wallpapers. A picture dealer would supply prints, paintings, and decorative mirrors in brightly gilded frames. The result generally was an inartistic hodgepodge of showy items. After 1870 a new ideal was widely promoted: the aesthetically integrated "home beautiful." This was a concept of interior decoration in which everything, from furniture to wall coverings, carpets to pictures was carefully selected so that, as an ensemble, they created a total, harmonious environment. This was a daunting challenge for the inexperienced home decorator. The popular press warned that the decoration of a home directly affected the moral character of the family: beauty ennobled but clashing colors and ugly objects degraded the occupants—especially impressionable children. "All parents are morally bound," declared the editor of *Beck's Journal of Decorative Art* in January 1886 "to instruct their children in the principles of beauty" and not inflict upon them "bewildering wall papers, flashy prints, and glaring chromos." All that stood between artistic salvation

Postcard View of the Basement of A. A. Vantine and Company, the "Oriental Store," New York, ca. 1910. *Courtesy of A Summer Place.*
In the aftermath of the Philadelphia Centennial Exhibition, there was an enormous vogue for decorative arts from the Orient. A. A. Vantine and Company on Fifth Avenue was the largest emporium in America for Chinese and Japanese objets d'art. Among the most popular imports were rattan chairs and tables made to order in Canton, China.

and moral damnation was the homemaker's "taste"—but how was she to acquire it?

By the mid-1870s the housewife could turn for much-needed instruction to an increasing flood

View from the Piazza, Dr. Frederick Hollister House, East Hampton, Long Island, *1912. Photograph from Albro,* Domestic Architecture, *1912, courtesy of the National Museum of American Art, Smithsonian Institution.*
Chinese hourglass chairs enjoyed a tremendous revival at the turn of the century. Examples could be found on the patios and porches of houses along the eastern seaboard and the West Coast. An Oriental chair and an American Bar Harbor—style chair furnish this Long Island, New York, piazza.

of literature on art-decoration. Published mostly between 1872 and 1900, these instructional books and articles were essential components of the household art movement that swept like a firestorm across the American domestic landscape. This popular movement was a middle-class American crusade within the framework of the international Aesthetic Movement and stressed the moral influence of artistic décors. To the Victorian, the beauty of art—in all its many applications—was spiritually uplifting; it had a "refining" influence. Thus, the more artful the home environment, the "finer, truer, and happier" were the lives of those who lived within its aesthetically sanctified precincts. Since the family home was the cornerstone of Victorian society, beautiful and harmonized interiors contributed directly to the moral and ethical health of the nation. In her widely read book, *Art Decoration Applied to Furniture* (1878), novelist and decorator Harriet Prescott

Spofford declared: "Furnishing, although largely woman's work in the direction, is really no trivial matter, to be left contemptuously to the women and girls of the family. Its study is as important . . . as the study of politics; the private home is the foundation of the state, subtle and unimagined influences moulding the men who mould the state."[12]

It was the stated goal of the Aesthetic Movement to bridge the gap between art and industry, to reunite the "beautiful" with the "useful" and in the process, elevate the status of the decorative arts to the level of the fine arts. The application of the term "art" to furniture had originated in England in the 1840s, was popularized there in the 1860s, and reached the shores of America in the early 1870s. In the United States, the art-

decoration movement was, to all intents and purposes, launched by a single, trend-setting publication: Charles Locke Eastlake's *Hints on Household Taste* (1868). Its impact on middle-class home decoration across the United States cannot be overestimated. In Spofford's view, "the book met a great want. Not a marrying couple who read English were without *Hints on Household Taste* in their hands, and all its dicta were accepted as gospel truths."[13] First published in London in 1868, it went through eight American reprints between 1872 and 1886. In 1882 *Harper's Bazaar* facetiously recalled how "Suddenly the voice of the prophet Eastlake was heard crying in the wilderness, 'Repent ye, for the Kingdom of the Tasteful is at hand!'"[14]

Eastlake's epoch-making book

Living Room of a Summer Home in Marion, Massachusetts, *early 1900s. Photograph courtesy of the Society for the Preservation of New England Antiquities. Wicker was the definitive vacation furniture, and summer houses such as this colonial-revival residence in the Buzzard's Bay resort town of Marion were furnished with more wicker pieces than were year-round city or suburban dwellings.*

instructed the masses in the principles of tasteful interior decoration. Strongly influenced by the English design reform movement, the author proposed the notion, radical at the time, that furniture should be functional and non-ostentatious. He decreed it should be simple, rectilinear, and "honestly" constructed, "without sham or pretense." Medieval principles of design and construction strongly influenced his ideas, and the new Eastlake-inspired art-furniture was called "Modern Gothic" in English

Above: Heywood Brothers and Wakefield Company, Gardner, Massachusetts, Tête-à-Tête, Model 6078F, ca. 1898–1904, rattan, wood, caning, and pigment. Courtesy of A Summer Place. Photograph by Kit Latham.

Opposite: Heywood Brothers and Wakefield Company, Gardner, Massachusetts, Reclining Chair, Model 6251, ca. 1898–1910, rattan, wood, and caning. Courtesy of A Summer Place. Photograph by Kit Latham.

Railroad Buffet Car with Reed Chairs Covered in Leather, ca. 1905. Photograph courtesy of the Prints and Photographs Division, Library of Congress.
From about 1885 to 1910, upholstered reed chairs were popular forms of seating in observation, smoking, and buffet cars on railway excursion routes. Their inherent comfort and associations with summer holidays made them popular with railroad car decorators.

circles. Like most reform-minded designers of his age, he detested the excessive and unnecessary curves of mid-century rococo-revival furniture. He believed a chair should look like a chair. It should be "chaste and sober" and composed of straight lines—not a gaudily upholstered, curvaceous assemblage of elaborately carved fruit and flowers. Since they enhanced construction, incised lines, shallow carving, and turned spindles were the only acceptable ornamentation. Visitors to the Philadelphia Centennial were deeply impressed by examples of Modern Gothic furniture on exhibit in the British decorative arts displays, and in the aftermath of the fair there was a boom in American-manufactured furniture stressing, with varying degrees of success, the essential Eastlake qualities—honesty, simplicity, functionalism, and appropriateness.[15]

The Aesthetic-era tastemaker Clarence Cook was Eastlake's most influential American disciple. In his avidly read book, The House Beautiful: Essays on Beds and Tables, Stools and Candlesticks (1878), Cook focused on decorating the parlor or what he called the "living room." The "largest, and pleasantest, and most accessible room in the house," he declared, "ought to represent the culture of the family—what is their taste, what feeling they have for art; it should represent themselves, not other people." As an important agent in education, "it will make a great difference to the children who grow up in it, and to all those whose experience is associated with it."[16] Therefore, its furnishing "deserved to be thought about a great deal more than it is." Cook's illustrated book gave homemakers much food for thought. In order to introduce the family to suitably beautiful and morally uplifting objects, the author recommended not only select plaster casts, paintings, and engravings, but both up-to-date and antique wooden chairs, and Oriental bamboo furniture. He strongly recommended the "deserving" furniture of the Wakefield Rattan Company— although with an Eastlakean warning against excessive curves— "whenever the designs obey the law of the material employed, and do not try to twist or bend it out of its own natural and handsome curves."[17]

Late-Victorian wicker was art furniture for the middle classes, and the voluminous literature of the household art movement constantly urged the use of rattan and reed furniture in artful home decoration. The Wakefield Rattan Company proudly described its furniture as "artistic"[18] and after 1885 introduced increasingly ornate forms that middle-class taste firmly equated with artfulness. Eclecticism was the order of the day. The housewife was advised to combine furniture of many different periods, styles, and materials in order to create a casual, unplanned environment. One tastemaker argued that an ideal parlor was full of "quaint, odd pieces instead of a regular set, as in days gone by."[19] Wicker was essential to the success of an eclectic room arrangement and was regularly introduced to achieve necessary variety and interest. In Constance Cary Harrison's popular book, *Women's Handiwork in Modern Homes* (1882), the housewife could learn the secrets of attaining a heterogeneous mix of wicker, wood, and bamboo chairs in the large, open living rooms of Queen Anne–style dwellings. "Chairs, like after-dinner coffee cups, [are] selected nowadays with a view to their harlequin effect," Harrison reported; "Gilt wicker . . . confronts the rigid dignity of a Tudor or Eastlake specimen in solid wood, while India teak and Wakefield rattan hob-nob most cordially. The Chinese bamboo chairs, gilded, are light and elegant when sparingly introduced, and the old mahogany three-cornered fireside chairs . . . bring back delightfully the old-time memories of our colonial homes in America."[20]

In order to display her personal creativity, the homemaker was urged to upholster and ornament her wicker chairs with cushions and fabrics. Harrison recommended introducing a black wicker chair "cushioned with sage-green stamped plush, and tied with numerous bows of sage-green and pale pink-satin ribbon" along with a comfortable, square-sided Wakefield Rattan Company reed chair called "the Oxford." The latter could be purchased already "ebonized" or picked out in "black and gold" and was just right, she advised, for soft cushions "of peacock blue, of old gold, or of garnet." The degree to which parlor wicker could be "bedizened" in the late nineteenth century is, in retrospect, quite extraordinary. Harrison approved cushions "embroidered with flaring scarlet poppies," which could be tied to a reed lounging chair by "knots of scarlet satin ribbons." Accenting wicker with brilliant red fabrics was clearly one of her favorite fashion statements and must have been followed by innumerable housewives. She even described how an otherwise lowly Wakefield Rattan Company wastepaper basket could be transformed into a suitably ornamental work of art with silk canvas embroidered with crimson trumpet-creepers, bands of crimson and blue plush, and, for good measure, a fringe of crimson chenille knotted with gold silk tassels.[21] It is hard to conceive of anyone attaching the word "waste" to such an extravagantly decorated basket. Harrison was only one of many writers on home handicrafts who advocated fabrics on wicker. The May 1897 issue of the popular *Godey's Lady's Magazine* declared that "Rattan couches, with a bright Bagdad thrown over them, look well mixed in with other furniture."[22]

The New York *Decorator and Furnisher* was likewise full of hints on decorating with natural and painted wicker. In June 1893 writer Virginia Shortridge suggested shellacked rattan for a parlor wainscoted with bird's-eye maple since its natural blond tonality harmonized with the color of the wood paneling. If, on the other hand, the living room was decorated in "green and old pink," it was also "very suitable for rattan furniture" since reed chairs could be purchased "already painted" in similar shades.[23] In its lavishly illustrated 1898–99 sales catalogue, the newly amalgamated Heywood

Unidentified Manufacturer, Round Table, *ca. 1890s, rattan and wood.*
Courtesy of A Summer Place. Photograph by Kit Latham.

Unidentified Manufacturer, Picture Frame, *ca. 1900–10, rattan and wood.*
Courtesy of A Summer Place. Photograph by Kit Latham.

Brothers and Wakefield Company published four-color plates of its "Fancy Colored" reed chairs. Painted an antique ivory, individual components are tinted green, pink, and tan. Shortridge explained how the manufacturers of wicker furniture recently had "exerted themselves to the utmost" to keep pace with advances in factory-produced, ornamental wood furniture: "nothing more dainty or comfortable can be conceived," she gushed, "than the many specialties produced nowadays in rattan and wicker fancy tables, settees, lounges, chairs of all varieties, workbaskets, music stands, tea tables, invalid chairs, cosey [sic] corners, overmantels, not to mention arbors . . . waste baskets, hat stands, gong stands, newspaper racks, linen baskets, bassinets, window blinds and baby carriage bodies." In chairs alone, she continued, "there is an ingenuity and freshness of fancy that is far too seldom met with in the generality of wood furniture."

Besides being "extremely artistic," Shortridge continued, reed and rattan furniture had the "great economic value" of being easily redecorated or refinished whenever the householder wished: "any lady can repaint her furniture with any of the ready made enamel paints on the market, which are to be had in any color." Spring was the season to refinish the household wicker in "robin's egg blue with silver, or pale pink with silver, or pale green"—even an eye-catching combination of "silver and gold bronze." And what could be a more appropriate gift for a June bride, declared a cost-conscious tastemaker in the November 1891 issue of *Decorator and Furnisher,* than "one of those low, delightful wicker chairs, which can be bought anywhere for two dollars. It can be painted to match the room it is destined to be used in with Aspinall's invaluable enamel paints, which have a gloss upon them and can be applied at home and wear beautifully."[24] If repainting was a bother, wicker chairs and tables could be "refreshed" seasonally by draping them with new fabrics, or giant bows, and by interlacing novel combinations of silk ribbons through the latticework. It was important to remember, yet another writer advised, to affix upholstery and fabric swatches to the backs so that they enhanced rather than obscured fanciful patterns.[25] By the mid-1890s, responding to the fad for dressing-up rattan and reed furniture, the major wicker manufacturers sold factory-upholstered parlor chairs and settees already adorned with bows.

Aesthetic-era tastemakers urged that large open rooms be broken up into smaller, more manageable areas by arranging chairs in intimate groupings. Informal seating arrangements were to be dotted around a living room affording discrete areas for privacy, gossiping, or tea-taking. Wicker was a perfect means of achieving the relaxed, seemingly spontaneous look so beloved of Victorians. In fact, with wicker, new arrangements could be formed simply by moving a lightweight rattan chair or tea table to join other, more stationary wood furniture. A slender reed rocker with a see-through back was a visual antidote to the heaviness of an upholstered sofa, and a

mix of wicker throughout a room—a table, a music stand, a sewing basket, a Turkish bench —provided a delicate foil and counterweight to overstuffed walnut furniture or tables draped with richly colored textiles. With its open latticework, the basket-weave or cane-backed chair was also a complement for the strongly patterned wallpapers commonly seen in late-nineteenth-century homes: it didn't conceal the two-dimensional design of the background as did upholstered furniture. Moreover, with its inherent transparency, wicker helped to lighten the visual heaviness and claustrophobic character of many Victorian rooms. Often, a wicker chair or bench was placed at the outer edge of an arrangement of furniture, providing a transition from one area to another within the room and helping to create a sense of spaciousness. In many respects, with its openwork patterns, rattan and reed furnishings performed the same functions inside a chamber that spindled or latticework screens and transom grills did in stairhalls and between rooms: they delineated psychological rather than physical limits to space, and allowed the eye to penetrate to the next zone. Victorians enjoyed being able to glimpse part of the room beyond, to look obliquely through an open doorway or lat-

Unidentified Manufacturer, Easel, *ca. 1890s, rattan and wood. Courtesy of A Summer Place. Photograph by Kit Latham.*

ticework divider to the next inviting space. It added to the sense of mystery and visual complexity they wished to foster in their interiors. Wicker, with its see-through quality, facilitated this perceptual playfulness.

American-made wicker furniture was essential to late-Victorian schemes of art-decoration not only for the formal and psychological roles it played in room arrangements, but because of its strong associational value. With its use of rattan from the Far East, its delicate, Oriental-inspired patterns of caning, and its relationship to Chi-

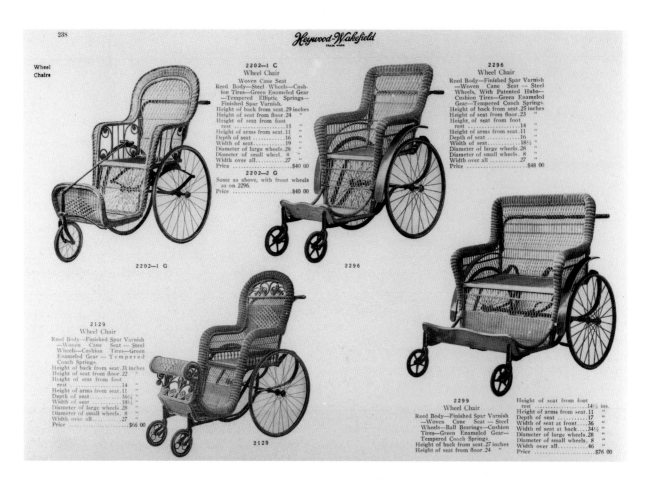

Wheel Chairs

2202–1 C
Wheel Chair
Woven Cane Seat
Reed Body—Steel Wheels—Cushion Tires—Green Enameled Gear—Tempered Elliptic Springs—Finished Spar Varnish.
Height of back from seat.29 inches
Height of seat from floor.24 "
Height of seat from foot
   rest ....15 "
Height of arms from seat.11 "
Depth of seat ....16 "
Width of seat...........19 "
Diameter of large wheels.28 "
Diameter of small wheel. 8 "
Width over all...........27 "
Price $40 00

2202–2 G
Same as above, with front wheels
as on 2296.
Price $40 00

2202–1 G

2296
Wheel Chair
Reed Body—Finished Spar Varnish—Woven Cane Seat — Steel Wheels, With Patented Hubs—Cushion Tires—Green Enameled Gear—Tempered Coach Springs.
Height of back from seat.25 inches
Height of seat from floor.23 "
Height of seat from foot
   rest ....14 "
Height of arms from seat.11 "
Depth of seat ....16 "
Width of seat...........18½ "
Diameter of large wheels.28 "
Diameter of small wheels. 8 "
Width over all...........27 "
Price $48 00

2296

2129
Wheel Chair
Reed Body—Finished Spar Varnish—Woven Cane Seat — Steel Wheels—Cushion Tires—Green Enameled Gear—Tempered Coach Springs.
Height of back from seat.31 inches
Height of seat from floor.22 "
Height of seat from foot
   rest ....14 "
Height of arms from seat.11 "
Depth of seat ....16½ "
Width of seat...........18½ "
Diameter of large wheels.28 "
Diameter of small wheels. 8 "
Width over all...........27 "
Price $66 00

2129

2299
Wheel Chair
Reed Body—Finished Spar Varnish—Woven Cane Seat — Steel Wheels—Ball Bearings—Cushion Tires—Green Enameled Gear—Tempered Coach Springs.
Height of back from seat.27 inches
Height of seat from floor.24 "

Height of seat from foot
   rest ....14½ ins.
Height of arms from seat.11 "
Depth of seat ....17 "
Width of seat at front....36 "
Width of seat at back....34½ "
Diameter of large wheels.28 "
Diameter of small wheels. 8 "
Width over all...........46 "
Price $76 00

Heywood Brothers and Wakefield Company, Wheeled Chairs from the 1909 Illustrated Catalogue of Reed Furniture. Courtesy of the National Museum of American History, Smithsonian Institution. Wheeled wicker chairs either for one or two occupants were popular not only with invalids. They could be found at resorts patronized by the wealthy as well as on seaside boardwalks frequented by working-class excursionists.

nese recliners and hourglass chairs, wicker provoked thoughts of the mysterious Orient. In the last quarter of the century, a vogue for Orientalism swept across the nation, inciting middle-class homemakers to incorporate art-decoration from the East into their homes. Americans long had been familiar with the silks, porcelains, and furniture of the Chinese, but until the epoch-making displays of Japanese products at the Centennial Exhibition, they were ignorant of the arts of Japan. However, in

the aftermath of the fair, Japanese objects became all the rage.

The cult of Japan had started at the London world's fair of 1862, the first to showcase Japanese products in the West, and had immediately spread to Europe. The art and architecture of the long-isolated island nation embodied many of the qualities English design reformers and Aesthetic Movement leaders yearned to reintroduce into Western society: unity, consistency, and simplicity. In fashionable homes and artists' studios, the simple display of a Japanese fan, paper umbrella, or folding screen signaled a firm dedication to new Aesthetic ideals. The passion for painted fans in the West was extraordinary. In 1884 alone, Japan exported to Europe almost four million of them.[26] In America, the craving was likewise

insatiable. In the 1870s and 1880s, household art apostles, including Clarence Cook and Constance Cary Harrison, urged their readers to introduce Japanese artifacts into their eclectic schemes of interior decoration and from coast to coast, Americans enthusiastically tacked paper fans to their walls or propped them up on their mantels. In 1884 the Wakefield Rattan Company, recognizing the popularity and significance of the fan, cleverly introduced a chair design with a delicately woven Japanese fan motif worked into the back. It became an instant hit, and by 1885 the idea was copied by most major wicker manufacturers. The fan fad lasted until 1894 when it was decreed by tastemakers to be passé.

The fervor for things Oriental in the late 1870s and 1880s also sparked a revival of interest in Chinese wicker. During the decade after the Centennial, many stores specializing in Oriental merchandise and Far Eastern wicker opened in cities across America. Most often they were called Japanese Art, Novelty, or Fancy-Goods stores since the term "Japanese" generally connoted anything Oriental, and Americans of the era did not distinguish between goods made in Japan and those made in China. Islamic art forms were also casually defined as Oriental. The most popular emporium for Chinese wicker in the late nineteenth century was the New York store A. A. Vantine and Company. It was located at Fifth Avenue and 39th Street, and from the late 1870s through the 1920s, Vantine's retailed tens of thousands of "chairs from Canton, China." For the most part, these were hourglass models, with or without arms. Celebrated as "cool, comfortable, and artistic," they were described as especially suitable for use on the lawn. Without legs, they could not sink into the ground like other Western-style chairs. Used indoors, on the porch, and in the garden, Chinese hourglass chairs had become so popular that by the late 1890s American firms designed and manufactured their own, better-constructed versions of the chairs.

Wicker was not only an essential component in the primary residences of Victorians but even more so in their second, summer homes. Cottages in rural retreats had been popular since the 1840s, but in the post–Civil War decades the number of vacation houses increased dramatically as the ritual of the summer holiday became

firmly established. By the late 1850s multitudes of middle-class urbanites regularly escaped the city in summer. During July and August, the heat, humidity, stench, and noise was too much for women and children to bear. At first, inland "watering places" were favored sites. By the eve of the

Civil War, however, middle-class Americans had discovered the salubrious effects of salty sea air. Spending a summer on the breezy peninsula of Nahant on Boston's north shore was like taking a months-long sea voyage. After the war, many city dwellers began to buy, rent, or build vacation hous-

Evalyn Walsh McLean and Her Son Vinson in a Wicker Rolling Chair, Palm Beach, Florida, ca. 1913. Photograph courtesy of the McLean Collection, Prints and Photographs Division, Library of Congress.
McLean, the daughter of mining magnate Tom Walsh and wife of the owner of The Washington Post and Cincinnati Enquirer, was famous for her purchase of the Hope Diamond. She and her son were photographed in Palm Beach, Florida, while riding with the family poodle in a wicker "rolling chair," often called an "Afromobile" because their drivers typically were African Americans.

The Fireplace, Grove Park Inn, Asheville, North Carolina, 1913. Photograph by
Herbert W. Pelton, courtesy of the Prints and Photographs Division, Library of Congress.
When the Arts and Crafts–style Grove Park Inn opened in Asheville, North Carolina, in 1913,
the ground-floor lounges were filled with comfortable willow chairs and rockers such as these
drawn up to the roaring fire.

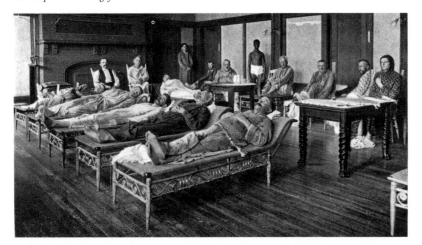

Postcard View of Gentlemen's Cooling Room, Mudlavia Health Resort, Kramer,
Indiana, ca. 1905. Courtesy of Steve Poole and Robert Evans.
After a therapeutic, hot-mud bath at the Mudlavia health spa in Kramer, Indiana, patrons cooled
off while stretched out on reed lounges.

es in seaside "cottage cities" scattered along the eastern seaboard. For the most part, they were modest wooden dwellings in the Gothic-revival style, or after the Centennial, the colonial-inspired Shingle style. In the 1880s and 1890s innumerable rustic summer residences, sheathed with clapboards and shingles and fronted on one or more sides by a veranda, sprouted along the coast.[27]

Wicker was the definitive vacation furniture.[28] Lightweight, airy, and comfortable, it was perfect for summer homes. Since the 1850s, when the Berrians' rattan sofas and Colt's willow chairs first appeared in rural homes, wicker had been firmly associated with the leisure and ease of country living. In the late 1870s the Wakefield Rattan Company extolled their furniture as "the most appropriate . . . for furnishing Sea-side cottages." Since it was "cool, comfortable, and elegant," it was "especially adapted for use at the seashore."[29] In the 1890s a wide variety of manufacturers and household art advocates fervently recommended the use of wicker in vacation homes. In July 1893 an article in *Decorator and Furnisher* declared that "in the furnishing of summer cottages, rattan must be insisted upon. The material satisfies all the requisites of the heated season. It harbors neither moths or dust. It is easily kept clean, and is light and portable, while its elasticity makes it adaptable to various uses and where upholstered furniture would be warm and stuffy."[30] In 1897 Boston's Paine Furniture Company issued an entire sales catalogue devoted to furniture for summer cottages. Its rationale was simple:

"with each recurring year there is a greater attention paid to summer pleasures. The hours of business have been shortened in all walks of life, and summer relaxation, which was once the luxury of the few, has become the law of the many." The catalogue gave five reasons why wicker was the furniture of choice: it was cool and practical; it was "luxurious"; it made the home "beautiful"; it lasted "for a quarter of a century"; and finally, it cost "almost nothing."[31] Among the pieces illustrated was a basketweave lounge with the evocative name, "Dreaming Wide Awake." Paine called it a "shape couch" and declared it to be "the most sumptuous single article of summer furniture ever devised." On one of its shelflike arms was a receptacle for a drinking glass. On the other was a deep pocket in which to store newspapers and magazines when the wind off the sea made reading on the veranda next to impossible or when the sitter dozed off.

In April 1903 the *Grand Rapids Furniture Record* noted the recent increase in summer furnishings. "More and more each season have the manufacturers put out special lines for the summer," the journal reported; "in no [other] branch of the furniture trade has a more remarkable advance been made." The reason was obvious: "the average family—especially in the East, and the custom is growing rapidly in the other sections of the country—spends a generous portion of each year in the summer home, either by the seashore, the lakeside, the mountains or in the country." Even suburban families content to remain in their wooded enclaves

during July and August often had a rustic garden house, gazebo, or tent in their gardens to which they could retreat on hot afternoons and lounge on outdoor furniture. And what kind of seating did they choose? According to the trade journal, "wicker or willow chairs [are] favored, for they are open enough to allow the air to circulate freely about the body, sufficiently pliable to be shaped to fit the figure and strong enough to bear a very considerable strain."[32]

Not everyone had a second home or garden gazebo to furnish. In fact, most vacationers in the last decades of the nineteenth century were city folks who stayed in hotels, inns, or boarding houses either at the seashore, in the mountains, at mineral springs, or in newly established national parks. The pressures of city living in the late nineteenth century demanded periods of rest and recreation in the countryside. Between 1870 and 1914 the number of Americans crowded into dirty, clamorous cities soared from nine to forty-five million. Most yearned to escape during the heat of the summer, and to satisfy the rising demand for vacations, public accommodations at seaside resorts burgeoned. The old barrackslike hotels of the antebellum era were renovated and enlarged, and vast new ones were constructed to house the hordes of city dwellers searching for fresh air, cool breezes, and a place to relax. For well-to-do Bostonians, the Nahant House just north of the city long had been a popular resort for those seeking ocean air and a chance to socialize with their peers. The rugged Isle of Shoals, a group of

seven small islands lying nine miles off Portsmouth, New Hampshire, on the other hand, was a favored destination for those more interested in health than fashionable society. Laighton's Hotel on Appledore and the Oceanic on Star Island catered to those who wished little more than ocean, sky, and salt sea air. The Isle of Shoals was also a summer retreat for artists, writers, and musicians who were attracted by the presence of the islands' most prominent resident, the poetess Celia Thaxter. During July and August her cottage on Appledore was a virtual literary salon. Thaxter's cultured visitors enjoyed not only picturesque views, thoughtful conversations, and informal musicales, but the comfortable rattan rockers in Mrs. Thaxter's sunny parlor. Block Island, Rhode Island, situated between Martha's Vineyard to the north and Long Island on the south, was another ocean resort popular with health-conscious vacationers. The poet John Greenleaf Whittier declared ". . . the pale health-seeker findeth there / The wine of life in its pleasant air." The Hygeia Hotel—built by a physician and named after the Greek goddess of health—specialized in holidays for the tired and run down. The fictional dialogue in an advertising brochure set the Hygeia's tone:

'Where are you going this summer?' 'Well, I don't know,' replied the Judge. 'I have a large family, and it is difficult to find any one place which will suit us all. My wife has a bad throat and catarrh; one of my daughters has been badly poisoned by malaria, another has nervous prostration

Fancy reed chairs in various styles were popular props in turn-of-the-century photography studios across the United States.

Above: Studio Photograph of Roger Tobey Wearing his Father's Baby Dress Seated on an Ornate Reed Bench with the Family Dog, *ca. 1895–1900. Photograph courtesy of Steve Poole and Robert Evans.*

Above left: Studio Photograph of Children Seated on a Heywood-Wakefield Fancy Reception Chair, *Woodstock, New York, ca. 1900. Photograph courtesy of Steve Poole and Robert Evans.*

Left: Studio Photograph of a Man Seated in a Reed Armchair with his Dog and Favorite Fishing Pole, *ca. 1905–10. Photograph courtesy of Steve Poole and Robert Evans.*

Above: Studio Photograph of Child in Fourth of July Regalia with a Fancy Wicker Fireplace Screen, *ca. 1895–1900. Photograph courtesy of The Historic New Orleans Collection, Museum/Research Center.*

Above left: Studio Photograph of an African-American Soldier Taken During the Spanish-American War, *1898. Photograph courtesy of the Savery Library, Talladega College.*

Left: Studio Photograph of General Douglas MacArthur as a Sixteen-Year-Old Cadet at the West Texas Military Academy, *1896. Photograph courtesy of the MacArthur Memorial, Norfolk, Virginia.*

Heywood Brothers and Company, Gardner, Massachusetts, Ladies' Reception Chairs and Square Table, With Sea-Shell Motif, *ca. 1890, rattan, wood, and caning. Courtesy of A Summer Place. Photograph by Kit Latham.*

from over study, and so on through the whole family. Our physician is trying to persuade us to go to Block Island for the summer.' 'Indeed? . . . we have spent several delightful summers there, and I shall be happy to tell you all about the place.'[33]

At the rival Ocean View Hotel, five hundred guests could be readily accommodated—not only in airy rooms but on the vast quarter-mile-long veranda. On this promontory fifty feet above the sea, they sat on rows of wooden and wicker rockers and gazed con-

tentedly at the mesmerizing ocean.

Verandas or "piazzas" were essential features of resort hotels everywhere. For those seeking the purity of ocean or mountain breezes, they served as "fresh air parlors" and oriented the visitor toward the best view. The porch was also the focus of guests' social life and was the special preserve of women. For middle-class families who lacked the advantages of a lavish urban social circuit, the hotel veranda was just the place for Victorian matrons to spot potential husbands for unmarried daughters. Matchmaking at Victorian resorts was serious business, and the piazza was the center of countless courtship dramas. The size of the veranda was an important factor in choosing a summer hotel. In the 1890s the famous

Churchill Hall in the Catskills boasted a continuous 650-foot piazza. Guests at the immense Grand Hotel on Michigan's Mackinac Island could sit in a wicker chair on the vast 880-foot-long veranda and watch the sun rise over one Great Lake and set on another.

After 1870 the summer exodus to resorts was facilitated by the rapid extension of railway lines, interurban transportation systems, and seasonal steamer routes. After boarding trains, passengers rushed for the rolled-arm wicker chairs that regularly furnished observation, dining, and lounge cars. Once they reached their destination, women and children typically stayed at hotels for six to ten weeks while working husbands and fathers often remained for shorter periods or simply visited on week-

Heywood Brothers and Wakefield Company, Gardner, Massachusetts, Set of White-Painted Chairs and Tête-à-Tête, With Sunflower Motif Backrests, ca. 1900. Private collection. Photograph by Kit Latham.

ends. By the turn of the century, such summer rituals were a fact of life for the middle classes.

In 1910 *The New York Times* put the burning question "How long should a man's vacation be?" to a series of prominent individuals. President Taft declared a period of two or three months was about right. A New York State Supreme Court justice decided that for doctors and lawyers two months was preferable, for businessmen it should be one month, while for office clerks two weeks was all that was needed.[34] Workers, on the other hand, had to be content with statutory holidays and only an occasional day off with pay. With such little free time at their disposal, the vast majority could only take day trips in the early 1900s to places like Coney Island or Atlantic City. On the boardwalks, they could take a ride in a wicker "rolling chair"—one of the most definitive experiences of such excursionists' "meccas." The wheeled wicker vehicle was a popular icon celebrated in the 1905 ditty, "Why Don't You Try? or, the Rolling Chair Song."

In the 1880s, 1890s, and early 1900s, a long vacation was viewed as essential to the mental health of educated professionals and their spouses. Urban Victorians suffered great psychological stress. A leading doctor declared that "neurasthenia"—or "the lack of nerve force"—was the leading malady of the age. Symptoms included "fear of responsibility, of open places or closed spaces, fear of society, fear of being alone, fear of fears, fear of contamination, fear of everything, deficient mental control, lack of decision in trifling matters, hopelessness."[35] The "great curse of American civilization," nervousness was declared a "national men-ace," and between 1890 and 1915, it was the topic of obsessive analysis in popular magazines and periodicals. In fact, turn-of-the-century families feared nervous breakdowns as much as a previous generation had dreaded cholera epidemics. For the businessman who experienced panic attacks when elevator doors opened, for the housewife bedridden with "the disease of the age"—nervous prostration—the best prescription was to take a long vacation. The wounded in spirit naturally avoided the crowded verandas of fashionable seaside resorts like the plague. The wicker chairs were filled with gossips. Instead, forest vacations were recommended. Mental hygienists firmly believed in the curative powers of trees, and after the mid-1880s they increasingly advocated summers in the Adirondacks, the Maine wilderness, or the Rockies to cure urban illnesses and restore psychic equilibrium.[36] Hotels in national parks and other wilderness areas blossomed. In such rustic settings as Yellowstone's Old Faithful Inn and Canyon Hotel, wicker was liberally used. For the physically infirm seeking hydrotherapy or mud cures for their ailments, sanitary reed and rattan furniture satisfactorily answered the need for comfort and hygiene. It was also the furniture of choice for tubercular patients in search of fresh-air remedies in Colorado Springs.

For those who were neither sick in mind or body but simply wanted a luxurious holiday in an expensive hotel, all manner of splendid new resorts opened in the Gilded Age. Among the best known was the chain built by Henry Flagler on Florida's east coast from St. Augustine down to the Keys. In porticoed courtyards, tiled lobbies, and lounges filled with potted palms, cool wicker chairs enticed guests to wile away the hot hours. But by the early 1900s reed and rattan furniture was just as likely to be found in bustling metropolitan hotels in the dead of winter. So strong was wicker's association with the leisured life of July and August vacations, it was specifically employed year-round in lobbies, lounges, and tea rooms precisely for its relaxed "summery" look.

NOTES

1. Thomas J. Schlereth, *Victorian America. Transformations in Everyday Life, 1876–1915* (New York: HarperCollins, 1991), 29. See also, Gwendolyn Wright, *Building the Dream: A Social History of Housing in America* (New York: Pantheon, 1981), 96–130; Clifford Edward Clark, Jr., *The American Family Home, 1860–1960* (Chapel Hill and London: University of North Carolina Press, 1986), 72–102.

2. Gavin Townsend, "Airborne Toxins and the American House, 1865–1895," *Winterthur Portfolio* 24 (Spring 1987): 29.

3. Ella Rodman Church, *How to Furnish a Home* (New York: D. Appleton, 1881), 83.

4. Helen Campbell, *The Easiest Way in Housekeeping and Cooking* (Boston: Roberts Brothers, 1893), 20.

5. E. C. Hussey, *Home Building* (New York: Leader and Van Holsen, 1876), iii. For discussions of the suburban idea in the late nineteenth century, see Gwendolyn Wright, *Building the Dream: A Social History of Housing in America*; Clifford Edward Clark, Jr., *The American Family Home, 1860–1960*; and John R. Stilgoe, *Borderland. Origins of the American Suburb, 1829–1939* (New Haven and London: Yale University Press, 1988).

6. James L. Garvin, "Mail-Order House Plans and American Victorian Architecture," *Winterthur Portfolio* 16 (Winter 1981): 321.

7. "American Architecture: Present," *American Architect* 1 (5 August 1876): 50. Quoted in James D. Kornwolf, "American Architecture and the Aesthetic Movement," in Doreen Bolger Burke, et al., *In Pursuit of Beauty: Americans and the Aesthetic Movement* (New York: Rizzoli, 1986), 346.

8. Arnold William Brunner, *Cottages; or, Hints on Economical Building* (New York: W. T. Comstock, 1884), 20.

9. Edward Hurst Brown, "Furnishing the Piazza," *Decorator and Furnisher* 24 (July 1894): 133.

10. "Furniture at the Centennial," *The Aldine* 8 (1876): 297.

11. Church, *How to Furnish a Home*, 87–88.

12. Harriet Prescott Spofford, *Art Decoration Applied to Furniture* (New York: Harper Brothers, 1878), 232. See also, Martha Crabill McClaugherty, "Household Art: Creating the Artistic Home, 1863–1893," *Winterthur Portfolio* 18 (Spring 1983): 1–26.

13. Spofford, *Art Decoration Applied to Furniture*, 147.

14. Quoted in Russell Lynes, *The Art-Makers of Nineteenth-Century America* (New York: Atheneum, 1970), 295.

15. Mary Jean Smith Madigan, "The Influence of Charles Locke Eastlake on American Furniture Manufacture," *Winterthur Portfolio* 10 (1975): 1–22.

16. Clarence Cook, *The House Beautiful: Essays on Beds and Tables, Stools and Candlesticks* (New York: Scribner, Armstrong, 1878), 49.

17. Ibid., 60.

18. Undated catalogue and price list, *Rattan and Reed Furniture* (Boston: Wakefield Rattan Company). This catalogue was located in the Library of the Cooper-Hewitt Museum in New York City.

19. Carrie May Ashton, "An Ideal Parlor," *Decorator and Furnisher* 21 (1892): 25. Quoted in Katherine Boyd Menz, "Wicker in the American Home" (Master's thesis, University of Delaware, 1976), 10.

20. Constance Cary Harrison, *Women's Handiwork in Modern Homes* (New York: Charles Scribner's Sons, 1882), 2:191. Quoted in Marilynn Johnson, "The Artful Interior," in Burke, et al., *In Pursuit of Beauty*, 137.

21. Harrison, *Women's Handiwork in Modern Homes*, 2:205.

22. "Summer Furnishings," *Godey's Lady's Magazine* 135 (May 1897): 660. Quoted in Menz, "Wicker in the American Home," 29.

23. Virginia Shortridge, "Summer Furnishings," *Decorator and Furnisher* 22 (June 1893): 109.

24. "Answers to Correspondents," *Decorator and Furnisher* 19 (November 1891): 72.

25. Virginia Shortridge, "Summer Furnishing," *Decorator and Furnisher* 22 (July 1893): 149. This article is illustrated with numerous engravings of trimmed and fabric-covered reed and rattan furniture.

26. "Notes and Clippings: Japanese Fans," *American Architect* 16 (18 October 1884): 190.

27. Clay Lancaster, *The American Bungalow, 1880–1930* (New York: Abbeville, 1985), 77ff.

28. See Katherine Menz, "Wicker: The Vacation Furniture," in *Nineteenth Century* 8 (1982): 61–67.

29. Undated trade catalogue, Wakefield Rattan Company. This catalogue was located in the Beinecke Rare Book Library, Yale University.

30. "A Summer Cottage," *Decorator and Furnisher* 22 (April 1893): 130.

31. Catalogue, Paine Furniture Company, *Summer Furniture* (Boston: Paine Furniture Company, 1897), introduction.

32. "Something About Summer Furniture," *Grand Rapids Furniture Record* 6 (April 1903): 440.

33. Quoted in Marie L. Aheran, "Health Restoring Resorts on the New England Coast," in *Nineteenth Century* 8 (1982): 45.

34. Schlereth, *Victorian America*, 213.

35. George Miller Beard, *American Nervousness. Its Causes and Consequences* (New York: G. P. Putnam's Sons, 1881), 8. See also, Jackson Lears, *No Place of Grace. Antimodernism and the Transformation of American Culture, 1880–1920* (New York: Pantheon, 1981), 47ff.

36. Stilgoe, *Borderland*, 189–90.

CHAPTER FOUR

The Search for New Materials, Styles, and Meanings in the Progressive Era, 1893–1914

In 1893 a trend-setting New York City decorator, Joseph Patrick McHugh, created an entirely new look by reintroducing willow as the material of choice for fashionable summer furniture. His chic, urban clientele were eager for novel furnishings for their resort homes, and McHugh offered them innovation and style. Factory-made wicker popular with middle-class suburbanites simply did not have the cachet the well-to-do sought for their country houses on Long Island, their retreats in the Berkshires, or their shingled cottages at Bar Harbor. McHugh was just the man to offer the wealthy and style-conscious something they couldn't afford to miss: voguishness. Vivacious, hard-working, and highly intelligent (at age eleven he entered college, where he majored in honors Latin, Greek, and French) McHugh had a sixth sense for detecting the slightest changes in the winds of fashion—inevitably just before they became apparent to other stylists—and thereby was able to establish and dictate a brand-new fad. Willow was only one of the trends he set. He was the first to promote Mission-style furniture, the definitive art furni-

ture of the reformist, Progressive era. McHugh even gave "Mission" its popular name.

McHugh grew up in the dry goods store his father Patrick owned and operated on Bleecker Street. As a youthful student at Holy Cross College in Worcester, Massachusetts, he had planned to enter one of the "learned professions," but reversals in the family's fortunes in 1869 forced him to limit his dreams to the dry goods business. Quick-witted and sharp-eyed, he proved adept at merchandising, adding a window blind and floor-covering section to the family emporium, which became so profitable that his father abandoned the dry goods business altogether, adding carpets and oil cloths to his son's more successful blind-making and matting operations. In 1880 Joseph struck out on his own, opening a store devoted to window shades, upholstery supplies, wallpapers, and odd bits of furniture for decorators. Ever alert to new swings in taste, he became, in 1882, the first New Yorker to sell reproduction colonial-era Windsor chairs. In 1884 he moved his now-thriving operations to a prominent, upscale address, 9 West 42nd Street, opposite the New York Pub-

lic Library and inside the precincts of a fashionable residential neighborhood. McHugh filled his new premises with an abundance of up-to-date and unique home furnishings, offering a one-stop interior decorating service to area householders, clubs, theaters, and churches. He called his store "The Popular Shop" (he was the earliest to use the stylish term "shop"), started a trend by painting the outside of the brownstone different colors, and used the front window as a constantly changing showcase for his latest decorating ideas. His window-dressing skills were legendary and attracted a large and enthusiastic clientele. Long familiar with things Japanese and Aesthetic, McHugh became increasingly fascinated by unusual art nouveau and Arts and Crafts decorations he encountered on buying trips abroad. Innovative art-decorations from Europe suddenly appeared in his casually arranged store, arousing great curiosity. At McHugh's, Manhattanites were exposed to the newest in William

Gustav Stickley, Craftsman Workshops, Eastwood, New York, Armchair, Model 64, ca. 1910, willow and wood. Courtesy of The Wicker Porch Antiques. Photograph by Kit Latham.

Joseph P. McHugh and Company, New York,
Advertisement, *"McHughwillow Furniture," 1914.*
Photograph from Arts and Decoration *(May 1914),*
courtesy of the National Museum of American Art,
Smithsonian Institution.
McHugh's stylish advertisements appealed to an affluent,
design-conscious clientele and helped make his plain-style
wicker fashionable in the years prior to World War I.

Morris chintzes and Walter Crane wallpapers, French metalwork, and Austrian art pottery—and the latest in European art furniture. He was among the first New York decorators to import goods directly from Liberty & Company in London, and by 1892, Joseph P. McHugh had influenced "in a very marked degree" advanced American tastes in home furnishing.[1]

Around 1892, with the assistance of a customer whose bank had a branch in China, McHugh arranged to purchase a load of Oriental wicker direct from manufacturers in Hong Kong. He selected the models he wanted from photographs and ordered a thousand or so hourglass chairs and rattan lounges. When the shipment arrived, he was cha-

grined by the inferior quality of its construction. Before he could sell it, he had to pay twenty-five percent of the wholesale purchase price just to make repairs. But demand for Oriental wicker among the well-to-do was skyrocketing and despite its flimsiness, the entire shipment quickly sold out. The brisk sales taught McHugh that there was a strong market for lightweight summer furniture. McHugh contemplated how he could best enter the crowded wicker field. To capture the buyers' jaded attention, he obviously needed a fresh approach to making attractive and comfortable furniture that satisfied the new interior design fashions he was promoting. He continued to import better quality Oriental wicker, but it remained only a minor sideline. With its agents in the Far East, A. A. Vantine and Company continued to dominate the booming market for Chinese chairs. Since McHugh wished to foster demand for unusual items that only he could supply, he had to decide whether he should retail American-made wicker, sell exclusive imports from Europe, or create altogether novel designs himself. The increasingly ornate and, from his point of view, outmoded designs of American reed and rattan furniture were simply not appropriate for his trend-setting Popular Shop. Neither were the

different patterns of rattan and willow chairs made in France, Germany, England, and the Madeira Islands. McHugh realized they were insufficiently adapted to American needs and tastes in the early 1890s. To capture a share of the lucrative summer furnishings market, he had to offer something entirely different and irresistibly appealing to his style-conscious clientele.

In early 1893 McHugh decided to produce his own wicker, employing willow rather than rattan as his medium. He was the first American furniture maker in a generation to use willow. Basketmakers employed osiers, but in the early 1890s no one in the United States was using willow to manufacture stylish furniture. McHugh's choice of willow would guarantee a degree of novelty—the essence of his general sales strategy. His next step was quite innovative and clever. Looking through his stock, he chose a select number of

Joseph P. McHugh and Company, New York,
The McHughwillow "Belknap" Chair,
ca. 1904. Courtesy of the National Museum
of American Art, Smithsonian Institution.
The "Belknap" was modeled on a standard wing
chair design. One of its arms contained a pocket
for storing reading material. In the early 1900s
it was copied widely by rival manufacturers.

upholstered chairs he knew would sell well and had them uncovered. He then carefully measured the wood frames and employed "a young artist, who knew nothing of furniture, to sketch them in perspective, substituting stakes for the frames, and filling in the vacant spaces with latticed windows."[2] The measurements and renderings were then taken to a New York willow-ware factory where basketweavers produced the first prototypes. They proved highly successful: "Everyone, including the basketmakers and the furniture dealers, was pleased." McHugh's new line was launched in 1893 and named "McHughwillow." Its simplicity of design and construction was to help redirect the course of American wicker away from fanciful shapes and toward a new plain style that suited the post–Victorian era. One of the early models was a traditional wing chair he called the "Belknap." It was an appropriate design for an emerging market. Eighteenth-century

The Piazza of a House at East Hampton, Long Island, *ca. 1912. Photograph from* Albro, Domestic Architecture, *1912, courtesy of the National Museum of American Art, Smithsonian Institution.*
This elegant outdoor setting on Long Island contains a set of willow furniture made by one of McHugh's strongest competitors, the Manhattan firm of Minnet and Company, whose factories were located in Carlstadt and Hoboken, New Jersey.

The Bar Harbor Chair

Designed by Jos P. McHugh & Co. New York.

Joseph P. McHugh and Company, New York, The McHughwillow "Bar Harbor" Chair, 1898. Courtesy of the Warshaw Collection of Business Americana, Archives Center, National Museum of American History, Smithsonian Institution.

furniture designs were then making a comeback as well-to-do homeowners outfitted their new Georgian-style residences with colonial-era furniture patterns. But while suitably old-fashioned in shape, the Belknap had a novel feature that made it an instant hit on Long Island loggias: one of its armrests had a deep pocket into which books and newspapers could be stored at tea time or whenever the occupant just wanted to sit and gaze into the distance and doze off in comfort. It became a best-seller and, for the following twenty-five years, the wicker wing chair with its convenient pocket regularly appeared, indoors and out, in stylish homes and resorts. The popular Belknap even materialized as a prop in magazine illustrations. But the most influential McHughwillow design was the "Bar Harbor" chair, another alum-

nus of the class of ninety-three. It proved one of the most popular and enduring designs and was imitated widely before the First World War. By 1915 McHugh and his son and business partner, James Slater McHugh, felt that their business was so threatened by all the look-alike Bar Harbor chairs flooding the market that they registered copyrights on the name and design with the Library of Congress.

Thirteen years earlier, on April 5, 1897, McHugh had been interviewed by the *New York Tribune* on the success of his new willow furniture. In "A Talk on Wicker Furniture," the proprietor of the Popular Shop extolled its obvious handmade quality — no two looked exactly the same—as well as its easy adaptability to changing fashions in design and color. Part of McHughwillow's trendiness was due, he declared, to the "undeni-

Above: Various Manufacturers, Large Armchairs and Child's Rocker, *ca. 1898–1920, rattan, wood, and caning. Courtesy of Charlie Wagner, The Wicker Lady, Inc. Photograph by Kit Latham.*

able fact" that a well-dressed woman always looked good in open-weave willow—no part of her outfit was obscured. As a result, "a clever hostess" was sure to place her fashionably attired, female guests on "seats of wicker in most artistic places." His ideas for designs came, he related, not only from upholstered furniture patterns but also from English and American illustration art. In the 1890s a variety of popular magazines on both sides of the Atlantic published pen-and-ink drawings of stylish

people in humorous situations seated on wicker chairs. When warranted, McHugh was quick to appropriate their novel designs—and certainly their modish associations—for his own willow chairs. Suggestions also came from friends and acquaintances as well as from clients who wanted customized features or designs which, if deemed attractive enough, were then added to his general line. Over the years, he also adapted numerous forms based on popular English, European, and even Oriental models.

Once a new design had been refined, a draftsman prepared a full-scale shop drawing of the piece. It was taken to the willow-

Opposite: Unidentified Manufacturer, "Bar Harbor"–Style Chair, *ca. 1905–20, willow, wood, and paint. Private collection. Photograph by Kit Latham.*

ware weavers who set the sketch in front of them and reproduced it in three dimensions. The wicker-workers began by weaving the seat on a frame made from thick wooden dowels. When this first step was completed, turned dowels forming the legs were inserted, and the skirt below the seat was woven, working upwards from the spirally braided feet. The framing posts for arms and backs were then joined to the seat, and following the drawing, the weaver filled in the sides and backrests with a widely spaced latticework of wil-

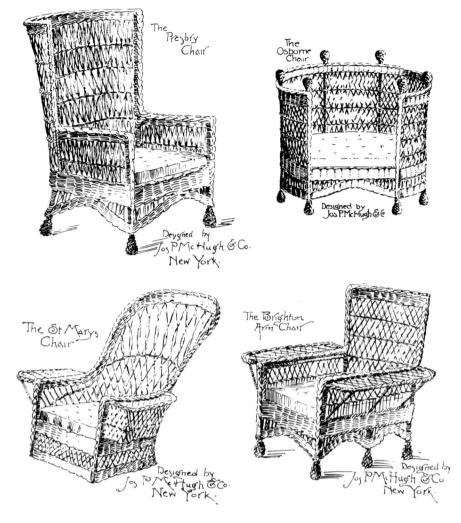

The Presbry Chair

The Osborne Chair

Designed by
Jos P. McHugh & Co.
New York.

Designed by
Jos P. McHugh & Co.

The St Marys Chair

The Brighton Arm Chair

Designed by
Jos P. McHugh & Co.
New York.

Designed by
Jos P. McHugh & Co
New York

Joseph P. McHugh and Company, New York, Designs from the 1898 Some Pictures of Quaint Things Catalogue. Courtesy of the Warshaw Collection of Business Americana, Archives Center, National Museum of American History, Smithsonian Institution. McHugh's draftsmen employed a deliberately crude drawing style that appealed to the contemporary taste for the handmade.

low rods. Finally, the untrimmed edges were often covered with decorative braidwork. McHugh's simple basketweave chairs were so resilient that they naturally adjusted to the weight and shape of the sitter's body and were exceedingly comfortable. At the Popular Shop they could be purchased already painted or ordered custom-toned in shades of forest green, nut brown, delft blue, ivory, or ebony. More dazzling colors were also available—sealing-wax red, Spanish yellow, indigo blue, and emerald green. To produce these brilliant hues, chairs and tables were dropped into steaming vats in which bright aniline dyes were boiled into the wood of the peeled willow. The colors were much more dramatic than those favored by the Wakefield Rattan Company's customers in the 1890s and anticipated the luminous tints of 1920s wicker. McHugh even created striking two-tone patterns by weaving black-painted osiers with brightly dyed rods.

By 1897 McHugh had his own master furniture designer on staff, the imaginative and highly versatile Walter J. H. Dudley. In 1896 Dudley had been responsible for originating the Popular Shop's Arts and Crafts–inspired Mission furniture—its most successful and critically acclaimed product line.[3] But at the same time as he was preparing drawings for straight-lined chairs in oak, Dudley produced even larger numbers of more relaxed designs in willow. Many of these were illustrated in two fashionably titled 1898 sales catalogues: *More than a Hundred Pen Sketches of Certain Very Picturesque and Agreeable Pieces of Furniture,* and *Some Pictures of Quaint Things.* Given the small size of his wickerwork operation and the limited production of individual designs, the line was unusually extensive. The 1904 McHughwillow catalogue included line drawings of 147 different functional items, from chairs, settees, swing seats, and lounges to wheeled tea carts, muffin-racks, picnic baskets, nesting tables, desks, songbird cages, and, for the sporting set, willow golf club hampers. In his own drawings for wicker, Dudley mimicked the crude and simplistic style of McHugh's original draftsman, self-consciously maintaining the stylish "quaint" feeling his boss was eager to preserve. To reinforce this mood McHugh christened his wicker with evocative names rather than model numbers, and each of Dudley's sketches is accompanied by a handwritten designation. Few stylish New Yorkers bound for a weekend on Long Island or a summer at Bar Harbor could resist stopping by the Popular Shop to pick up an "Oolong Muffin Rack," an "Oxford Smok-

er," or a "Tillbury Tea Cart." In 1915, to supply the resort market more directly, the McHugh Summer Shop was opened on Narragansett Pier: willow chairs were advertised as "cool and pleasing for the country house."

In 1916, in recognition of his business accomplishments, McHugh was invited to give the commencement address at his alma mater. He happily returned to Worcester for the first time since 1869 and was fêted at a college banquet in his honor. But the originator of McHughwillow never

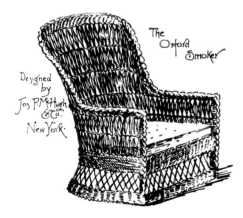

Joseph P. McHugh Company, New York, McHughwillow "Oxford Smoker," ca. 1904. Courtesy of the National Museum of American Art, Smithsonian Institution. With its enclosed skirt, the "Oxford Smoker" was based on a popular English willow basket chair style. In design and construction, the chair is rooted in traditional Roman-era wicker.

gave his inspirational speech to the graduating seniors. Before dawn on commencement day, he died in his sleep in a Holy Cross College dormitory room. An obituary published in the December 1916 edition of *The Upholstery Dealer and Decorative Furnisher* reported that "Mr. McHugh was naturally bright and extraordinarily adept in learning things. . . . He had a wonderful gift of expression and an individuality that reflected itself in everything he did or undertook. He numbered among his friends authors, artists, newspaper men, explorers, politicians and others of note. He did things differently from other people, and was alive to the spirit of his times."[4] The Popular Shop continued under the able direction of James Slater McHugh and Walter Dudley, and McHughwillow remained fashionable into the 1920s. Ironically, almost no labeled examples of McHughwillow have survived. Simply explained, when painted, osier rods tend to dry out, become brittle, and eventually the basketweave structure disintegrates. But if few models actually remain, their influence persists in the numerous extant imitations produced by McHugh's competitors

Sons-Cunningham Rattan Company, New York, Advertisement, The Upholstery Dealer and Decorative Furnisher, December 1901. Courtesy of the Library of Congress. The Sons-Cunningham firm was one of several manufacturers of specialty wicker in New York who mimicked the trend-setting designs and drawing style of McHugh and Company. Instead of willow, the firm employed reed, which they colored in "rich shades."

who, after 1900, endlessly repeated the simplicity of his willow designs. In 1905 the magazine *Ideal House* noted the dramatic evolution that had recently occurred in the design of wicker furniture:

In reed . . . rattan, willow, and fibre rush chairs there is . . . a most notable advance in design, largely tending toward greater simplicity. The scrolls and whirlygigs of rattan that were inevitable in these chairs a few years ago are being discarded in the better furniture. It is being appreciated that these finicky twists and whirls add nothing to the beauty or the stability of such furniture.[5]

The materials for plain-style McHughwillow came from York County, Pennsylvania, one of the most productive areas for willow culture in the eastern United

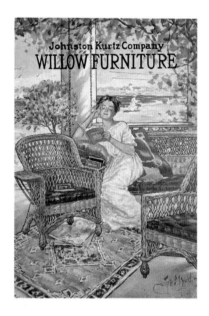

States. Although willow was easy to grow and harvest, and was a proven cash crop, Anglo-American farmers remained resistant to growing it. It fell to immigrant Germans to foster its cultivation. In the 1880s, Liverpool, New York, had the largest population of German willow farmers and basketmakers, but in the 1890s osier growing began to be vigorously promoted all across the United States—not only for traditional basketware but for woven furniture as well. On January 25, 1893, the *Wooden and Willow-Ware Trade Review* reported that the wetlands along the Missouri River near Sioux City, Iowa, were just right for cultivating osiers in order to supply the growing western mar-

ket for willow manufactures of all kinds. "Eight or ten years ago," the journal stated, "a Willow-Ware factory meant merely a place where baskets were made, now it represents the place where an indefinite variety of articles of furniture are produced." Wild native willow was of little use to wicker weavers: it was too stiff. The skeins of imported species cultivated especially for delicate basketware were so pliable they could be used as shoe laces. But for the type of rod used in McHughwillow, a much thicker and more rigid shoot was needed, the sort cut from the *Salix viminalis* that Samuel Colt had first planted along his Connecticut River dike in the 1850s. Forty years later, this species was grown commercially in Pennsylvania and Maryland. Expanding cultivation notwithstanding, most basketweavers' supplies came from Germany or France, both of which did a roaring business in North America with exports of both processed willow shoots and woven goods. To promote greater local growth and more American-made willow-ware, the U.S. Department of the Treasury instituted higher tariffs on imported willow. In 1895 basketweavers' supplies were taxed thirty percent and finished goods forty percent ad valorem. Federal intervention seems to have helped. The *Wooden and Willow-Ware Trade Review* reported in late 1898 that a Clyde, New York, farmer had sold 114 tons of willow rods, the largest single crop ever recorded, to one George Dietz, a prominent Liverpool, New York, basket manufacturer. But as demand for flexible osiers surged in the early 1900s, local suppliers could never keep up. One of the most active willow-ware factories was operated in Milwaukee by the Wisconsin Workshop for the Blind. In 1906 an administrator reported that he had to import nearly all the workshop's stocks: "our country does not grow enough willow to supply a few dozen shops of the size of ours, each using between 40,000 and 50,000 pounds per year. We are therefore obliged to look for our main supply to the foreign countries, especially Germany and France."[6] European supplies cost seven to eight cents a pound whereas the charge for locally grown willow, the official believed, would amount only to four or five cents. Since it thrived on land otherwise unfit for crops, he could not account for American farmers' continued reluctance to plant willow. Neither could the U.S. Department of Agriculture. Washington bureaucrats constantly

Postcard View of the Willow Furniture Factory at Paine's Furniture Company, Boston, *ca. 1910. Courtesy of Steve Poole and Robert Evans.*

urged willow cultivation. They even sent out free pamphlets and brochures on the subject. But "The Basket Willow, Bulletin 46" proved to be an insufficiently inspiring document. In 1908 there were more than 160 willow-ware manufacturers active in the United States, but only one-tenth of them grew their own stock. Another ten percent raised at least part of their supplies; but all the rest relied upon imported osiers. The cost of European materials, even with the additional tariff charge, was nevertheless low enough to encourage the growth of willow furniture manufacturing, and, in the early 1900s, the number of new firms escalated sharply. Among the leaders in the New York City area—the heart of willow furniture making in America—were Minnet and Company (founded in 1898), Bielecky Brothers, F. Debski, Grand Central Wicker Shop, and the Walter J. Brennan Company. Boston-area manufacturers included the long-established Paine's Furniture Company, Willowcraft, The Bolton Wil-

Johnston-Kurtz Company, Buffalo, New York, "Bar Harbor Suite" side chair from the 1911 Willow Furniture Catalogue. *Courtesy of the Warshaw Collection of Business Americana, Archives Center, National Museum of American History, Smithsonian Institution.*

American Grass Twine Company, St. Paul, Minnesota, Advertisement, "Crex" Prairie Grass Furniture, ca. 1903. Photograph courtesy of A Summer Place. Prairie grass was a tough, long-bladed wire grass native to wetlands in the Midwest. In the early 1900s it was harvested by the American Grass Twine Company and used at their Long Island, New York, plant to weave extensive lines of wicker furniture retailed under the trade name "Crex." Naturally green-toned, Prairie Grass furniture was praised for its durability. Production ended during the First World War.

low Shop, and the Boston Willow Furniture Company. In Philadelphia and Buffalo, Charles Schober and Johnston-Kurtz produced extensive lines of willow furniture—including Bar Harbor chairs. The trend started by McHugh was not interrupted until the autumn of 1914, when the outbreak of World War I suddenly halted large shipments of European osiers and seriously set back the willow-ware industry in the United States. In the war-torn fields of western France, local willow was used to weave baskets for artillery shells.

At the turn of the century, willow had not been the only viable alternative to rattan and reed for weaving lightweight furniture. The search for inexpensive, locally grown supplies had turned up a novel material—wire grass or *Carex stricta*. This wild plant thrived on thousands of square miles of prairie wetlands in Minnesota and Wisconsin and was regarded as a pest. Individual blades grew to a height of several feet and were so tough and fibrous that even livestock would not consume it. For years, the American Grass Twine Company of St. Paul, Minnesota, had woven extremely durable carpets from wire grass. In 1900 the firm decided to exhibit its wares at the *Exposition Universelle,* the epoch-making world's fair held that year in Paris. The ever-vigilant *Wooden and Willow-Ware Trade Review* report-

ed in March 1900 that they would show a number of newly introduced articles "made of Marsh Grass . . . in lieu of Reed, Rattan, or Willow." These included folding screens, baskets, and baby carriages, and their appearance marked a breakthrough into a new realm of woven furniture. In June 1900 the trade journal revealed that the American Furniture and Manufacturing Company of Brooklyn, a subsidiary of the St. Paul firm, was now producing wire-grass furniture that they hoped would altogether replace rattan and willow furniture. The novel goods proved an immediate sensation, and in 1902 a vast new factory was built in Glendale, Long Island, especially for the manufacture of Prairie Grass furniture. The same year, Montgomery Ward and Company offered a selection of the new chairs to their vast mail-order clientele in a catalogue titled "High

Grade Furniture." The pieces were described as similar to those woven from reed but "handsomer in color" and more durable.

In 1903 the American Grass Twine Company issued its first color trade catalogue illustrating more than 260 models. For the most part, the chairs, divans, lounges, benches, music stands, tables, hampers, and screens mimicked popular designs in reed and rattan. Many were twine-wrapped, fanciful forms in the ornate style of Heywood Brothers and Wakefield Company, but there was also a Belknap-type chair as well as several other forward-looking, simplified designs. Grass furniture was retailed by dealers under the trademark "Crex," which was accompanied by the advertising jingle, "From the Prairies of America to the Homes of the World." The company advertised heavily, and its products were well known to consumers throughout the United States. Copywriters praised the soft, green tonality for its ability to blend harmoniously into its surroundings. Prairie Grass furniture was extolled not only for its durability but also for its hygienic quality. In trade literature, it was regularly advertised as germ-free—an important factor in the hygiene-obsessed early 1900s. By 1913 the Crex line had grown to an astonishing four hundred items that were now available in two shades, "Nature Green" and "Baronial Brown." The last Crex catalogue appears to have been issued in 1916, and by the close of World War I grass furniture had gone out of style, having been replaced by a surprising new man-made material. As a curious aside, the St. Paul

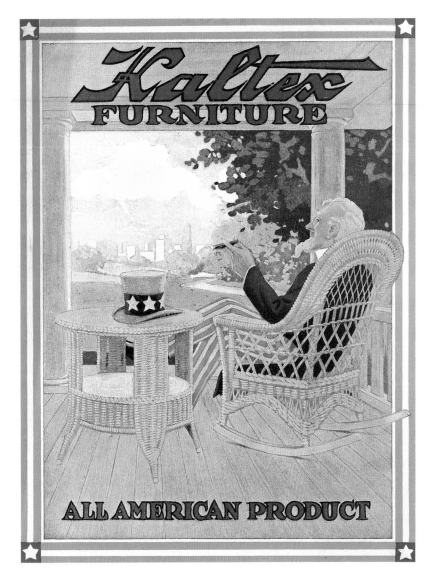

Michigan Seating Company, Jackson, Michigan, Cover of the 1917 "Kaltex" Furniture Catalogue. Courtesy of Frog Alley Antiques/Merry P. Gilbert, New York City. The Michigan Seating Company was one of the first to manufacture furniture from man-made "fiber." During World War I, when supplies of Asian rattan and European willow were seriously disrupted, increasing numbers of firms turned to the inexpensive "All American Product."

firm had not been the only enterprise to use native vegetation to manufacture wicker. In 1904 the somewhat mysterious H. and W. Company of Leominster, Massachusetts, had set about making imitation reed furniture from wild grasses and plants gathered from southern states. According to the *Wooden and Willow-Ware Trade Review*, the New Englanders had a secret formula for mashing up and chemically treating the flora, then pressing the sodden mass into "desired shapes."[7] Precisely what these forms were is anybody's guess. Nothing further is known about the product.

Also in 1904, another entirely new material for weaving furniture had been invented that, after the outbreak of the First World War, proved so wildly successful that it eventually supplanted both reed and rattan as the most common material for wicker furniture. The

Grand Rapids Fibrecord Company, Grand Rapids, Michigan, Manual Training Class Weaving Furniture from Fiber, ca. 1925. Photograph courtesy of A Summer Place.
In 1904 a new man-made wicker material was developed. Made of long, thin strips of paper which were mechanically twisted and sized with glue, it was called fiber, or "fibre." Inexpensive and easier to use than reed or willow, the new material revolutionized the wicker industry. Fiber ushered in the age of classroom and homemade wicker created from kits sold by handicraft companies. By 1930, fully eighty-five percent of even manufactured wicker furniture was made of fiber.

substance was man-made and cleverly called "fibre." Also commercially known as "fiber," "fibrecord," "art-fibre," "fiber-rush," or any other combination or spelling of the word, the modern product was simply a thick string made of mechanically twisted paper. The term fiber, of course, sounded more elegant than paper—after all, who would want furniture made of paper? And most consumers never really knew its source. Fiber furniture first appeared in 1904, when the otherwise unremarkable Western Cane Seating Company introduced a fiber-woven chair with a wood-and-rattan frame.[8] However, the credit for inventing and perfecting the machinery to twist rolls of paper into long, tough cords—and thus really sparking the mass-production of fiber furniture—goes to one H. Morris, an employee of the long-established Ford Johnson Furniture Company of

Chicago that called its new wicker line "Fiber-Rush." The patented Morris machines became the industry standard and were soon installed by the Michigan Seating Company of Jackson, Michigan, producers of the famous "Kaltex" line of fiber furniture; P. Derby and Company of Gardner, Massachusetts; and the Ypsilanti Reed Furniture Company of Ionia, Michigan. By 1912 only these four firms were using fiber, yet their market share of wicker sales amounted to fifteen percent. With the sudden disruption of foreign supplies of reed and willow that followed the outbreak of the war in Europe, a majority of American wicker factories were forced to use the inexpensive man-made material or go out of business. After 1918 the imposition of high import duties on foreign products solidified the industry's dependence upon fiber, and by 1921 its production in the United States was a

five-million-dollar-a-year business. It was so inexpensive and easy to use that, by 1930, fully eighty-five percent of all wicker manufactured in the United States was made of strands of twisted paper.[9] Fiber was also widely used in high-school manual training classes and by a generation of handicrafters who filled their living rooms with homemade chairs, lamps, wastepaper baskets, and ferneries. An unsung hero of American wicker, Morris belongs, along with William Houston of the Wakefield Rattan Company, Gardner A. Watkins of Heywood Brothers and Company, and later Marshall B. Lloyd, to that elite group of inventive American engineers who mechanized the age-old craft of furniture weaving into a modern industry, pushing the mass production of wicker to ever greater heights. With Morris's inventions, however, the altitude reached proved too precarious to maintain a critical balance between art and mass production. As the manufacture of fiber furniture skyrocketed, prices fell dramatically, and quality declined. Only the larger firms such as Heywood-Wakefield and the Lloyd Manufacturing Company, who manufactured the best grades and used newly invented power looms, maintained high standards. By 1930 general run-of-the-mill fiber furniture had become bargain-basement goods, and as a result, woven furniture lost much of its stylishness.

Fiber was made from coniferous wood that had been reduced to pulp using the sulfite process. In this procedure, the shredded timber was "slow cooked" in a solution of sulfuric acid to produce paper of superior strength. Under

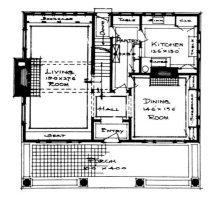

Gustav Stickley, Floor Plan and Rendering of a "Craftsman" Cottage, 1909. *Photograph from Stickley,* More Craftsman Homes, *1912, courtesy of the National Museum of American Art, Smithsonian Institution.*

The simple bungalow replaced the multiroomed Queen Anne–style house as the preferred residence for progressive-minded, middle-class Americans in the early 1900s. Stickley was one of the chief proponents of the bungalow, and each issue of his monthly magazine, The Craftsman, *published floor plans and sketches of different models.*

a microscope, the grain looked as if it were composed of long strands of silk floss. The alternate "soda" process of papermaking produced a wood pulp with a short grain that could not stand up to the stress of machine spinning into cord. In design and operation, Morris's machinery was quite simple. A large roll of fifty to sixty-pound stock, measuring between thirty-six and forty inches, was first placed on the splitting machine. The paper sheet was then passed under a roller containing a set of adjustable circular knives that sliced the single roll into a series of smaller, individual ones: four-, three-, or one and three-eighth-inches wide, depending on the diameter of the fibercord desired. The spools were next placed on a machine that moistened the narrow strips by pulling them through a trough of water. During

this procedure, if desired, the paper could be tinted with dyes. Slightly wetted, the sulfite paper was even tougher and was ready for the lathelike spinning machine. The operator of this device placed the spool of damp paper on a shaft in front, pulled the strip through two tension-creating rollers and then, tearing off a corner, fed this curled angle through a circular hole in the machine that could be set to

produce fiber strands of different thicknesses. The manually twisted end was then passed through a set of disklike guides and finally attached to a spool on the other side. With the machine in operation, the spool revolved and the moistened strip was automatically drawn through the die and twisted into a tightly wound cord. In the stake-spinning machine, glue could be applied, so that when air-

Living Room of a Bungalow Furnished with Gustav Stickley's "Craftsman Willow Furniture," ca. 1912. *Photograph courtesy of Steve Poole and Robert Evans.*
The antithesis of the over-decorated, late-Victorian parlor, this spare Craftsman–style living room is furnished with Gustav Stickley's angular Craftsman Willow furniture. First introduced in 1907, it was modeled on modern Austrian and German wicker furniture.

Various Manufacturers, Tête-à-Tête, Round Table, and Lidded Basket, ca. 1898–1920, rattan, wood, pigment. Private collection. Photograph by Kit Latham.

dried the twined fiber was given greater stiffness. It could then be cut in lengths and used as the rigid, vertical stakes in the weaving process. Not only was fiber easy to make, but it was easy to use. Unlike reed, it did not have to be soaked to become pliable. Moreover, it neither splintered nor broke. When properly manufactured, the sulfite-paper fiber actually proved hardier than natural materials. Its only problem was that it unraveled slightly when left too long in the rain.

Between 1893, when McHugh-willow first appeared, and 1914, when the use of fiber began to

escalate, American social and cultural values underwent massive change, deeply affecting the design and use of all woven furniture. The late-Victorian era with its love of exaggerated sentiment and ornamentation rapidly faded to be replaced by a new, tough-minded era that valued science and economy in thought, action, and industrial design. The sheer magnitude of the financial collapse following the Panic of 1893 and the resultant human misery forced Americans to rethink many of their collective values. Was capitalism a fair economic system? Could the flood of immigrants be properly assimilated? Were Congress, the courts, schools, and the police capable of solving social problems? Once-cherished Victorian beliefs came under harsh attack as icono-

clastic politicians, social reformers, philosophers, labor leaders, muckraking journalists, novelists, artists, and photographers, cut through the veneer of appearances to expose the harsh realities of turn-of-the-century America. In the search for new, rational standards of living, the design of the ideal middle-class home and its furnishings in the Progressive era underwent a total metamorphosis.

Beginning in the 1890s, social and architectural reformers attacked the eclectic, late-Victorian house as inartistic, inefficient, and unhealthy. Progressives criticized the embellished Queen Anne–style dwellings as architectural "monstrosities" that were poorly built and contained too many rooms filled with too much bric-a-brac. To maximize architectural decoration within set budgets, the late-nineteenth-century builders often had skimped on construction quality, and as a result the roofs leaked, plaster cracked, and the window frames and ornamental shingles came loose. Inside, the plumbing systems were outdated and unsanitary, and the multiroomed dwellings could not be properly heated. By 1900 the Victorians' passion for display was also decreed by a new breed of Progressive tastemakers to be morally and aesthetically repugnant. Instead of expressing ennobled taste, tough-minded reformers believed it expressed nothing more than vanity and deceitfulness. Ornamentation was out. Simplicity was in—and with a vengeance. One arbiter declared in the February 1900 issue of *Good Housekeeping* that "simplicity is three-fourths of beauty" while another article published in the June 1901 issue of the same magazine harshly criticized the "plague of ornateness" that had infected all moderately priced household articles in the 1890s. The author asserted that housewives with good taste were ashamed to have "vulgarly ornamented" things in the home and warned manufacturers that the "fatuous craze for the crudely ornate" was over.[10]

The florid art-decoration beloved by late Victorians was also denounced as unsanitary. Decorative clutter, heavy draperies, textured wall surfaces, and elaborate, machine-cut ceiling moldings, were strongly censured for harboring germ-laden dust. Dust certainly had been the bane of Victorian housewives and parlor maids. Before the invention of the vacuum cleaner, when feather dusters

Heywood Brothers and Wakefield Company, Gardner, Massachusetts, Swinging Crib, Model 6278, ca. 1898–1904, rattan, wood, and metal. Private collection. Photograph by Kit Latham.

and brooms had been the only tools, dust had been almost impossible to remove from mantel displays, upholstered furniture, and rugs. Every surface in the parlor was covered with films of dust to some extent—except the wicker. Manual cleaning methods simply stirred up interior dust storms. While bothersome and cough-provoking, dust had not been characterized as infectious and a serious hazard to health. Until the dawn of the new century, "carbonic acid" remained the householder's most dreaded enemy. But in the early 1900s, dust took its place as sanitarians broadcast the

dangers of germ-infected, airborne particles. An all-out campaign for home hygiene now replaced the household art movement as the most powerful force in shaping the middle-class dwelling. A popular 1917 book, *The Healthful House*, advocated the new ideal of a dustless residence. "The dangers of dust are not a product of the imagination of scientists," the authors warned. Dust was often made up of "the organic filth of the street, of decayed vegetable and animal substances" that blew into the house through open windows or cracks in the walls. Such offensive particles afforded "a splendid medium

Photograph of the 1905 Secessionist Art Exhibition, Vienna. *Photograph from International Studio (July 1905), courtesy of the National Museum of American Art, Smithsonian Institution.*
On display at the exhibition was a set of basketweave chairs made by the Viennese firm Prag-Rudnicker, the leading manufacturer of willow art furniture.

for the collection and development of germs . . . of a disease-producing type." In the "crusade" against dust, the homemaker's first action, they declared, was to banish "all gewgaws and unnecessary furniture."[11] The authors were not alone in attacking dust-attracting furnishings and ornament. Beginning in the 1890s and extending through the 1920s, streams of articles in such popular magazines such as *Good Housekeeping, Cosmopolitan,* and *House Beautiful,* fostered a national obsession with domestic cleanliness and simplified surroundings. McHughwillow and other plain-style, open-weave wicker escaped the condemnation of sanitarians. Unlike carved and upholstered wood furniture, wicker was viewed as naturally hygienic, and many manufacturers and retailers of willow, rattan, and Prairie Grass furniture in the new century were quick to point out to health-conscious consumers that wicker was airy, vermin-free, and thoroughly sanitary.

The reformers' constant demands for unpolluted, easy-to-clean, and efficient homes resulted in the creation of a new type of functional dwelling for the middle classes—the bungalow. In the early 1900s, it was the all-American dream home[12] and untold thousands of these practical, inexpensive dwellings were constructed in outlying suburban developments, some just beyond the fringe of Queen Anne–style neighborhoods, others further out and connected to city jobs by rail lines and, as the years progressed, paved roads for automobiles. They were also to be found deep in the countryside and at resorts. Like the eclectic, late-Victorian house before it, the modern bungalow exerted an enormous influence on the design and use of wicker furniture during the first two decades of the twentieth century. Simple, uncluttered, and minimally embellished, the new type of suburban dwelling suddenly made ornate reed and rattan furniture look utterly ridiculous and out of place.

The rush to the suburbs after

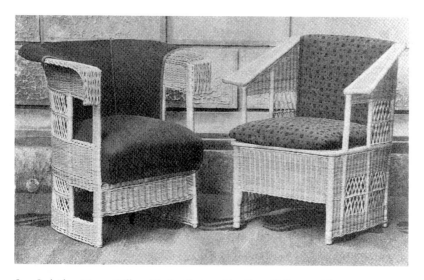

Prag-Rudnicker, Vienna, Willow Chairs Designed by Hans Vollmer with Upholstery by Josef Hoffmann, *1904. Photograph from International Studio (January 1904), courtesy of the National Museum of American Art, Smithsonian Institution. Before the First World War, avant-garde Austrian and German woven furniture was imported and sold by leading New York decorators, including McHugh. The abstract designs influenced a variety of American manufacturers to restyle their wicker in the modernist manner.*

the turn of the century was even greater than it had been during the previous three decades. It was now the turn of lower-middle-class apartment renters to flee the city—and the modest bungalow was their means to a better life. In 1900 more than seventy-five percent of urbanites lived in rented apartments or flats, and by 1917 their average annual income more than doubled, rising from $651 to $1,505.[13] During this same time, it cost between eight hundred and three thousand dollars to build an affordable two-bedroom bungalow. In this new dwelling, the Victorians' belief in the authority of art and beauty was supplanted by reformist ideals of "domestic science." Instead of art-decoration, women's magazines and housekeeping journals stressed the importance of home economics in influencing the character of the family home and the lives within it. In the middle-class residence, as well as in the office and factory, the modern watchword was efficiency, and theories of "scientific management" fired the imaginations of zealous reformers of domestic living standards. The post-Victorian homemaker was to be a sober household economist, not an artistic decorator.

The bungalow was a very different house than its Victorian predecessors. For one thing, it was much smaller in size. The 1880s house priced at three thousand dollars might contain twenty-five hundred square feet of interior space, while its 1905 counterpart comprised roughly fifteen hundred square feet.[14] Higher costs in land, building materials, and plumbing, heating, and electrical systems helped account for this reduction in overall size. But what the householder lost in space, he or she gained in efficiency. The typical bungalow was a rectangular one- or one-and-a-half-story building with a wide, sloping roof, dormer windows, and a prominent front porch typically furnished with plain-style wicker. Gone were picturesque turrets, wraparound piazzas, projecting gables, recessed balconies, and intricate detailing. Exterior decoration was kept to an absolute minimum, and simple, inexpensive building materials such as concrete, cement block, fieldstone, and wood were used in an "honest" and forthright manner. The goal was to harmonize with nature by blending into the landscape, not to stick out ostentatiously like the Queen Anne–style house. Inside, the ground-floor layout was elemental and compact. Generally, it was made up of three rooms—living, dining, and kitchen—sometimes a front hall was added. Each of these spaces was multipurpose: the Victorian ideal of numerous, single-purpose rooms was rejected as wasteful. Rather than a specialized space for the aggressive display of art decoration, the new living room was to be a simple backdrop for relaxed family activities. In his popular *Bungalow Book* (1910), H. L. Wilson described the homey living room as "the room where the family gathers, and in which the visitor feels at once the warm, homelike hospitality. Everything should suggest comfort and restfulness." This new social space combined the separate functions of the Victorian dwelling's front parlor where visitors were received, the family's informal sitting room, the library, and living hall. Following a strong minimalist aesthetic, the decoration of the multipurpose living room was restricted to plain-painted walls, possibly a chair rail or wood wainscotting, and dark, oak-framed windows and doors. The room might have a beamed ceiling or a stenciled frieze. The severity of the bungalow's living room was truly the converse of the riotous overdecoration of the late-Victorian parlor. To preserve space, furniture was reduced to a minimum and bookcases, mantels, and inglenook seats were typically built-in. The multiplicity of specialized pieces so beloved by Victorians was now eliminated. The plethora of whatnot shelves, tête-à-têtes, reception chairs, window benches, tea tables, music and newspaper stands, and other limited-use furniture was banished, replaced instead by a few pieces of austere and strictly functional Arts and Crafts–style furniture—a reclining Morris chair, a rocker or two, a plain-style willow chair, and an oblong library table. The modern dining room, entered from the living room through a wide arch or doorway, was also free from elaborate ornamentation and unnecessary furnishings. Leaded art-glass windows with geometric designs and a wicker fernery might help decorously screen the sight of the house next door, but simple buffets and china closets were built into the walls. The room did double duty: with the chairs pulled back, the dining table typically served as a work surface for dressmaking and other handicraft activities. It might also contain an upright piano and function as the

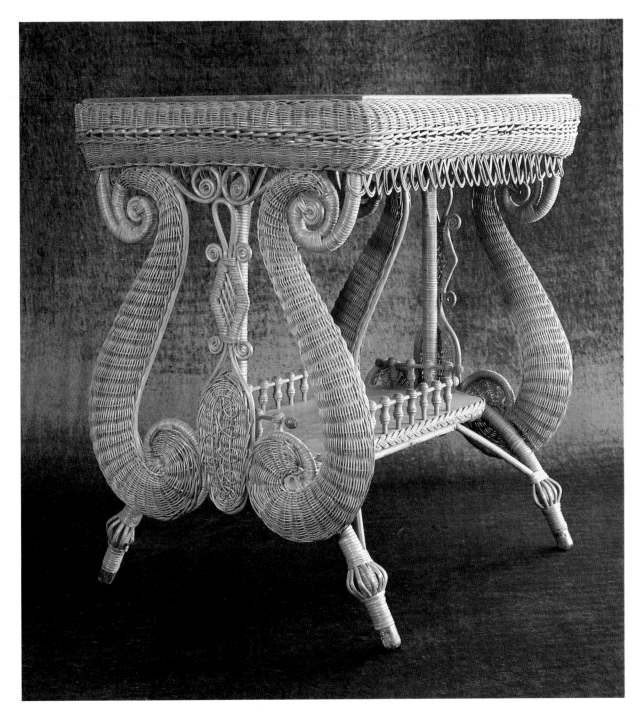

music room. The kitchen was a paragon of cleanliness and efficient design. Since the modern family was always on the go, the kitchen often had an eat-in area for quick, informal meal-taking. Throughout the ground floor, space flowed unrestrictedly, facilitating a convenient, circular pattern of movement. Since family size had diminished over the decades, there were only two or three small bedrooms upstairs, along with a hygienic, tiled bathroom with up-to-date fixtures and plumbing.

After 1905 post-Victorian architectural plan-books heavily promoted bungalow-style dwellings, just as earlier ones had championed the eclectic Queen Anne house. Mail-order designs for simple, comfortable homes proved immensely popular and numerous firms and individuals offered

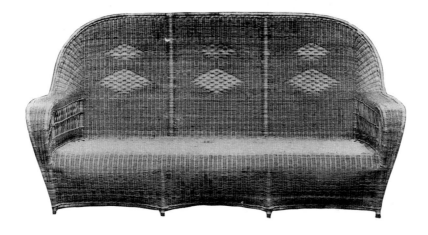

a wide variety of inexpensive models. If the middle-class homebuilder chose to circumvent a local contractor and go it alone, he could now order a totally prefabricated dwelling that could be shipped in crates anywhere by rail and assembled on site by amateurs. The largest purveyor of build-it-yourself houses was the Alladin Company of Bay City, Michigan, which was founded in 1904.[15] Everything one needed to construct and decorate a house was machine-cut, numbered, and packed at the factory. Plumbing, heating, and electrical systems were also included in the total package—even nails. At the site, the owner was responsible for all necessary excavations and foundation work, and as long as he and his helpers carefully followed the detailed assembly instructions, the prefab Alladin house would last for decades. In 1908 the mighty Sears, Roebuck and Company, already a leader in nationwide wicker sales, entered the house-by-mail field. Their first catalogue included twenty-two styles selling between $650 and $2,500. By 1939 a hundred thousand families had ordered "Honor Bilt Modern Homes" from Sears.[16] The giant mail-order firm was soon followed by its rival, Montgomery Ward—and a host of smaller, prefab firms proliferated across the United States before the First World War. The A. C. Tux-

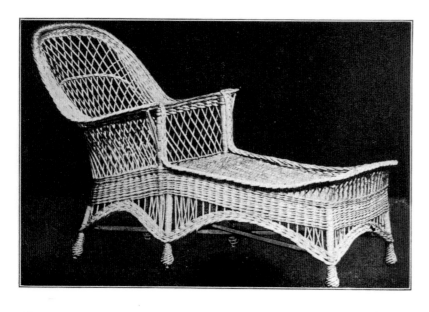

Above, below, and opposite: F. Debski and Company, New York, Designs from the ca. 1923 Willow and Reed Furniture Catalogue. Courtesy of Frog Alley Antiques/Merry P. Gilbert, New York City.
Debski produced not only American Bar Harbor–style willow lounges, but designs for chairs and settees based on European wicker styles—boxy willow furniture from Germany and Austria and tightly woven reed seating with flaring arms made by the English firm, Dryad.

bury Lumber Co. of Charleston, South Carolina, proudly advertised that their "Quickbilt Bungalow" could be erected in seven and a half days with only five men.

Among the most ardent champions of the functional bungalow and the simple, wholesome life advocated by Progressives was Gustav Stickley, among the foremost spokesmen for the values of the American Arts and Crafts movement. As a design philosophy, Arts and Crafts was the antithesis of late-Victorian aestheticism, shifting the emphasis from ornate surface decoration to primary form and structure. The old Victorian principle of "art for art's sake" was abandoned for a new, socially oriented goal of "art for life's sake." Art—defined minimally as fine handcraftsmanship—was to be incorporated naturally into everyday activities. Stickley's influential monthly magazine, *The Craftsman* (1901–15), was the principal voice of this democratic movement and was proudly dedicated to the "Simplification of Life." Stickley is best known as the originator of Craftsman Furniture, the architectural oak furniture that set the design and construction standards for other mass-produced Arts and Crafts furnishings in the first two decades of the twentieth century. But he also had a fervent interest in reforming the entire fabric of the middle-class residence, and each issue of his journal contained plans and sketches of bungalow-style and other simple houses. *The Craftsman* also provided sketches of interiors outfitted with austere Craftsman Furniture. Stickley's goal was to create a total unity in architectural and interior design that clearly embodied the "art for life's sake" philosophy. The dark-stained oak chairs, tables, bookcases, sideboards, and bedroom furniture produced in his Craftsman Workshops outside Syracuse, New York, between 1900 and 1915, and similar-styled pieces by his many competitors and imitators, was the new art furniture for the progressive-minded middle classes. Just as the bungalow was the antithesis of the Queen Anne dwelling, so Stickley's geometric furniture was the opposite of florid designs in reed and rattan.

Around 1906 Stickley decided to enter the wicker field. To off-set the massive qualities of his architectonic oak, he realized that he needed to offer a line of similarly designed, yet lighter furniture. Clearly, he had been impressed with the success of McHughwillow

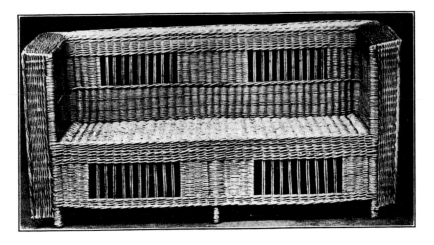

and its off-shoots. In July 1907 he introduced the readers of *The Craftsman* to the boxy, basketweave forms of his new Craftsman Willow Furniture. It was perfectly suited to the simplicity of the country bungalow and the back-to-nature philosophy of the Arts and Crafts Movement. "Everybody knows willow furniture," he wrote, "and nearly everybody uses it, especially in country homes where delicate and elaborate furnishings are out of place, and where the need is for something that naturally belongs to the comfort and simplicity of country life, and that brings into the house a pleasing suggestion of the out of doors."[17] In both design and construction, it was Stickley's intent to remain faithful to the nature of his material: willow simply had to be used in a natural, willowlike way.

"When a [willow] chair," he continued, "is designed after some fantastically ornate pattern, constructed so that it is stiff and unyielding and given a solid color and a hard enamel finish, it has lost every characteristic of the thin, flexible willow withes which belong naturally to basket work. Hence, a willow chair is most nearly right when it resembles straight basket work in its construction, when it is flexible and yielding, and when it is so finished that it looks like willow and nothing else." Craftsman Willow was also aesthetically appealing because the natural tones of the osier rods had "all the intangible silvery shimmer of water in moonlight." But like other manufacturers of the era, Stickley also stained his peeled willow skeins. In keeping with the nature-based artistic ideals of his

Wicker-filled Sun Room in Winter, 1919. *Photograph from* Arts and Decoration *(August 1919), courtesy of the National Museum of American Art, Smithsonian Institution.*

age, he dyed them a soft green or golden brown, which harmonized with the earth-tones he recommended for the interior color schemes of his suburban Craftsman homes. Every room, he felt, should have one or two pieces mixed in with the darker oak furniture. But Stickley particularly stressed the suitability of Craftsman Willow for the summer home, seaside cottage, or country bungalow: "for the veranda, balcony, and open-air living room it would be difficult to find anything more comfortable and appropriate, particularly in States where the warm sunny climate permits more outdoor life."[18]

In design, Craftsman Willow differs dramatically from other American wicker made in the early 1900s. McHugh and his imitators based their openweave designs in large part on traditional English and Madeiran basket chairs. But in the late 1890s, Stickley, the child of German immigrants and fluent in his ancestral language, was aware of the new winds of artistic change sweeping across central Europe and turned to a more innovative source of design inspiration—the modernist willow art furniture created by avant-garde German and Austrian designers at the turn of the century. He may have first encountered their work on an early study abroad, but after 1900 he had ample opportunities to examine models reproduced in the pages of German-language design journals. The popular American edition of the progressive English art and decoration magazine *The Studio* published numerous reproductions and several landmark articles on the new Austrian and German wicker.[19]

The Austrian government had long promoted basket making as a profitable winter activity for poor peasant farmers scattered throughout the middle European Austro-Hungarian Empire. It long had sponsored the propagation of better species of basket willow and regularly trained students at the Imperial School in Vienna to teach the craft of basket weaving to rural families in Austrian Poland, Bohemia, Croatia, and Moravia. In the late 1870s an important private enterprise, Prag-Rudniker, was established specifically for the large-scale production of willowware. In the 1880s the firm produced basket chairs expressly for the English market. But by the early 1900s the weavers were making high-style art furniture from patterns supplied by leading industrial designers and architects of the

Vienna secession.[20] Stickley was attracted by the pure geometry of these forms. They resembled his Craftsman oak furniture and influenced his early wicker designs. However, not all of Stickley's nationwide customers enjoyed the stark, rectilinear aesthetic, and among the more than twenty-five patterns of Craftsman Willow seating he produced by 1915 are relaxed designs based on English basket chairs and the then ubiquitous American Bar Harbor model. Imported Austrian willow along with similarly styled German wicker woven from reed was retailed by McHugh's Popular Shop and other fashionable outlets in New York, and the modernist, Missionlike designs with their square "cutouts" influenced production models by several leading American wicker manufacturers.[21]

Another transatlantic influence on the design of modern American wicker was the tightly woven reed furniture made by the English firm Dryad. Founded by the headmaster of the Leicester School of Art in 1907, the company produced a variety of functional forms inspired by the success of Austrian-German wicker and the ideals of the English Arts and Crafts Movement. Dryad rejected the harsh geometry of the secessionists and instead created graceful and springy forms that evoked the sense of movement found in art nouveau design.[22] Dryad furniture was particularly well made. The workers used ash frames and wove

Heywood Brothers and Wakefield Company, Gardner, Massachusetts, Dressing Stand, Model 6445, ca. 1898–1904, rattan, wood, mirror glass, and metal. Courtesy of A Summer Place. Photograph by Kit Latham.

Above: W. and J. Sloane and Company, New York, Advertisement, Dryad English Cane Furniture, *1914. Photograph from* Country Life in America *(May 1914), courtesy of the National Museum of American Art, Smithsonian Institution.*

Dryad, a British firm, offered a line of well-constructed wicker that was sold exclusively in the United States by W. and J. Sloane in New York. The close weave favored by the firm became the standard for upscale American wicker in the 1920s.

Opposite: Unidentified Manufacturer, Child's Go-Cart, *ca. 1905–10, rattan, wood, metal, porcelain, and rubber. Courtesy of Richard Moulton. Photograph by Kit Latham.*

their strands of reed (called "cane" by the English) so tightly that they could dispense entirely with tacks or nails. Dryad wicker was sold exclusively in New York by the upscale department store W. and J. Sloane.

During the 1890s the giants of the industry, Heywood Brothers and Company and the Wakefield Rattan Company, had paid little or no attention to the revolutionary changes in design philosophy that were beginning to transform the domestic landscape. Both firms

had offered lines of simplified reed seating since about 1880, but they remained firmly committed to the Victorian ideals of ornately rendered art-decoration. Little could their directors have imagined in 1893 the threat McHugh's crude Bar Harbor willow chair would pose to the immense reed and rattan furniture industry in the new century. After their corporate merger in February 1897, the two former rivals moved quickly to consolidate their separate factories in Wakefield, Gardner, Chicago, and San Francisco. A year later the new company rushed its first joint sales catalogue into print.[23] Handsomely produced, it contained 388 exquisitely engraved images of rocking, arm, reception, and conversation chairs; divans, tête-à-têtes, couches, and lounges; all manner of children's chairs and cribs; and a diversity of tables, tabourets, and ottomans. There

were also baskets of all sorts, music stands, fancy display cabinets, and suites of three to five ornately designed pieces of furniture. The new catalogue included a stunning array of decorative forms—the finest yet produced. In keeping with current fashions, they even offered Oriental-style hourglass chairs. Both firms put forward their best-selling models. The Wakefield Rattan Company contributed fifty from its 1895 catalogue and more from its final 1897 register while Heywood Brothers offered forty-one patterns from its 1895–96 sales catalogue. The vast number of designs, however, were new. Many pieces illustrated in the original 1898–99 catalogue survive today—a testament to the remark-

Heywood Brothers and Wakefield Company,
Fancy Display Cabinet from the
1898–99 Catalogue of Reed and Rattan
Furniture. *Courtesy of the National Museum
of American Art, Smithsonian Institution.*

able skill of the anonymous designers and fabricators and the durability of the wooden frames. The quality of turn-of-the-century Heywood-Wakefield reed and rattan furniture is unsurpassed. Given the scale of its production and the number of plants, it is remarkable that such high standards were maintained. With four large factories devoted to reed and rattan products, the firm was the largest manufacturer of wicker furniture in the world. And the world took notice of that fact. In May 1898 the *Wooden and Willow-Ware Trade Review* reported that the newly amalgamated company had received a single order from an Australian retailer for nearly forty thousand chairs![24] The former Heywood Brothers' warehouses

already established in Liverpool and London must also have boosted sales of Victorian-style wicker abroad. At home, the only real threat to their nationwide sales network was provided by the giant mail-order firm Sears, Roebuck, that in 1898 began to retail ornate reed and rattan furniture.

In 1905 the Heywood Brothers and Wakefield Company published an all-new sales catalogue of wicker furnishings. It was very different from the one they had printed in 1898. A comparison reveals that in the interim the giant manufacturer had been forced to adapt to the new post-Victorian design ideals. The illustrations in the

Heywood Brothers and Wakefield Company,
Children's High Chair from the
1898–99 Catalogue of Reed and Rattan
Furniture. *Courtesy of the National Museum
of American Art, Smithsonian Institution.
The first combined Heywood-Wakefield
catalogue was issued for 1898–99 and contained
388 exquisitely engraved images of Victorian-
style reed and rattan furnishings. Most were
ornate models that appealed to suburban tastes.*

1905 catalogue show that the firm had struggled to catch up with changing fashions. The number of ornate models was drastically reduced; only a few old favorites remained. In place of fanciful, curvilinear models, there were massive, Mission-style pieces upholstered in red, green, or brown leather, their woven frames stained a newly popular "weathered oak." Other examples clearly were related to McHughwillow designs. Some are even direct copies of contemporary French wicker with its distinctive fields of two-toned, enameled caning; others are simply odd hybrids combining old Victorian flourishes with new, severe shapes. The aesthetic unity of the late 1890s continued to erode. The company's reed and rattan furniture catalogue of 1909 displayed an even greater hodgepodge of miscellaneous styles. On one page, there are illustrations of chairs in French, Chinese, Mission, and Victorian modes—there is even a cane wing chair. But the firm's more up-to-date line of "Reedcraft" furniture, designed for simple bungalow living rooms, was also showcased in the 1909 catalogue. Introduced in 1907, Reedcraft was Heywood-Wakefield's first serious essay in the Arts and Crafts style. According to the Chicago *Furniture Journal,* the reed chairs were based on the contemporary German furniture exhibited to wide acclaim at the 1904 St. Louis World's Fair and represented "possibilities in reed weaving along the latest 'Modern Art' lines, the aim being to produce forms which are more in keeping with the prevalent thought of the architect and

1916 C
Large Arm Chair.
Berlin Green, Weathered Oak or Shellac
Finish.
With Seat Cushion in Linene Tap-
estry $18 00
With Seat Cushion in Panama
Cloth, Jute Tapestry or Taffeta. 18 50
Chair Without Cushion............ 15 50

1918
Reading Chair.
With Shelves and Pockets for Books and
Papers.
Berlin Green, Weathered Oak or Shellac
Finish.
With Seat and Back Cushions in
Linene Tapestry $28 00
With Seat and Back Cushions in
Panama Cloth, Jute Tapestry or
Taffeta 28 50
Chair Without Cushions 24 00

1919
Reading Chair.
With Shelves and Pockets for Books and
Papers.
Berlin Green, Weathered Oak or Shellac
Finish.
With Seat and Back Cushions in
Linene Tapestry $30 00
With Seat and Back Cushions in
Panama Cloth, Jute Tapestry or
Taffeta 30 50
Chair Without Cushions 26 00

6800 D
Large Arm Rocker.
Leather Cushions in Plain or Spanish Leather. Red,
Green or Brown. Frames—Weathered Oak Finish. $36 00
Same as Above, Without Cushions................. 22 00
6800 C
Large Arm Chair to match above.   Same prices.

6800 F
Tete-a-Tete.
Seat 42x21 inches.
Leather Cushions in Plain or Spanish Leather. Red,
Green or Brown. Frames—Weathered Oak Finish. $64 00
Same as Above, Without Cushions................... 36 00

Heywood Brothers and Wakefield Company,
Upholstered Reed Furniture from
the 1905–06 Catalogue of Reed
and Rattan Furniture. *Courtesy of*
the National Museum of American
History, Smithsonian Institution.
In the early 1900s Heywood-Wakefield
was forced to adapt to changes in taste
and relinquish its reliance on ornate designs.

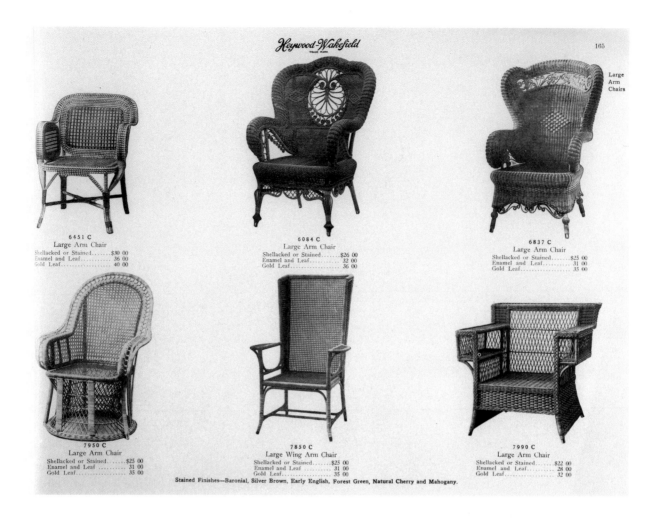

6451 C
Large Arm Chair
Shellacked or Stained.......$30 00
Enamel and Leaf...........36 00
Gold Leaf.................40 00

6084 C
Large Arm Chair
Shellacked or Stained.......$26 00
Enamel and Leaf...........32 00
Gold Leaf.................36 00

6837 C
Large Arm Chair
Shellacked or Stained.......$25 00
Enamel and Leaf...........31 00
Gold Leaf.................35 00

Large Arm Chairs

7950 C
Large Arm Chair
Shellacked or Stained.......$25 00
Enamel and Leaf...........31 00
Gold Leaf.................35 00

7850 C
Large Wing Arm Chair
Shellacked or Stained.......$25 00
Enamel and Leaf...........31 00
Gold Leaf.................35 00

7990 C
Large Arm Chair
Shellacked or Stained.......$22 00
Enamel and Leaf...........28 00
Gold Leaf.................32 00

Stained Finishes—Baronial, Silver Brown, Early English, Forest Green, Natural Cherry and Mahogany.

Heywood Brothers and Wakefield Company, Armchairs from the 1909 Catalogue of Reed and Rattan Furniture.
Courtesy of the National Museum of American History, Smithsonian Institution. By 1909, Heywood-Wakefield had abandoned a single philosophy of design. This page from the company catalogue shows a surprising diversity of styles: on the left is a contemporary French-style enameled cane chair and an Oriental-inspired hourglass model; to the right, Victorian-era designs with fluid serpentine arms and backs contrast sharply with a pair of severe, rectilinear chairs, including an up-to-date Mission design.

the interior furnishers."[25] The company realized that the days of the Queen Anne–style house were over. Middle-class consumers clearly were undismayed by Heywood-Wakefield's extraordinary diversity of wicker furniture styles. They obviously welcomed it. In July 1909 the Chicago factory announced that it had sold more reed furniture in the previous six months than it had during the whole twenty-two years it had been in business.[26]

In the early 1900s, with the rattan trust terminated, Heywood-Wakefield was one of only a handful of American wicker manufacturers that imported its rattan directly from the Far East. Since the late 1890s rising business costs in the United States had forced most smaller companies to import supplies of already-cut cane and reed from Germany, where labor was far cheaper. In July 1901 Lionel J. Salomon, treasurer of the American Rattan and Reed Company of Brooklyn, New York, went so far as to threaten publicly to move the entire operation to Germany unless the federal government dramatically increased its tariffs on imported reed. But supplies of raw rattan shipped directly to the United States were still enormous. During September 1906, Singapore alone shipped 958,733 pounds to America—versus 339,333 and 1,752,133 pounds to England and Europe. Five years later, Taiwan, a newly emergent Far Eastern source, exported just over a million pounds to the West.[27] The commerce in Oriental cane started more than four centuries earlier by Portuguese mariners had now turned into an international commerce of truly vast dimensions. With such demand, it is surprising that *Calamus rotang* was not threatened with extinction throughout

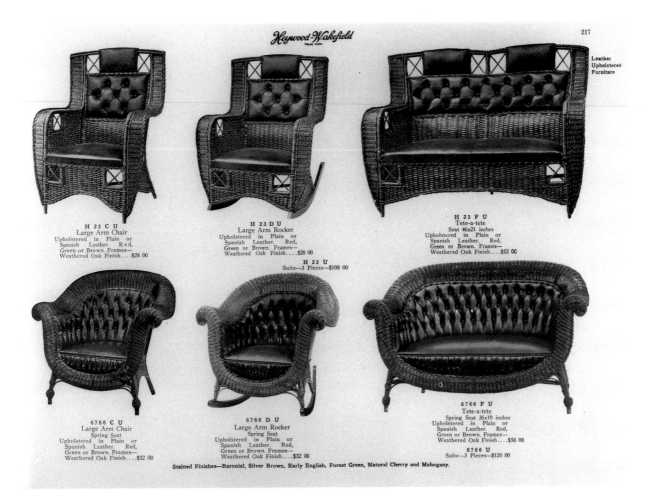

Heywood-Wakefield
TRADE MARK

217

Leather
Upholstered
Furniture

H 23 C U
Large Arm Chair
Upholstered in Plain or
Spanish Leather. Red,
Green or Brown. Frames—
Weathered Oak Finish....$28 00

H 23 D U
Large Arm Rocker
Upholstered in Plain or
Spanish Leather. Red,
Green or Brown. Frames—
Weathered Oak Finish.....$28 00

H 23 U
Suite—3 Pieces—$108 00

H 23 F U
Tete-a-tete
Seat 46x21 inches
Upholstered in Plain or
Spanish Leather. Red,
Green or Brown. Frames—
Weathered Oak Finish....$52 00

6766 C U
Large Arm Chair
Spring Seat
Upholstered in Plain or
Spanish Leather. Red,
Green or Brown. Frames—
Weathered Oak Finish....$32 00

6766 D U
Large Arm Rocker
Spring Seat
Upholstered in Plain or
Spanish Leather. Red,
Green or Brown. Frames—
Weathered Oak Finish....$32 00

6766 F U
Tete-a-tete
Spring Seat 36x19 inches
Upholstered in Plain or
Spanish Leather. Red,
Green or Brown. Frames—
Weathered Oak Finish....$56 00

6766 U
Suite—3 Pieces—$120 00

Stained Finishes—Baronial, Silver Brown, Early English, Forest Green, Natural Cherry and Mahogany.

Heywood Brothers and Wakefield Company, Seating from the 1909 Catalogue of Reed and Rattan Furniture. *Courtesy of the National Museum of American History, Smithsonian Institution. In 1909 massive wicker chairs upholstered in Spanish leather found popularity. Like the Mission furniture of the period, the woven reed was toned with a weathered oak stain. The three models presented on the top share a squared-off Arts-and-Crafts design aesthetic, while the curvilinear shapes of those below are inspired by older Victorian aesthetic ideals.*

the Malay Archipelago. Had the war in Europe not intervened, it might well have been overharvested. Hostilities on the Continent had, as already noted, an immediate impact on the American willow-ware industry. Imports of French and German willow sharply declined, and in mid-August 1914 the *Wooden and Willow-Ware Trade Review* reported that the Heywood-Wakefield Company even anticipated a severe shortage of reed in the United States if the war lasted more than a few months. Since most reed stocks had been imported from Germany for years, few American factories had bothered to install their own rattan-splitting machines. With its huge reserves and extensive machinery, the Heywood-Wakefield Company was virtually the only firm now capable of making large amounts of reed and rattan furniture. For the rest, as the war dragged on beyond Christmas 1914, fiber, the new, locally manufactured product proved a godsend.

War clouds were not the only problems looming on Heywood-Wakefield's corporate horizon. In 1914 labor strife seriously dislocated activities at the Wakefield complex. Wicker production dropped dramatically. At the beginning of the year everything seemed rosy: the company's treasurer reported assets of $9.7 million and a cash surplus of $2.6 million. In mid-April, the company's shares listed on the New York Stock Exchange advanced to a record 110.5 points. But later in the month, seventy-five Wakefield mat weavers walked off the job demanding a ten-cent-an-hour increase in pay. They were followed by a handful of teamsters who likewise demanded more wages and shorter hours. Soon some one thousand hourly employees—virtually the entire work force—went out on strike. The workers at Wakefield in 1914 were different than those who had suffered through the labor troubles of the 1890s. They were no longer solidly Irish. Recent Italian immigrants had been attracted to Wakefield in the early 1900s by construction jobs and then had stayed on to work at the rattan plant as the older generation of Irishmen retired.[28] As negotiations dragged on through April and May, the directors closed the plant. After six weeks, the strike was finally settled. On June 2 the factories started up, but six days later, after management reneged on an agreement and fired the strike leaders, the outraged workers struck once again. On June 11 the plant was shut down indefinitely, and the mechanical looms that wove the cane webbing for trolley and railroad car seats—one of the firm's best-selling products—were moved out hastily to rented factory quarters in Worcester, Massachusetts, where they were operated by strike-breakers. This only exacerbated tension. On July 8, Richard Stout, the longtime superintendent of the cane-splitting department, narrowly escaped death when someone threw a firebomb through his kitchen window. By July 15, the value of Heywood-Wakefield stock had fallen to ninety-eight points, but just as the guns of August 1914 began to roar on the Continent, some four hundred members of the Rattan Workers' Union voted to return to work, and the remainder of the employees, tired of the three-month strike, soon followed suit. So ended one of the most bruising chapters in Wakefield's history.[29] Not until the 1950s did the company again experience such labor strife. But by that time, it no longer made wicker.

NOTES

1. "Joseph P. McHugh—His Shop," *The Upholstery Dealer and Decorative Furnisher* 29 (October 1915): 48.

2. Ibid., 53.

3. Matlack Price, "A Study of the Work of Walter J. H. Dudley," *Arts and Decoration* 15 (July 1921): 167.

4. "Obituary," *The Upholstery Dealer and Decorative Furnisher* 30 (October 1915): 47.

5. "Recent American Furniture," *The Ideal House* 1 (October 1905): 15.

6. "Wisconsin Blind Making Willow-Ware," *Wooden and Willow-Ware Trade Review,* 26 July 1906, 74.

7. "W. and H. Company to Make Imitation Reed Goods," *Wooden and Willow-Ware Trade Review,* 11 August 1904, 85.

8. Emil Gandre, *Fiber Furniture Weaving* (Milwaukee: Bruce Publishing, 1930), 1. See also, Lloyd F. Hyatt, *Furniture Weaving Projects* (Milwaukee: Bruce Publishing, 1922), 21ff, for information on fiber making.

9. Gandre, *Fiber Furniture Weaving,* 1.

10. James Buckham, "The Parade of Cheapness," *Good Housekeeping,* June 1901, 452–53.

11. Lionel Robertson and T. C. O'Donnell, *The Healthful House* (Battle Creek, Mich.: Good Health Publishing, 1917), 155–56.

12. See Gwendolyn Wright, *Building the Dream: A Social History of Housing in America* (New York: Pantheon, 1981), Chapter 9; Clifford Edward Clark, Jr., *The American Family Home, 1800–1960* (Chapel Hill and London: The University of North Carolina Press, 1986), Chapter 6; and Clay Lancaster, *The American Bungalow, 1880–1930* (New York: Abbeville, 1985).

13. Clark, *The American Family Home, 1800–1960,* 182.

14. Ibid., 163.

15. Alan Gowans, *The Comfortable House, North American Suburban Architecture, 1890–1930* (Cambridge, Mass. and London: MIT Press, 1986), 48–50.

16. Katherine Cole Stevenson and H. Ward Jandl, *Houses by Mail, A Guide to Houses from Sears, Roebuck and Company* (Washington, D.C.: Preservation Press, 1986), 19.

17. "Craftsman Willow Furniture," *The Craftsman* 12 (July 1907): 477.

18. *Craftsman Furniture* sales catalogue, April 1912, 63.

19. A. S. Levetus, "Modern Austrian Wicker Furniture," *The Studio* 21 (January 1904): 323–28; "Dresden—Studio Talk," *The Studio* 25 (June 1905): 364–66. See also, *The Craftsman* 21 (February 1912): 577–78.

20. See Eva Ottillinger, *Korb Moebel* (Salzburg and Vienna: Residenz Verlag, 1990): 99ff.

21. See Edward H. Aschermann, "New Ideas for Interior Decoration," *Arts and Decoration* 4 (June 1913): 279–81; 290; G. Mortimer Marke, "The Informal Note in Summer Furniture," *Arts and Decoration* 6 (April 1915): 232–33. F. Debski and Bielecky Brothers of New York City manufactured Secessionist-inspired willow and reed furniture.

22. Roger Caye, "Decorative Value of Woven Cane Chairs," *Arts and Decoration* 5 (May 1914): 266–67; Pat Kirkham, "Willow and Cane Furniture in Austria, Germany and England, c. 1900–14," *Furniture History* 21 (1985): 127–31; and Ottillinger, *Korb Moebel,* 129–37.

23. Reprinted as Heywood Brothers and Wakefield Company, *Classic Wicker Furniture. The Complete 1898–1899 Illustrated Catalog* (New York: Dover, 1982). Introduction by Richard Saunders.

24. "Heywood Brothers and Wakefield Company's Large Export Order," *Wooden and Willow-Ware Trade Review,* 26 May 1898, 45. The number was described as "thirty-two hundred dozen."

25. Chicago *Furniture Journal,* 25 October 1907, advertisement, n.p.

26. Ibid., 12 July 1909, 102.

27. "Rattan Exports from India in September," *Wooden and Willow-Ware Trade Review,* 27 December 1906, 61; "Rattan Exports from Formosa in 1911," *Wooden and Willow-Ware Trade Review,* 27 June 1912, 61.

28. Richard Saunders, *Collecting and Restoring Wicker Furniture* (New York: Crown Publishers, 1976), 57.

29. "Heywood Brothers and Wakefield Company Weavers Strike," *Wooden and Willow-Ware Trade Review,* 23 April 1914, 29; 28 May 1914, 45; 11 June 1914, 53; 9 July 1914, 69; 23 July 1914, 77; and 27 Aug. 1914, 93.

CHAPTER FIVE

Novel Uses, Technologies, and Designs in the Modern Age, 1915–1930

Before the First World War, the bungalow was not the only design popular with home builders. The two-story classic box, or four-square, was a common model in post-Victorian suburbs. Another middle-class favorite was the gabled temple-house.[1] Both types were roomy and had prominent front porches suitable for wicker chairs. Another, more traditional, dwelling, the Georgian colonial, found favor with those who sought stronger historical and symbolic associations. The Georgian-revival mansion, with its aristocratic roots, proclaimed wealth and power and was the fashionable style among the rich and the upper middle class from 1890 to 1930.[2] But, in more modest guise, it was also popularized through mail-order architecture and thus often appeared in unassuming suburbs. In its high-style form, the two-story building was symmetrical in elevation, had side gables, a center-hall plan, and was made of brick. Typically, it had a Palladian window or portico and louvered wooden shutters. Significantly, there were porches at either end. One opened from the dining room and served as an open-air dining

porch. The other, on the opposite side, was enclosed by windows and entered from the living room. Commonly called the "sun parlor," this glassed-in room was one of the most important developments in early twentieth-century domestic architecture. One architect called it "the most valuable asset of the entire home."[3] Usually, it was outfitted with plain-style wicker furniture. It was the only room in a pre-1920s house in which wicker was used exclusively. Elsewhere, one or two pieces of willow or reed might be mixed in with wooden and upholstered furniture. In cold weather, the heated solarium was a homeowner's delight. Filled with plants, sunlight, and "summery" wicker furnishings, it served as a winter garden. Sun rooms were essential features but not unique to Georgian and other colonial revival–style houses. By 1915 they were also being regularly retrofitted to Queen Anne houses and bungalows. With advances in central heating, portions of Victorian piazzas and entire bungalow front porches could be enclosed, warmed with radiators, and made available for year-round use. From 1910 to 1930, wicker-filled sun par-

lors were also popular amenities in hotels, country clubs, and resorts.

In an article, "Among the Wicker Shops," published in *Country Life in America* in May 1914, James Collier Marshall noted the vogue for woven furniture. It was suitable not only for porches and sun parlors, he reported, but also for use in other fashionably decorated rooms. Unlike ornate Victorian wicker, plain-style, fitch-weave wicker was the perfect complement for antiques and simplified colonial-revival interiors which, in the period from 1910 to 1930, were favored in well-to-do, Georgian-style homes:

In going about the shops one is impressed by the quantity of wicker furniture on display everywhere. . . . This indication of the rapidly growing popularity of wicker is easily accounted by the fact that the public has come to consider it a legitimate article of interior decoration rather than a makeshift for porch and lawn use during the summer. . . . From the decorative viewpoint,

Unidentified Manufacturer, White-Painted Lounge, *ca. 1925, rattan, wood, and paint. Private collection. Photograph by Kit Latham.*

Colonial-Revival Living Room with Willow Furniture, 1916. *Photograph from* Good Furniture *(April 1916), courtesy of the Library of Congress.*
In the early 1900s, many upper-middle-class houses were furnished in the aristocratic colonial style, with antiques or reproduction pieces. Plain-style willow chairs also were included.

the chairs particularly rank very high since they are the one modern manufacture that harmonizes well with any type of antique furniture. Perhaps this is because wicker work is older than history itself. Whatever the reason, a wicker chair will find an agreeable niche for itself in any setting and often proves a softening leaven in a group of forbidding Ancients!

Willow and reed chairs and lounges were not only used in architectural settings. They proved particularly popular on yachts. From 1910 to 1930 several manufacturers specialized in yacht wicker. After World War I, when commercial airlines burgeoned, passengers often sat on rows of lightweight wicker chairs. In 1927, when Charles Lindbergh made his solo flight across the Atlantic, his plane, the *Spirit of St. Louis,* was out-

fitted with a woven-reed seat. By that date, however, the age-old tradition of handweaving using natural materials had waned significantly: a new technological means of weaving fiber sheets by machine had all but taken over.

The man responsible for transforming the wicker industry was Marshall Burns Lloyd (1858–1927), an inventive baby carriage manufacturer based in Menominee, Michigan. On October 16, 1917, he was assigned United States patent number 113,608 for a new method of wicker weaving. Lloyd's innovation was simple yet revolutionary. Abandoning five thousand years of continuous tradition, he proposed to weave wicker independent of its final shape—the frame. Up to this point, every wickerworker had either woven his weft of willow or reed by hand either on a warp of rigid vertical stakes, directly on an inflexible wooden framework, or,

like a basket chair maker, created a unitary structure as he diagonally fitched his materials and then braided the edges for stiffness. In a radical revision of the ancient process, Lloyd proposed to separate the procedure into two independent operations—weaving and frame making—and leave the weaving entirely to machines.

In March 1920 the editor of *Scientific American* commented on the breakthrough: "It is hard to believe that in all these ages of industrial advancement, since the coming of man, there could be one art handed down without change from generation to generation. And yet that is what has happened in the wicker weaving line. Century after century has found this ancient art handed down and down and down without development. Many have tried to improve it and failed, until it became an accepted fact that the method of producing wicker goods was a supreme gift to mankind and that no improvements were possible. Today it is being improved." An article in the magazine explained Lloyd's remarkable improvement:

From the very first he realized that no loom could be built to weave wicker if the original and only known method of weaving on the frame in the final shape were used. . . . Finally . . . Lloyd produced a method whereby the wicker is woven as desired, and the frames are built according to patterns, absolutely independently. The one is constructed at one end of the factory and the other is woven at another end. Each is improved as it travels toward the middle where the fabric is slipped over the frame and attached thereto. Simple indeed, and yet never thought of before. No man ever dreamed he could weave wicker and build the frame of the desired article apart from each other and yet that is just what is now done.[4]

The Lloyd Loom was the logical outgrowth of years of experimenting by one of the most inventive individuals to enter the wicker field. The story of his rise from untutored obscurity to prominence as an industrial tycoon is fascinating.

Lloyd was born in 1858 in Minneapolis to a British father and Canadian mother. His family emigrated to Ontario, Canada, and settled on a farm near Meaford on the southern shore of Georgian Bay while he was still an infant. He had an onerous boyhood. At an early age he was forced to quit school and work at a wood-roofing-shingle mill his father had set up. At the mill, he demonstrated his innate inventiveness by making and selling gutters from hollow cedar trunks. He also supplemented his family's meager income by selling fish he had caught with a specially adapted spear. A subsequent stint as a successful store clerk in the village of Meaford was short-lived when the proprietor moved his operations to Toronto. Thrown back on his own devices, the youthful Lloyd next invented "an improved hamper"—probably a wickerwork item—that he bartered locally for necessities and food. His fortunes blossomed when the departed storekeeper offered him a job, room, and board in Toronto for eight dollars a month.

Marshall Burns Lloyd (1858–1927).
Photograph courtesy of Frog Alley Antiques/Merry P. Gilbert, New York City.

But the merchant again decided to move on, leaving his erstwhile assistant to fend for himself in the city. Young Lloyd acquired a stock of soap, and pulling it along in a small wagon, went back to selling door-to-door. He proved a successful salesman. In his next venture, he stood atop one of his soap boxes on Toronto's major thoroughfare, Yonge Street, and hawked cheap costume jewelry to the passing crowds. The teenager soon became a downtown fixture, holding up one of his baubles and shouting such slogans: "If you give this to your Isabella, she will never leave you for another fella!"[5] With proceeds from his street-vending enterprise, he bought a horse and buggy, stocked up with new merchandise, and tried his luck selling to homeowners on the outskirts of the city. At eighteen, Lloyd left Toronto, settled in Port Arthur, Canada, on the rugged north shore of Lake Superior, and took a job as a postman. His winter route took him through the snowbound wilderness by dogsled to the Minnesota border town of Pigeon River. He readily aban-

doned the huskies after hearing that fortunes were to be made by speculating in farmland on the prairies of Manitoba. Settlers poured into the province, creating a boom in land sales. Eager to cash in, Lloyd sold his watch to raise the price of a train ticket to Winnipeg. He arrived penniless, found a job as a waiter in a local hotel, and soon had saved enough to buy an option on a parcel of land. Within an hour, he had sold it for a $150 profit. Lloyd peddled real estate as energetically as he had previously hawked soap and cheap jewelry—but far more successfully. He left Winnipeg fifteen thousand dollars richer. Traveling south to North Dakota, he bought a farm for his unprosperous parents and siblings near the town of Grafton and turned his attention to selling insurance. One day, while out on his rounds, he idly watched as two North Dakota farmers struggled to fill and weigh a single sack of grain. The task was simple but, to his eyes, the procedure followed was utterly inefficient. One held the bag open as the other poured in the grain and then they both had to heave the heavy sack up onto the scale. As he observed the scene, a mechanical solution to the problem of filling and weighing grain sacks popped into his head, and he soon created the first of a number of inventions that ultimately made him a millionaire. The initial device was a combination bag holder and scale which would enable one man easily and efficiently to complete the chore. Renting a blacksmith's shop, the thirty-year-old entrepreneur now channeled all his resources into the Lloyd Scale Company of St. Thomas, North Dakota. The former insurance salesman ironically had refused to take out a policy against fire. When disaster struck, Lloyd lost everything. Undeterred, he took a job as a shoe salesman to make ends meet, but spent his free time tinkering with mechanical devices, patenting some of his inventions. In 1890 he created a process for weaving door mats out of wire, and joined forces with an established Minneapolis manufacturer to put them into production. By 1894, with several more patents to his credit, he had risen to become president of the C. O. White Company, a firm that made one of his Minneapolis inventions—mechanically woven wire bed springs and mattresses. These proved so profitable that he was able, in 1900, to buy out his part-

Lloyd Manufacturing Company, Menominee, Michigan,
Shaped and Flat Fabric Power Looms, 1922.
Photograph courtesy of Frog Alley Antiques/Merry P. Gilbert, New York City.
The loom at left produced the shaped forms for baby carriage bodies while the one at right wove sheets of fabric which were nailed to frames to make Lloyd Loom furniture.

ner White and rename the now-booming Minneapolis enterprise the Lloyd Manufacturing Company. In 1903 he patented an advanced wire wheel for boys' wagons and subsequently added wagons and reed baby carriages to his product lines. According to Lewis Larsen, the Lloyd Manufacturing Company's chief engineer, machinist, and designer from 1903, "the only reason [Lloyd] wanted to get into the baby carriage business was because it had four wheels, and he had a patent on a new way of making wheels."[6] Within a short time, Lloyd's "Princess" line of wicker go-carts and baby carriages—"Fit for the Child of a King"—were renowned.

On December 27, 1906, the *Wooden and Willow-Ware Trade Review* reported a short, seemingly inconsequential news item that later would be of supreme significance to the wicker industry: "the Lloyd Manufacturing Co. will move its rattan goods plant from Minneapolis to Menominee, Michigan." The town of Menominee, on the shores of Green Bay on Michigan's Upper Peninsula, had once been a leading lumber center, but with the depletion of nearby forests, business leaders were anxious to recruit new industries and made Lloyd an investment offer he could not refuse. It was a godsend; as it had become increasingly difficult to raise capital in Minneapolis to expand his business. Lloyd reincorporated his

company under the Michigan laws, built a factory near the shore of Green Bay in 1907, and, once the building was complete, transferred his machinery and supplies to Menominee. The firm was initially capitalized with four hundred thousand dollars and employed 125 workers.

In his new office, Lloyd had a couch on which he stretched out and did his best thinking. A framed maxim prominently displayed urged him on: "I never do what anyone else can do." One novel thing he did do was to invent, in 1913, the Lloyd Oxyacetylene Method, a revolutionary manufacturing process that produced thin-gauge steel tubing that he fashioned into continuous pushers for his baby carriages. He approached Pittsburgh Steel with the idea of funding it, but they ridiculed his invention. Undeterred, Lloyd turned around and patented the process. Soon, the steel company was forced to pay Lloyd a high price whenever it employed the patented procedure that had quickly proved to be very valuable. Already wealthy, the new industrial procedure made him richer—and all the more determined to find new solutions to old manufacturing problems.

Lloyd turned his attention to the craft of weaving wicker. While everyone believed it was beyond improvement, the Menominee inventor remained unconvinced. Known as "Efficiency Lloyd," he was chagrined that it took one of his skilled workers an entire day to weave the body of a reed baby carriage. Persuaded there must be a faster and more practical way to produce carriage bodies, he began

to rethink the problem from its first step to its last. Lloyd's solution to the time-consuming procedure of shaping the form while weaving was to divide the work into two separate operations: one employee made a wooden frame while another independently handwove a wicker cover for it. At first, he created temporary wooden forms or dies around which unskilled workers wove reed carriage bodies. Once the weaving was complete, the die was removed, and the woven shell was then attached to a permanent frame. This speeded up the process considerably, but Lloyd was still not content. The dream of weaving by machine obsessed him. Others had tried to make mechanical looms, but had failed. Lloyd, however, already had considerable experience in machine-weaving wire. A basic question was what wicker materials would be best suited for mechanical looms? Reed was out.

It splintered easily and was not long enough. Willow had the same restrictions. Lloyd turned to a new product—man-made paper fiber.

At the Menominee factory, fiber was made from rolls of brown kraft paper cut into one-inch-wide discs. These were fed into spinning machines much like the ones invented at the Ford, Johnson

Lloyd Manufacturing Company, Menominee, Michigan, Sulky, Pullman Baby Carriage, Stroller, and Doll Buggy from the 1922 Lloyd Loom Products Catalogue. *Courtesy of Frog Alley Antiques/Merry P. Gilbert, New York City.*

Company in Chicago: paper ribbons entered the machine at one end and emerged at the other in long, thin strings. Lloyd made two

Workers at the Lloyd Manufacturing Company Inserting Wooden Frames Into Prewoven Baby Carriage Bodies, *1922. Photograph courtesy of Frog Alley Antiques/Merry P. Gilbert, New York City.*

types of fiber. One, used as the flexible, horizontal filler strands, or weft, had a glue sizing. The other, employed as the rigid vertical stakes, or warp, in the weaving process, also was sized as it was spun, but—and here was Lloyd's real innovation—it was twisted around a wire core. Both were fine, tightly twined strands—thinner, harder, and more uniform than other manufactured fiber. Once they had been spun, the continuous lengths were wound onto large, heated drums to dry the glue and then rewound into huge spools ready for the looms. These revolutionary machines had been rushed into service in 1917 when Lloyd's reed workers went on strike, forcing the plant to close for five weeks. The manufacturer and his engineers worked night and day during this period to perfect the design and build the first looms. When the factory reopened after the strike, many of the employees discovered that their jobs had been abolished. One loom did the work of thirty weavers.[7]

The original Lloyd Loom was a tall, vertical device with a cylindrical body and half-conical top. It was created specifically to weave seamless, basketlike bodies and hoods for baby carriages—then the most profitable part of Lloyd's lines. Workers affixed a warp of vertical rods made of wire-core fiber around the conical top, and then fed strands of regular fiber from huge coils through stationary shuttles affixed to the machine. In 1920, *Scientific American* described the mechanics of the process:

The wicker [i.e., fiber], wrapped in spools at the side of the loom is threaded into it over a tension wheel [above]. Before starting the loom in its rotary movement the stakes or warp are placed in permanent positions much as they are fitted on to the patterns when the Lloyd Method is used for hand weaving. Both ends of the warp are fastened before the loom begins to operate. As the machine revolves the weft is drawn from the spools on each side over the tension wheel and into the stationary shuttles, there being two weaving devices on each loom. A star-shaped wheel meets the warp as it turns on the loom and just before it reaches the shuttle the wheel presses alternate strands to either side of the shuttle. After the weft is drawn through the shuttle and woven, an automatic finger attached to a flexible arm grasps the weft and presses it downward to its proper place. Each arm has a uniform weight attached to it so that the weaving must necessarily be even. These weights travel on a stationary cam and operate uniformly at all times. The arm with a small wheel . . . at the front of the machine holds the warp in shape while it passes over or behind the shuttle. The machine is extremely simple, can be operated by an ordinary man with no skill required and weaves just thirty times more fabric than the best hand expert can weave. When the body has been woven the top of the machine is raised and the article taken off. The top and bottom ends of the warp are bent over by hand and the carriage body is completed.[8]

As an aside, none of the patents for which the Lloyd Manufacturing Company applied between 1917 and 1930 make any mention of a "loom."[9] Rather, they refer to methods of weaving independent of a frame. Although integral to the process, the Lloyd Loom was simply a means to this end.

The baby carriages that streamed out of the newly enlarged Menominee factory in 1918 caught the public's fancy. The weave was tight, absolutely uniform, and, with the use of wire-core fiber, virtually indestructible. No other wicker manufacturer could match the expensive look of Lloyd's fine carriages at the prices he charged, and the basketlike vehicles with their large, rounded hoods were phenomenally successful. For the first two years the looms were in operation, the firm concentrated solely on carriage production—producing up to one thousand a day. In 1920, however, Lloyd was ready to make machine-loomed furniture as well. His own analysis of consumer demand assured him it would be an extremely profitable venture. According to his calculations, only one in ninety-six Americans needed a baby carriage—and then usually only one. Furniture, on the other hand, was required by at least one in twenty-four. In his view, published in the factory newsletter, *Lloyd Shop News,* in March 1920, "every person wanting furniture needs from thirty to seventy-five pieces of which six to twenty are made of wicker. It must then follow that demand for furniture is forty times greater than the demand for baby carriages." Who could argue against such figures?—especially when the boss was convinced that "the demand for wicker [was] constantly increasing."[10] In 1920 the design of the conical, shaped-fabric loom was modified to weave sheets of flat fabric for furniture. The new drumlike looms were extraordinarily fast. If a carriage body could be made on a shaped-fabric loom thirty times faster than one woven by hand, flat fabric could be machine-made two hundred times as swiftly! If Lloyd Loom furniture caught on, many thought, it soon would put every large manufacturer of handwoven wicker out of business.

In 1918 the directors of the Heywood Brothers and Wakefield Company had been forced to take note of their Michigan rival as sales of Lloyd Loom baby carriages suddenly caught on. Carriages, go-carts, sulkies, and children's strollers made from tightly woven reed were an important part of Heywood-Wakefield's business, and with its new high-speed weaving technology, the Lloyd Manufacturing Company presented serious competition. In 1916 the Massachusetts company had put out an extensive catalogue devoted to its handwoven wicker vehicles. Three years later, to boost sales, it issued yet another catalogue, but Lloyd's machine-made fiber models were cheaper and better looking. The market for Heywood Brothers and Wakefield's reed buggies was now seriously threatened. The huge corporation shrewdly and swiftly resolved to counter the threat by buying out the smaller company and thus obtaining the rights to its patented technology. Lloyd had no objection and the lucrative deal was signed in 1921, the same year Heywood Brothers

and Wakefield Company, originally chartered in 1897 in New Jersey, was legally dissolved and reincorporated as the Heywood-Wakefield Company in Massachusetts. Heywood-Wakefield's acquisition of the rights to the Lloyd Loom was to be of tremendous commercial advantage to the company in the years ahead. It was also not a bad arrangement for Lloyd. He did not retire but joined the board of the corporation and remained in control of his Menominee factory. All its merchandise retained the "Lloyd Loom Products" label and was shipped directly to dealers nationwide. Only rarely were Lloyd Loom baby buggies and furniture sold through Heywood-Wakefield's network of warehouses. Lloyd also maintained the prerogative to license foreign firms to use his patented looms. In 1920 he had sold the rights to an Australian company, and in 1921 he licensed a French firm, Duval et Mouronval, and the London manufacturer, W. Lusty and Sons, to make Lloyd Loom merchandise. The following year, the manufacturer assisted his German-born workers to set up the Lloyd Cello Fiber Company at Fulda, near Frankfurt, Germany. This factory employed Menominee-trained Germans, but given the nation's disastrous inflation, the enterprise was short-lived.[11] In 1921 Heywood-Wakefield set up a small Canadian factory in Orillia, Ontario. After the merger with Lloyd, it assembled baby carriages, from parts shipped from Menominee, for the Canadian market. The Orillia plant was outfitted with two shaped-fabric looms and, with fiber-making machinery installed, was able to

make its own baby carriages.

In 1922, with Heywood-Wakefield's blessing, Lloyd introduced his first full line of Lloyd Loom furniture for the American market. The initial color catalogue illustrated thirty-four models of chairs, davenports, tables, lamps, ferneries, hampers, and wastepaper baskets. The designs were immediately successful, and in 1923 the plant was enlarged for furniture-making on a grand scale. During the decade of the 1920s—the golden age of American Lloyd Loom—upwards of a hundred different designs were offered annually in catalogues. Typically, vast amounts of unfinished furniture were stockpiled in Menominee before peak buying periods—Christmastime and spring—and when orders came pouring in for specific colors or upholstery patterns, they could be made rapidly and shipped out by rail—usually within a week.

In the late 1920s visitors were encouraged to tour the state-of-the-art Menominee factory. According to the company's promotional booklet, *My Trip Thru the Lloyd Plant,* tourists were guided first through the cavernous stockroom piled with all sorts of supplies and then into the wood room where dowels cut from rough lumber were steam-bent and kiln-dried for furniture frames. The "real magic" of the Menominee plant, however, took place on the second floor. Upstairs, deafening batteries of fiber-spinning and drying machines manufactured flexible filler strands and more rigid wire-core fiber. Others cut the latter into measured lengths to be fixed on the looms as warp. Enormous coils of newly made fiber and bundles of

No. D 61—Davenport
Seat—Width 72; Depth 23.
Back—Height from seat 24.
Finish—Enamel, choice of any two tone.
Upholstering—Velour or tapestry to match finish.
Springs—Marshall springs in cushion over spring seat.
Crated—One to a crate.

No. C 61—Chair
Seat—Width 20; Depth 18.
Back—Height from seat 26.
Finish—Enamel, choice of any two tone.
Upholstering—Velour or tapestry to match finish.
Springs—Marshall springs in cushion over spring seat.
Crated—Two to a crate.

No. R 61—Rocker
Seat—Width 20; Depth 18.
Back—Height from seat 26.
Finish—Enamel, choice of any two tone.
Upholstering—Velour or tapestry to match finish.
Springs—Marshall springs in cushion over spring seat.
Crated—Two to a crate.

No. C 61—CHAIR

No. R 61—ROCKER

Lloyd Manufacturing Company, Menominee, Michigan, Davenport and Chairs from the 1922 Lloyd Loom Products Catalogue. Courtesy of Frog Alley Antiques/Merry P. Gilbert, New York City. Lloyd launched his first line of machine-loomed furniture in 1922.

steel-hearted stakes were transported hourly to the weaving room next door. In this vast space, one section was devoted to the whirling looms that produced the shaped fabric for rounded carriage bodies and hoods, while another contained the larger flat-fabric looms. Other specialized weaving machines churned out long, ornamental figure-of-eight fiber braids used to trim the edges of buggies, chairs, and tables. Next on the factory tour was the enormous room in which the furniture frames were assembled from finished bentwood dowels—a single Lloyd Loom chair frame might need up to a dozen separate parts. Once the frames were put together, they were decoratively wrapped with strands of fiber, just like wicker made from reed and rattan. From the assembly area, the tourist moved to the room where skilled workers, the highest paid of the factory employees, stretched the flat fabric over the skeletal frames and fixed it in place with nails. The labor was divided. One man carefully fitted precut sections over the seat frame while another stretched the woven sheets over backs and sides. To facilitate the process, the flat-fiber fabric was cut into sections, and the ends were clamped with metal plates so that they would not unravel. Secondly, the tension of the stretched woven sheets had to be adjusted precisely to achieve the taut, clean look characteristic of Lloyd Loom furniture before it was nailed to the frame. Finally, braidwork was tacked along the edges to conceal the ends of the fiber sheet. After construction, each piece was dipped in a bath of colorless glue. When dried, the glue solution not only sized and strengthened the entire structure but provided a nonabsorbent undercoat for painting. In the paint department, workmen spray-painted the individual pieces in booths and loaded them onto carts that were wheeled into drying ovens. It was a twenty-four-hour operation.

Color was an essential feature of

Lloyd Loom furniture. The company offered more decorative finishes than any other wicker firm: the 1922 catalogue illustrated sixteen shades. Half were plain enamel colors—ivory, brown, dark blue, white, dark gray, black, and pink. The others were frosted tones—light colors sprayed over darker ones and then wiped off, leaving a pale residue in the crevices of the weave. In the 1920s most manufacturers produced lines of brightly painted and decorated wicker. In fact, by mid-decade, reed and fiber furniture "revelled" in color.[12] The Chicago firm of S. Karpen and Brothers, for example, used slim wire-core fiber for its handwoven furniture, and not only painted it in uniform and frosted tones, but highlighted it with more brilliant colors in diamond-check patterns specially woven into the backs of chairs. In 1924 a brightly painted lozenge design was a fashion fad in handwoven wicker, and the abstract pattern soon became a standard feature for Lloyd Loom furniture as well. By 1925 the looms were regularly fitted with a device adapted from automated jacquard looms which, at set intervals, automatically wove diamond shapes, ribbon patterns, or other, more elaborate motifs into the sheets of flat fiber.[13]

The only other American factory to install the patented looms in the early 1920s was Heywood-Wakefield's Chicago works.[14] The fiber furniture made in Chicago was similarly spray-painted, and the geometric motifs and braidwork strips later handpainted. Color toning became increasingly popular. By the late 1920s Heywood-Wakefield's machine-loomed

wicker was offered with novel shaded effects and further ornamented with airbrushed stencil designs. The range of deluxe color coatings—described as "bright, sparkling, and up-to-the-minute in style"—was quite extraordinary. In the company's 1929 furniture catalogue, thirty-nine different fiber finishes were divided into three price categories. Level "A" included uniform enamel tones such as Black Gloss, Jade Green, and Café au Lait. Finishes "B" and "C" were more costly and diverse. They included "Harvest Shade Decorated," described as "Yellow-Green Bronze; Shaded Red-Gold Bronze, Decorated in Green and Red," and "Beryl," composed of "Green Enamel with Lavender Overtone, Gold Highlight, Decorated Red and Black."

Heywood-Wakefield's reed furniture was also brightly painted. According to the decorative arts journal *Good Furniture* in July 1925, "reed furniture permits every possible type of coloring from black to scarlet and gold, and any color combination conceivable. . . . The most popular colors in the New York market are green, orange, red, black, and decorated greys . . . dark colors are the best liked for all-year city use because they do not show wear and soil."[15] Wicker, of course, was only one of many consumer products of the 1920s to be brightly painted. In order to sell, just about everything had to be colored—from radios to toothbrushes.

During the decade of the 1920s Americans attained an unparalleled standard of living. Between 1919 and 1929, the gross national product grew by forty percent and

the purchasing power of individuals increased by a full twenty percent.[16] The decade was the first great age of consumerism. Wartime production had resulted in new, standardized and highly efficient manufacturing techniques that by the end of the decade had doubled the nation's industrial capacity. Restrictive immigration quotas established in 1921 suddenly reduced the number of unskilled foreign laborers streaming through Ellis Island which, during the 1920s, forced the burgeoning industries to mechanize even faster. It was truly the Machine Age, and consumer goods of all kinds rolled off assembly lines in unprecedented numbers—and colors. With the widespread institution of buying on credit, cars, radios, and household appliances were now no longer available only to the well-off. The installment plan proved a great social leveler. By 1929 two-thirds of all American homes had electricity, a quarter boasted vacuum

Lloyd Manufacturing Company, Menominee, Michigan, Lloyd Loom Products Paper Labels, 1922. Courtesy of Frog Alley Antiques/Merry P. Gilbert, New York City.

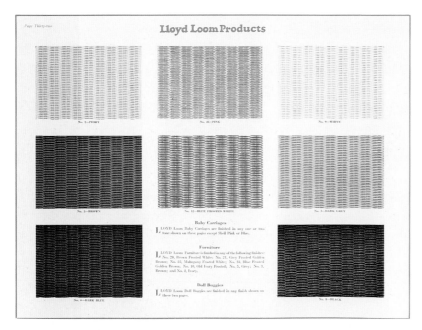

Lloyd Loom Products

No. 2—IVORY   No. 26—PINK   No. 9—WHITE

No. 3—BROWN   No. 12—BLUE FROSTED WHITE   No. 5—DARK GREY

No. 4—DARK BLUE   No. 8—BLACK

Baby Carriages
LLOYD Loom Baby Carriages are finished in any one or two tone shown on these pages except Shell Pink or Blue.

Furniture
LLOYD Loom Furniture is finished in any of the following finishes: No. 20, Brown Frosted White; No. 21, Grey Frosted Golden Brown; No. 22, Mahogany Frosted White; No. 18, Blue Frosted Golden Brown; No. 10, Old Ivory Frosted; No. 5, Grey; No. 3, Brown; and No. 2, Ivory.

Doll Buggies
LLOYD Loom Doll Buggies are finished in any finish shown on these two pages.

Above: Lloyd Manufacturing Company, Menominee, Michigan, Color Finishes from the 1922 Lloyd Loom Products Catalogue. Photograph courtesy of Frog Alley Antiques/Merry P. Gilbert, New York City.
Lloyd offered more factory finishes than any other wicker firm. In 1922 Lloyd Loom products came in sixteen colors. Half were plain enamel colors, the others frosted tones.

Below: S. Karpen and Brothers, Chicago, Suggested Color and Fabric Combinations for Fiber Furniture, 1923. Photograph courtesy of the Warshaw Collection of Business Americana, Archives Center, National Museum of American History, Smithsonian Institution.
In the 1920s, color was a successful sales tool for all consumer goods—including wicker furniture. Karpen offered colored lozenge designs in the backs of painted handwoven fiber chairs and sofas, as well as specially coordinated fabrics.

cleaners, and one fifth had electric toasters. By 1931 two-thirds of families in Pittsburgh owned a washing machine. The most significant product of the era, however, was the automobile. In much the same way as the proliferation of railroads had altered late-Victorian demographic patterns, the family car revolutionized American society. It offered unparalleled freedom of movement and soon became a cult object for people of all economic levels. In 1923 there were 108 different manufacturers offering a spectrum of enticing models. By the end of the decade, the number of privately owned automobiles soared to thirty million—one for every five people.[17] The ownership

of a car allowed city families by the tens of thousands to relocate in suburbs and new bedroom communities beyond city limits. Except for southern cities, urban growth across America peaked in the 1920s. During the decade, suburbs outside Chicago, Los Angeles, and Cleveland grew five to ten times as fast as did city neighborhoods. Many of the new outlying communities were preserves of the upper middle class and wealthy, filled with Georgian and neo-Tudor mansions. However, with the spread of paved roads, innumerable small towns sprouted beyond the suburbs that were soon filled with prefabricated Sears houses, which were home to middle-class commuters and their families. In the 1920s the white collar work force increased by forty percent, and, like the mushrooming middle classes of the late nineteenth century, this sector of the population proved the most avid consumer of mass-produced wicker furniture—especially Lloyd Loom. It is estimated that the number of machine-woven pieces manufactured in the United States and Britain before 1940 was more than ten million.[18]

Fiber furniture was inexpensive and meant to be so. According to *Good Furniture,* "fiber furniture is at base a 'price' product. It has been invented as a cheaper article to be used in place of the more expensive reed."[19] Increasingly in the 1920s, fiber furnishings were sold to lower-income Americans in multiple-piece sets or "suites"— typically, a rocker, armchair, sofa, table, and lamp. Newlyweds on limited budgets were eager purchasers of sets, but they were not the only ones to participate in the vogue. One East Coast furniture dealer reported that his sales of Lloyd Loom suites for 1924 were double what they had been the previous year. Similarly styled groupings had been introduced in the Victorian era but had not become popular until after 1910, when centrally heated sun rooms began to be outfitted entirely with "summery" basketweave furniture. The wicker-filled solarium influenced the 1920s practice of furnishing middle-class living, dining, and even bedrooms not only with fiber suites but with sets of more costly reed and willow as well. Sometimes, small houses were almost completely furnished with wicker. Cashing in on the trend started by manufacturers, department stores in the early twenties often displayed wicker suites in enticing room settings geared to attract higher income buyers. In June 1925, *Good Furniture* declared that so many different pieces were available that "it is now possible to furnish many rooms entirely in reed." No longer did the upscale retail industry consider wicker a product for summer use only:

The all-year use of reed furniture is a theme in process of development. Some New York stores have as yet no winter sale for reed, but the increasing attention given to the designing of reed furniture suitable for rooms used year 'round, and the fine and costly suites procurable for the complete furnishings of a room, are evidence that the only need remaining is that of educating the public in the year 'round

use of this type of furniture.[20]

In the "Roaring Twenties," taste in home furnishings was extremely conservative. Except for wicker, an eclectic historicism pervaded virtually every aspect of American design. After the First World War and the demise of the Arts and Crafts Movement, wood furniture manufacturers produced little more than pseudo-antiques or reproductions of historical styles. By the mid-1920s period furniture was all the rage. Department stores like Lord and Taylor, Abraham and Straus, and Macy's—as well as less stylish outlets such as Sears—were filled with contemporary versions of Louis XV, Louis XVI, Jacobean, Chippendale, Sheraton, and Adam designs. Colonial-revival furniture had been popular since the 1890s, but when the Metropolitan Museum of Art opened its Early American Wing in 1924, the

Heywood-Wakefield Company, Armchair and Footstool, ca. 1925. Photograph courtesy of the Chicago Historical Society. In 1921, Heywood-Wakefield purchased the Lloyd Manufacturing Company, acquiring the rights to its patented looms. Several of the machines were installed at Heywood-Wakefield's Chicago plant, where this painted fiber chair and stool were manufactured. The upholstery with its vivid floral pattern is original.

public's familiarity with and demand for colonial and Federal-era furniture styles increased dramatically. In July 1925, *Good Furniture* reported that "five years ago in New York City there was little heard of period furnishings. . . . [while] today every department and furniture store makes constant use of the names of the decorative periods in advertising, displaying, and selling. There has been no single development in the house furnishing business more significant than the broad spreading of information regarding period styles in so short a space of time."[21] Each

Barker Brothers and Company, Los Angeles,
Living Room Set from the 1921
Quality Reed Catalogue. *Photograph
courtesy of A Summer Place.*
*In the early 1920s, wicker firms began to
offer coordinated sets of wicker furniture for
living, dining, and bedrooms. Barker Brothers
was among the first to provide suites suitable
for southern California bungalows.*

historical period was deemed to have its own personality or symbolism. The French Renaissance signified luxury, English Tudor represented somber dignity, English Georgian connoted individual creativity, while early American suggested sincerity and hospitality.[22] The wealthy rejected contemporary period furnishings and instead scoured Europe for authentic antiques. Dark, heavily carved furniture of Italian or Spanish heritage and somber Renaissance and baroque textile wall hangings were especially prized acquisitions. The ahistorical, geometric logic of modernist European design movements—de Stijl in the Netherlands, the German Bauhaus, and Le Corbusier and Purism in France—was largely unknown in the United States and, when encountered abroad, the abstract forms were generally dismissed as aberrations by tradition-minded Americans.

America's deeply rooted conservatism resisted change. According to one critic writing in 1927, "The modern movement has taken stronger hold in Europe than here [in the United States], owing to the fact that the Europeans have been willing to experiment. Europeans were not so sure as we were that the decorative arts were dead and buried and that the best anyone could get, if he could not afford originals, were expert copies of the antique. It is curious that the inquiring American mind should have developed this rapid spirit of antiquarianism and so remain insensible and even hostile to the new spirit of design."[23] Another observer decided America was simply too young to be "surfeited" with tradition as were the Europeans: "We are so young that we are the most conservative nation on the face of the globe. We cling to what little traditions we possess. One of these days we may become so bored with early American furniture that we'll do something desperate, but that day is still far off."[24]

The epoch-making *Exposition Internationale des Arts Décoratifs et Industriels Modernes* held in Paris in 1925 proved to be a major catalyst for design reform in the United States. By 1928 the new aesthetic had changed the look of contemporary American furniture—and totally revolutionized the wicker industry. Even though the French government had set aside a special site, the United States had refused officially to exhibit at the "Art Deco" world's fair on the grounds that, as a nation, it had no modern decorative or industrial arts worth exhibiting. However, realizing that there might be important economic lessons to learn from the application of art to industry, Secretary of Commerce Herbert Hoover invited representatives of American furniture manufacturers to attend the fair and sent a three-man committee to make a full report. Over 108 industry delegates, as well as many artists, designers, critics, and other interested Americans visited the Paris fair. For the most part, they were shocked by what they saw. Isolated from Europe by the war and only minimally aware of the radical changes in industrial design brought about by the modern movements, they were quite unprepared for the international exhibition's modernist architecture and home furnishings exhibits. One writer described the scene as "a cubist dream city or the projection of a possible city on Mars, arisen overnight in the heart of Paris."[25] So disorienting were the angular forms and bright colors, another American visitor felt he had entered "a kaleidoscope." A member of Hoover's commission described it unofficially as "the most serious and sustained exhibition of bad taste the world has ever seen."[26] Whether outraged or enthusiastic—and many, indeed, responded warmly to the new decorative styles—all the visiting Americans recognized that the Paris show marked a clear break with the past. There simply were no period reproductions. The sources of Art Deco—the term is a recent one; at the time it was known popularly as "modern art" or "art moderne"—included the revolutionary fine arts movements of the pre–World War I era: Fauvism, Cubism, Futurism, and Expressionism. However, in the early 1920s, the French furniture makers modified these earlier influences by adding a stylized vocabulary of forms derived from Egyptian, Greek, Mayan, and other ancient civilizations, even producing creative reinterpretations of historical furniture styles. Yet another, far more stringent modernism was also on view at the

ЈUGGEЅTED DAVENPORT FOR 40Ј ЅUITE
BY FRED ЅTRATTON.
THE THREE HUMP, INDIVIDUAL BACK IS VERY UNPOPULAR.

exposition—the minimalist forms of Le Corbusier. His model apartment in the *Pavillon de l'Esprit Nouveau* astonished Americans with its simplicity of form and its rejection of decoration and precedent. Along with the anti-representational geometry of the Bauhaus designers, Le Corbusier's rectilinear designs would dominate the modern movement and, in the guise of the 1930s International Style, reshape America's decorative arts and architecture.

During 1926 four hundred pieces of deluxe French furniture, metalwork, ceramics, textiles, and glass selected from the exposition toured eight cities in the United States under the auspices of the American Association of Museums. This was the public's first exposure to the modern movement. In New York, the Metropolitan Museum hosted the show, and the new Art Deco aesthetic, already championed by *Good Furniture* and the *American Magazine of Art,* delighted upscale Manhattan designers and retailers searching for a way to break the stranglehold of historicism. In New York, Boston, Chicago, Los Angeles, and other centers, major department stores led the

Sketch for a Reed Davenport from a Heywood-Wakefield Company Designer's Notebook, 1925. *Courtesy of Steve Poole and Robert Evans.*

way. During the post-war economic boom, these urban emporia had increased dramatically in number and size. Housewives, newly liberated from time-consuming home chores by all manner of electrical appliances and not yet forced to take jobs to sustain the family's income level, engaged in a popular 1920s pastime—shopping. Many of the department stores initiated decorating services and housewives regularly visited the home furnishings departments to examine the latest trends. In early May 1927, building on the Metropolitan Museum's exhibition, R. H. Macy and Company staged its landmark "Exposition of Art-in-Trade," a dazzling pageant of modern-style furniture and decorative arts. During its first week, the show attracted forty thousand visitors. In Manhattan, Lord and Taylor, B. Altman, Abraham and Straus, and John Wanamaker soon followed suit, actively promoting "art moderne" fashions through exciting window and floor displays of modern French and American

These HEYWOOD-WAKEFIELD Finishes Are Particularly Adapted to Fibre Furniture.

THE six new Heywood-Wakefield finishes shown on this page have been particularly developed for fibre furniture, although they are suitable to some of the reed pieces as well. These finishes bring out unusual shaded effects and color combinations that lend a new sparkle and lightness to fibre and increase its eye and sales value. On your popular price fibre furniture for 1930 be sure to include an assortment of these exclusive Heywood-Wakefield colors.

Cream De Luxe

Tan De Luxe

Pearl Blue De Luxe

Brown De Luxe

Grey De Luxe

Green De Luxe

Heywood-Wakefield Company, "Deluxe" Color Finishes for Fiber Furniture from the 1930 Furniture Catalogue. Courtesy of A Summer Place.
In 1930, the Heywood-Wakefield Company offered a total of nineteen "deluxe" finishes on its popularly priced fiber furniture.

products. Lord and Taylor's own extravaganza, "An Exposition of Modern French Decorative Art," opened on February 29, 1928. It was a sensation: during its first ten days, 130,000 spectators crowded into the Manhattan store to view the luxury objects from France. Before the show closed on April 1, it was estimated that half a million visitors had viewed the exotic furnishings.[27] A senior executive of Boston's Jordan Marsh boldly declared that "since they reflect good taste and act as a great educating force in the community . . . department stores are the museums of today."[28] To a large extent he was right: from 1927 to 1929 there were thirty-six department store exhibitions of modern furnishings in as many months.[29] Retail buyers across the United States remained in the vanguard of the new movement, showcasing the latest developments in wood and wicker furniture and influencing the design evolution of American home furnishings. In May 1928 Pittsburgh's Gimbel Brothers displayed a series of "art mod-erne" model rooms. A brochure declared: "the world has reached a new age—a complete renaissance—nothing is as it was a generation ago. The modern apartment house, labor-saving devices, mass production, automobiles, airplanes—our economic and social lives are bringing it about—creating a new people that demand a new setting."[30]

For the most part, however, decorative arts manufacturers were hesitant about joining the "new age" and wholeheartedly embracing the modern movement. Popular taste remained conservative, and the luxury furniture from France typically was handmade by cabinetmakers using rare and costly materials. American furniture manufacturers were dependent on machines and mass-production techniques. French methods and standards clearly were inappropriate models. As *Good Furniture* noted, "All European attempts so far made to create furniture strictly of the present, with no allegiance to historic precedence, involve effects possible only by costly labor processes that do not lend themselves to quantity production."[31] Nevertheless, American market forces dictated change. By mid-decade, industrial capacity had increased dramatically but consumption had not kept pace. The furniture trade was in the doldrums; sales of even early American were declining noticeably. The modern style thus offered a much-needed means to stimulate new sales—not only for wood furniture but also for wicker. In March 1928 the editors of the trade journal *Furniture Record* posed the question to furniture dealers, "Art Moderne—Shall We Take It Seriously?"

'If I had to live with that for two weeks, I'd go crazy'—that's a common reaction to Art Moderne furniture as exhibited in many market centers and stores. It isn't just a small divergence from the furniture we're used to. It's a jump off the bridge! However, you'd be amazed how some furniture stores are selling it. 'Modernistic' furniture is supposed to be brilliant, alive, dynamic—a perfect epitome to the age in which we live. . . . Nowadays furniture must be easy to keep clean, because we have so little time for housework. It

Heywood-Wakefield Company, Painted Reed Furniture from the 1929 Catalogue. *Courtesy of A Summer Place.*
With its dramatic shape and colorful patterns, this reed chair reflects the influence of French Art Deco style. Heywood-Wakefield offered extensive lines of reed furniture only until 1929. With the Depression and the institution of a new, modernist design philosophy, the costly, time-consuming practice of weaving wicker by hand was abandoned.

must be free from dust-catching turnings and carvings. Period furnishings reflects the glory of the hand artisan and craftsman; 'modernistic' furniture glorifies the machine. To appreciate it, one must discard all previous concepts of what is beautiful in furniture.[32]

After 1928 a variety of established furniture companies realized the new style was "serious" and introduced new lines of angular, veneered furniture that they promoted as "modernistic"—among them was Heywood-Wakefield.

Three years earlier, however, Heywood-Wakefield's wood and woven furniture designs, like those of its competitors, were highly conservative. Wicker designers' notebooks reveal their ideas in reed furnishings to be utterly conven-

tional. Clearly, the firm anticipated no need for radical design changes: tight weaves with lozenge designs predominated. In 1926, a hundred years after Levi Heywood and his brothers started their wood chair factory on the family farm, Heywood-Wakefield published its centennial history, *A Completed Century.* The celebratory book not only detailed the early years of both Heywood Brothers and the Wakefield Rattan Company and the period since their merger in 1897, but also provided an in-depth look at the corporation's current organization and industrial operations. In the mid-1920s, it was a large and complex business under the direction of Levi H. Greenwood—a member of the third generation of Heywoods to manage the firm. A total of seven factories employed 3,706 workers. In Gardner, 1,226

Two Views in the Heywood-Wakefield Company's Chicago Factory, *1926. Photograph from* A Completed Century, *1926, courtesy of the National Museum of American Art, Smithsonian Institution. Heywood-Wakefield manufactured handwoven reed and machine-loomed fiber furniture. Workers wove wicker in the traditional fashion (top), while skilled workers nailed machine-made fiber fabric to wooden frames (bottom).*

employees made cane and wood seat chairs, wicker, school furniture, and reed and metal baby carriages. At the Wakefield complex, 822 men and women processed supplies of raw rattan still imported by the shipload from the firm's Singapore "godown" into chair caning and reed, machine-wove cane fabric for railway and street car seats, made cocoa matting, and handwove reed furniture. In Chicago, 674 employees manufactured reed and fiber furniture, produced wooden and upholstered seating for theaters, sports stadiums, and movie houses, and made fiber, reed, and metal baby carriages. The other company-owned factories in Menominee and Orillia manufactured Lloyd Loom furniture and carriages, while two smaller plants in Portland, Oregon, and Erving, Massachusetts, turned out wood, and in Portland's case, wicker, furniture. There were also thirteen large company warehouses with 1,601 employees scattered across the United States and Canada. The largest was the New York building. Constructed in 1911, it rose thirteen stories next to Pennsylvania Station. The Heywood-Wakefield warehouses were the firm's commercial backbone. They functioned as retail stores and stocked inventories of home and office furniture for regional markets, assembled chairs shipped knocked-down from the factories, and custom-upholstered and spray-painted wicker furniture on order for customers. Spread from coast to coast, they decentralized the firm's operations and in the 1920s were essential keys to its economic success. Furniture dealers visited the warehouse showrooms and Heywood-Wakefield salesmen set up displays at the semi-annual or quarterly furniture trade shows in Chicago, Grand Rapids, Michigan, Jamestown, New York, and High Point, North Carolina, and aggressively sought contracts from school boards and other clients for public seating. In 1926 no firm matched its output in seating—either in wood or wicker.

A Completed Century detailed the manufacture of reed furniture at the Chicago plant. First, wooden dowels were steamed until they were soft and pliable and then bent into desired shapes and left to dry. Finished bentwood dowels next went to the machine room where they were cut and assembled into frames. After being inspected for quality and accurate size, the frames were sent to the winders who wrapped strips of flat reed around the legs and structural braces. Once the winders had completed their task, the skeletal forms were taken to the reed shop where skilled Swedish, Polish, Lithuanian, Dutch, Czechoslovakian, Irish, and Italian workers, "some singing, others reticent," handwove individual pieces. Many took two days of hard work to complete.

The men work in individual stalls with long reeds lying on the floor or hanging from the walls—each stall the reed worker's private domain. Stacks of frames stand in front of the weaver, and by his side is a pail of water into which the reed is dipped to make it pliable for weaving and to prevent splintering. The ends of the reed are pointed with a small knife so that they may be concealed

when the piece is finished. Small benches with swivel forms help to hold the frame in position as the work progresses.[33]

Next door, a younger generation of workers fitted sections of fiber fabric onto the same bentwood frames constructed for reed furniture. The room resounded with the noise of their hammers as they tacked the machine-loomed wicker onto the wooden forms. Once completed, each piece of reed or fiber furniture was inspected before being shipped out to the company's warehouses to be painted and upholstered.

Heywood-Wakefield's clientele for reed and fiber furniture generally was conservative and of moderate means. The company's warehouse showrooms were filled on Saturdays with middle-class homeowners in search of sets of woven furniture, and the firm advertised in color in such popular magazines as *Saturday Evening Post, Ladies' Home Journal,* and *McCall's.* Well-to-do urban trend-setters, on the other hand, turned to upscale department stores for their wicker needs and leafed through *Good Furniture, Country Life in America,* and *Arts and Decoration,* looking for the latest fashions in living-room, sun-room, and terrace furniture. In the mid-1920s city dwellers no longer considered wicker for summer use only. "Reed furniture has progressed far beyond the former demand for chairs for the open porch," declared *Good Furniture;* "its indoor use keeps pace with its attention to indoor requirements. The downstairs all-year living room, the up-stairs sitting room, the bed room, the breakfast room are all considered in the new designs for reed and rattan furniture."[34] Nonetheless, wicker sales were seasonal, and each spring department stores showcased the newest in reed, willow, and high-quality fiber furniture. The manu-

Heywood-Wakefield Wicker Furniture on Display in Chicago, 1926. *Photograph from* A Completed Century, 1926, *courtesy of the National Museum of American Art, Smithsonian Institution.*
After 1925, Heywood-Wakefield joined other midwestern furniture manufacturers in displaying their products year-round at the American Furniture Mart Building in Chicago.

facturers who dominated the spring shows—and whose pieces were most often reproduced in high-style journals—included the Ypsilanti Reed Company of Ionia, Michigan; S. Karpen and Brothers from Chicago; F. A. Whitney of Leominster, Massachusetts; and from New York City, Bielecky Brothers, F. Debski, Sons-Cunningham, Mastercraft Reed Corporation, Manhattan Wicker Shop, and Grand Central Wicker; the Northfield Furniture Company of Sheboygan, Wisconsin; Ficks-Reed of Cincinnati; and, from Los Angeles, Barker Brothers. In addition, American firms specializing in

Barker Brothers and Company, Los Angeles, A Breakfast Room Set from the 1921 "Quality Reed" Catalogue. *Courtesy of A Summer Place.*
The success of the wicker-filled sun room led manufacturers and decorators to suggest, in the 1920s, using sets of woven furniture throughout the home. Barker Brothers illustrated several different suites of handwoven reed, including this white-painted set for a breakfast room, in its 1921 catalogue.

Asian wicker exhibited and advertised their latest imports.

Generally, *Good Furniture* would preview the new season's offerings in an illustrated article. In April 1927 the magazine noted that "although woven furniture is being used increasingly inside the house, its principal use is still confined to the sun room and porch."[35] For the uninitiated, the writer distinguished five different types of wicker by materials employed: "peel (sometimes called cane) and reed, which are made from rattan . . . fibre, similar to reed in appearance but less expensive; willow; and sea grass." So-called "peel" furniture was Chinese-made and included traditional peacock chairs in natural tones with black weave patterns. However, most Oriental wicker of the 1920s was made for a sophisticated urban clientele and came in familiar Western designs. Fiber, the magazine noted, was an inexpensive product for the cost-conscious and, with several coats

of disguising enamel paint, might easily be mistaken for more costly reed furniture. According to the author, supplies for American-made willow furniture were still imported from France and Germany. However, large commercial shipments of peeled osiers also came from Argentina—a new source developed during the war years when trade with Europe was reduced. Sea grass, harvested in the coastal marshes of China, was a relatively new weaving material for American consumers. Frames for Oriental grass furniture were made from rigid poles of Malacca rattan, while vertical strips of attached cane supplied the warp for the weavers. Before interlacing the strands, the Hong Kong craftsmen moistened two separate blades of sea grass and then twisted them into one long, thick filament. Like the Crex Prairie Grass furniture of the prewar period, Oriental sea grass had a rough texture and a natural green tone.

As illustrations revealed, designs for the 1927 season were surprisingly diverse. Ypsilanti Reed offered period-style woven furniture—a wood and reed Duncan Phyfe desk and chair in orange; a Biedermeier-inspired armchair with turned wood legs and arms and a woven reed back; a fiber chaise longue with colorful Egyptian motifs stenciled on wood medallions affixed to the frame. Seasonal offerings that year also included Oriental peacock chairs and French Empire-style reed settees. Even traditional Bar Harbor chairs were available. To stimulate the use of wicker in formal living rooms, manufacturers often combined reed with turned hardwood frames suggestive of period designs and upholstered chairs and settees with luxury fabrics—mohairs, velours, and silk damask. In 1927 color was a continuing wicker fashion fad:

. . . colors are gayer and more brilliant this year than ever before—both in the reed and fibre and in the upholstery. Green, suggesting the grass and leaves of spring, is the most popular color. There are also sets in orange, red, blue, orchid and light rose color. Some, sprayed with gold or silver, are particularly brilliant, and many have fascinating two-tone effects . . . gained by twisting together two strands of different colored fiber . . . and by spraying a painted set with an additional color.[36]

The fabric-covered seats and backs of the latest models were particularly dazzling: "futuristic art with its flaming colors and queer fantastic designs is evident in most of the upholstery . . . vivid stripe patterns, block designs, and colorful plaids are most often used."

Wicker for 1928, however, was markedly different. Modernist "stick" wicker was all the rage. *Good Furniture* reported on the development: "certainly one of the most interesting tendencies in this line of furniture . . . [is] the increased popularity of stick reed and stick willow. Although it had an important season last year its display now is far more extensive. Furthermore, the feature suites in various manufacturers' exhibits—those displayed in an especially prominent position on the floor and upholstered in particularly novel fabrics—were very often made of stick willow or reed."[37] The nonwoven designs were not recent innovations. "Contrary to frequent opinion," the magazine reported, "this stick reed and willow furniture is not new, but it is simply enjoying a great revival in popularity." The rectilinear mode appears to have emerged around the turn of the century in secessionist Vienna and in Switzerland. Examples had been included in the 1904 catalogue of McHughwillow, and in 1917 The Reed Shop of Manhattan had prominently featured stick-style furniture in their new catalogue, *Suggestions in Reed Furniture*. In 1928 the Michigan Seating Company—which had originated the Kaltex line—added thick rods of wire-core fiber to the list of materials used. As its name suggests, the rigid furniture was stick-like: composed of parallel rows of vertical—or sometimes horizontal—rods fastened to perpendicu-

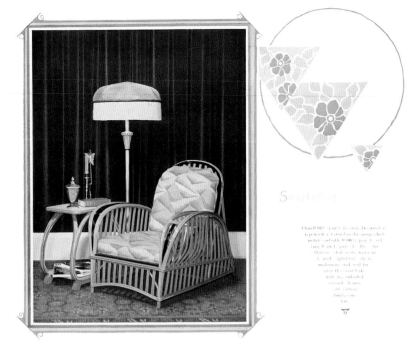

Heywood-Wakefield Company, Painted Stick Reed Chair, End Table, and Fiber Lamp from the 1929 Furniture Catalogue. *Courtesy of A Summer Place.*
Stick-wicker was described as "modernistic." Painted orange with jade and black trim, this deep-seated armchair was modeled on a Chinese boat chair fashionable in the 1920s.

lar members or tied together with paired lengths of woven reed. The sleek, geometric look was very up-to-date and, unlike traditional woven wicker, mimicked the "art moderne" design aesthetic in wood furniture. In the view of *Good Furniture:* "Modern art does not seem to have had, as yet, a marked influence on the woven furniture styles. . . . But when the modernistic feeling in the shape of pieces is noted it seems inevitably to be in furniture of the stick willow type."[38]

One of the companies that had rushed an extensive line of stick-wicker to the market for the 1928 season was Heywood-Wakefield. A growing interest in the modern movement among well-to-do consumers had convinced the firm to be-

gin to update its designs. A new, lucrative market had developed: the style-conscious New Yorker living in a modern high-rise apartment. Heywood-Wakefield was eager to appeal to this new consumer. In the late 1920s Manhattan was deemed "the nation's style pulse," and the skyscraper was considered its inspirational symbol.[39] Multistory urban towers had

Heywood-Wakefield Company, Stick-Wicker Tables from the 1929 Furniture Catalogue. *Courtesy of A Summer Place.*
In its 1929 catalogue, the Heywood-Wakefield Company showcased its stick-reed furniture in the dramatic "art moderne" style popular from 1927 to 1930.

Ficks-Reed Company, Cincinnati, Stick-Wicker Chairs Designed by Paul Frankl. *Photograph from Frankl,* New Dimensions, *1928, courtesy of the Library of Congress. In the late 1920s, industrial designers were employed by several wicker manufacturers to create new styles. In 1928 Frankl, famous for his "skyscraper" furniture, was hired by Ficks-Reed to restyle its stick-wicker line.*

been a fact of life in Chicago and New York since the late nineteenth century, but in the 1920s there was an extraordinary boom in skyscraper construction both for commercial and residential use. In 1916 a zoning ordinance required all new towers to be stepped back as they rose, to ensure that sunlight and fresh air reached pedestrians on the sidewalks below. As a result, the skyscrapers looked, in elevation, like stretched ziggurats. Familiar beaux arts and Gothic architectural detailing on buildings nearby was soon confronted by stylized "art moderne" decoration. The setback towers erected between 1922 and 1932 altered the Manhattan skyline, and to many artists, writers, and sensitive observers they symbolized the Machine Age and America's modernity.

Skyscrapers inspired new forms of decorative art and design. One leading designer declared:

Some architects call this spirit in our new architecture the spirit of democracy, others call it the result of the machine age . . . . The modern skyscraper is a distinctive and noble creation. It is a monument of towering engineering and business enterprise. . . . Decorative arts and furniture design are already under the powerful modern architectural influence. This can only resolve into one thing: a decorative art that is in keeping with the country and the people who live in it. It will resolve into an American decorative art, original and at the same time satisfying.[40]

The high-rise apartment and how to furnish it was, in the late 1920s, a subject of much interest and debate in progressive decorative arts journals. In space and layout, the skyscraper residence posed a series of problems. It was more modest in scale than its predecessors. Standard ceiling heights had dropped from fourteen to twelve feet, and since windows were restricted usually to one wall of a room, rooms were narrowed. As families moved into skyscrapers, their old furniture was clearly out of place. Just as Victorian wicker had looked ridiculous in the setting of a bungalow, so the period furniture from Georgian-style residences appeared inappropriate in modern high-rise settings. The simple geometry and functional requirements of the late-1920s apartment demanded something up-to-date. Clean lines and pristine surfaces of modernist furniture were perfect complements. Since rooms were smaller, most of the

Ficks-Reed Company, Cincinnati, Stick-Wicker Furniture Set Designed by Paul Frankl, *1930. Photograph from Deskey,* "Style in Summer Furniture," Good Furniture *(April 1930), courtesy of the Library of Congress. By 1930, Frankl's designs for Ficks-Reed had evolved into simple geometric forms based on his "new classicism" design philosophy. Outlined in his manifesto* Form and Re-Form *(1930), it stressed the square, circle, and horizontal line as essential components.*

furniture designed for apartment use was multipurpose. In the view of one writer in 1929, "a large fraction of us live in cities where room becomes more and more at a premium. This has made the apartment house our typical living arrangement, with the tendency toward smaller and fewer rooms. Furthermore, household service . . . becomes increasingly difficult to afford. All these things require that we have fewer and smaller pieces of furniture. We no longer have space for the chaise longue or for couches. . . . What furniture we have must function effectively."[41] In the late 1920s, the high-rise residence of a middle-class businessman or professional might contain just a single room for living, dining, and sleeping, so that every piece of furniture had to have a double life. The doors of a compact cabinet might conceal a desk and store a telephone, typewriter, and stationery; a well-designed sofa could be transformed into a bed by removing the cushions.

The most celebrated American designer of high-rise furnishings was Paul Frankl. He was one of a new breed of professionals who emerged in the aftermath of the Paris exposition—free-lance industrial designers. For the most part they were European immigrants or Americans trained as architects and influenced by Continental design. In the late 1920s and the depression years of the thirties, these individuals transformed the look of America. From railroad engines to salt shakers to porch furniture, virtually every industrial product was reconfigured to fit the functional—and symbolic—needs of the streamlined age. In

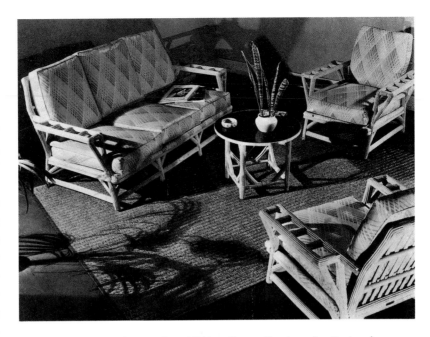

Ypsilanti Reed Furniture Company, Ionia, Michigan, Rattan Furniture Set Designed by Donald Deskey, *ca. 1929. Photograph from Deskey, "Style in Summer Furniture,"* Good Furniture *(April 1930), courtesy of the Library of Congress.*

1928 *Good Furniture* enthusiastically reviewed a "modernistic" apartment library Frankl had created as a model room for a department store. According to the magazine, he was an "enthusiastic sponsor" of the "so-called 'skyscraper' furniture of today." Among his signature pieces were "huge, towering bookcases reaching ceiling-ward in a series of set-back terraces."[42] These were decreed to be as "American and New Yorkish as Fifth Avenue itself."[43] Case furniture, however, was only one of Frankl's angular productions. In 1928 he turned his attention to designing reed and willow furniture in the modern manner. Walter J. H. Dudley, the creator of McHughwillow, had been the only other professional to design wicker. Everyone else had been a stylist or draftsman employed by a manufacturer. These individuals had responded only to market pressures. The design of Frankl's modernist stick-wicker, on the other

hand, was based on his commitment to ideals set forth in his manifestoes, *New Dimensions* (1928) and *Form and Re-Form* (1930). "Modernism has been called the style of reason," Frankl declared, "its appeal is an appeal to the intelligence. Its emphasis on simple forms, its return to mathematical axiom and the fundamentals of form, confer upon it a classical rather than romantic beauty. . . . By line, proportion and inherent relations, the new classicism makes a direct appeal to the vision and the mind. Modern forms are simple: the square, the circle, the horizontal line, skillfully and dynamically coordinated—these are a return to the Greek ideal."[44] The stick-wicker that Frankl created for Ficks-Reed from 1928 to 1930 evolved from "art moderne" stylishness to Spartan forms that adhered to his design philosophy.

In 1928, another leading designer, Donald Deskey, responsible in 1932 for designing the interiors of

Model Reclining on a Stick-Wicker Chair, *1930. Photograph from* Furniture Record *(July 1930), courtesy of the Library of Congress.*

Manhattan's Radio City Music Hall, was employed by Ypsilanti Reed to update its lines of woven furniture. The Ionia, Michigan, firm wished to appeal to a more sophisticated and affluent class of consumers. For Ypsilanti Reed, Deskey created a variety of wicker designs. Some were boxy forms in machine-woven fiber with horizontal bands of black, gray, and natural colors.[45] Others were elegant rattan, stick reed, or cane designs. Another line of chairs, which heralded the coming revolution in furniture, used cantilevered tubular steel frames with handwoven reed seats and backs.

In an illustrated article, "Style in Summer Furniture," published in *Good Furniture*, Donald Deskey observed that reed, rattan, cane, and fiber could adapt naturally to the new Machine Age aesthetic:

No matter how strong may be the resistance to contemporary developments in furniture and in decoration, one must accept modernism in relation to outdoor furniture. We may cling tenaciously to Italian Renaissance or to Colonial as models of architecture, or we may battle valiantly for the maintenance of Queen Anne or Louis Quinze in other pieces of furniture; but without challenge sun room furniture gains admittance, even in the very stronghold of the traditionalist. . . . [Wicker] furniture . . . [is] free of precedent. There are no period forms to direct the designer's pencil. . . . The designer of reed furniture does not go to the museum and to text books to copy meticulously . . . but into the factory itself. In no other branch of furniture design—not even in metal furniture—does the material dictate its design so emphatically. Form and function, functional decoration —these popular terms must be considered by one who would work with the materials used in the manufacture of outdoor furniture.[46]

Deskey declared that woven reed was sadly susceptible to the "malformations" that result when a material can be easily worked. The craftsman's virtuosity, he claimed, naturally lead to design "atrocities." However, because it was stretched over such simple frames, machine-loomed fiber furniture was "a particularly interesting matter in the hands of a modern designer." For the same reason, he declared that machine-woven cane fabrics—either with an open or close weave—were likewise suitable for contemporary sun-room furniture. The designer reported that the merchandising of wicker had undergone a welcome revolution: "At one time the $3.95 Bar Harbor chair served all purposes for outdoor or porch use; now we find a demand for style, a demand for better quality and the one element which for many years was the pivot of every business transaction—price—is relegated to the background, let us hope for ever!"

Like earlier woven furniture, modernist stick-wicker was used indoors in sun rooms and living rooms and outside on porches and patios. But it was also to be encountered in a new location—the landscaped "sky gardens" of residential towers built in the late 1920s. According to *Arts and Decoration,* "the newest apartment houses with their set-back style of architecture are furnishing ideal settings for the development of terrace and roof gardens, where high above the turmoil of crowded city streets, far removed from the ceaseless roar of city sounds, these oases of greenery, with their miniature trees, shrubs, vines and flowers seem to flourish and bloom as luxuriantly as in their native gardens."[47] The high-rise terraces typically were tiled, shaded by awnings, and separated from neighbors by wrought-iron gates, palisade and picket fences, and vine-covered trellises. An article in *House Beautiful* noted that "the number of these enchanting sky gardens, hung on ledges at dizzying heights above the ground, has increased as

skyscraper apartments have multiplied. . . . Here, in the cool seclusion of the upper air, remote and aloof from disturbing realities, are assembled gay furnishings and the little accessories of an intimate sort, where much of the social life of the owners is spent. . . . One may while away the hours with no fear of unwelcome interruption."[48] On wide parapets overlooking Central Park, affluent apartment residents placed marble urns, garden statuary, and Tuscan strawberry jars filled with trailing or blossoming plants. These sky gardens were delightful warm-weather aeries, and were made all the more attractive by the addition of chairs, lounges, and tables in up-to-date bent rattan and stick-wicker. The new, contemporary-style outdoor furniture was also regularly to be found on flag-stoned patios and manicured lawns of Long Island or Greenwich, Connecticut, estates. Many wealthy

Various Manufacturers, Stick-Wicker "Fan Tail," Chairs, and Table, *ca. 1929, rattan, wood, and paint. Courtesy of A Summer Place. Photograph by Kit Latham.*

owners of Manhattan apartments actually lived in the city only during the fall and winter social season and otherwise enjoyed a relaxed life in sumptuous countryside retreats. Stick-style willow and rattan was also favored on the

Ypsilanti Reed Furniture Company, Ionia, Michigan, Tubular Steel and Woven Reed Furniture Designed by Donald Deskey. *Photograph from* Home and Field *(May 1930), courtesy of the Library of Congress. Ypsilanti Reed pioneered the American manufacture of tubular steel furniture. Designed by Deskey, the cantilevered chair frames with reed backs and seats were inspired by examples created in Germany in 1927 by Mies van der Rohe.*

afterdecks of luxury yachts. Modernist wicker furniture designed by Frankl and Deskey often found considerable favor with the very rich. Many of the younger generation recognized the status it conferred on them. At the same time, the design-conscious middle-class homeowners who built modern-style residences also fully appreciated these contemporary outdoor and sun-room pieces. More conservative householders, who in the late 1920s lived in comfortable, four-square dwellings in the suburbs, remained fully content with their outmoded woven reed sets.

In March 1929, when Herbert Hoover, the newly elected president, took up residence in the White House, everything seemed rosy. What the former Secretary of Commerce—in private life a wealthy mining engineer and businessman—called "the American system" appeared to offer unlimited promise to all. In his inaugural address, Hoover declared a "New Day" and reported that the nation's future was "bright with hope." The members of the Cabinet were mostly businessmen like the President, and included six millionaires. Devotees of capitalism and the status quo, they could not be expected to offer much in the way of innovative programs for social or economic change. Yet deep-seated problems in the United States cried out for daring solutions. In 1929 minorities and women regularly were denied equal opportunities and almost sixty percent of families lived at or below the poverty line of two thousand

dollars. One percent of Americans owned fifty-nine percent of the nation's wealth, while only ten percent of the population owned a staggering eighty-seven percent. Hoover realized that the economic system produced inequities in the distribution of wealth but was unwilling to consider alterations. "The only trouble with capitalism," he grumbled, "is capitalists. They're too damned greedy."

On Wall Street, get-rich-quick was the order of the day for millions of enthusiastic investors, who bought stock on credit. In the early autumn, a surging bull market fueled an unprecedented speculative binge. In late September and early October, however, prices fell markedly, but the decline was viewed as a necessary market correction. On the morning of Thursday, October 24, 1929, a record number of shares were sold— many below list price. Frightened, bank executives gathered at noon to halt the sudden erosion in value and put up twenty million dollars to help restore confidence. In the afternoon, the market rallied but news of deep reversals on the New York Stock Exchange panicked nervous shareholders nationwide. On October 29, 1929, "Black Tuesday," prices plummeted to new depths. The stock market crash ultimately led to the depression of the 1930s. The national economy, however, had been soft for several years: overproduction had led to declining sales in all sectors—including the wicker industry. Wages in the 1920s simply had not kept pace with the increase in

industrial production. There simply were not enough buyers for the flood of new consumer goods rolling off assembly lines and, as supply outstripped demand, inventories stacked up, workers were laid off, and business investments fell. With income concentrated at the top, much of the nation's wealth went into savings, stocks and bonds, and luxuries.

The drop in consumption and investment after the crash was precipitous and dealt the economy a staggering blow. Between 1929 and 1933 one hundred thousand businesses failed and corporate profits dropped from ten to one billion dollars. Banks across the United States collapsed by the thousands. By 1933, the year Franklin D. Roosevelt became President, nine million individual savings accounts had been wiped out.[49] The Great Depression was far deeper and longer lasting than the economic chaos provoked by the Panics of 1873 and 1893. Unlike those business reversals, the depression had a catastrophic effect on the wicker industry. As the income and savings of the middle classes evaporated, the production of hand-woven furniture declined rapidly. Not only were there fewer dollars available to purchase it, the furniture now was too costly to make. Economics, however, provides only one of the reasons for the demise of traditional wicker. During the 1930s new design philosophies and industrial materials contributed strongly to the end of the great age of American woven furniture.

NOTES

1. See Alan Gowans, *The Comfortable House, North American Suburban Architecture, 1890–1930* (Cambridge, Mass., and London: MIT Press, 1986), 84ff.

2. Ibid., 146.

3. Glenn L. Saxton, *The Plan Book of American Dwellings* (Minneapolis: Privately Printed, 1914), 11.

4. George W. Rowell, "Wicker Weaving by Machine," *Scientific American*, 6 March 1920, 242.

5. Lee J. Curtis, *Lloyd Loom Woven Fiber Furniture* (New York: Rizzoli, 1991), 15.

6. Ibid., 26.

7. *A Completed Century, 1826–1926: The Story of the Heywood-Wakefield Company* (Boston: Printed for the Company, 1926), 38.

8. Rowell, "Wicker Weaving by Machine," 242.

9. Curtis, *Lloyd Loom Woven Fiber Furniture*, 21.

10. Quoted in Curtis, *Lloyd Loom Woven Fiber Furniture*, 32.

11. Ibid., 23–24.

12. "Summer Furniture," *Good Furniture* 24 (May 1925): 225.

13. Curtis, *Lloyd Loom Woven Fiber Furniture*, 51.

14. By 1928 the Ypsilanti Reed Company of Ionia, Michigan, and the Metropolitan Chair Company of New York were manufacturing machine-loomed, fiber furniture, presumably under license.

15. G. Glen Gould, "Rattan, Willow, Grass, and Fiber Furniture; Part I: American Reed and French Cane," *Good Furniture* 25 (July 1925): 305.

16. Thomas G. Paterson, "The New Era of the 1920s," in *A People and A Nation: A History of the United States* (Boston: Houghton Mifflin, 1984), 362.

17. Ibid.; and Jeffrey L. Meikle, *Twentieth Century Limited. Industrial Design in America, 1925–1939* (Philadelphia: Temple University Press, 1979), 7.

18. Curtis, *Lloyd Loom Woven Fiber Furniture*, 7.

19. G. Glen Gould, "Rattan, Willow, Grass, and Fiber Furniture. Part II. Willow and Fiber, Chinese Peeled Rattan and Sea Grass, Bamboo," *Good Furniture* 25 (July 1925): 32.

20. G. Glen Gould, "Rattan, Willow, Grass, Fiber Furniture. Part I. American Reed and French Cane," *Good Furniture* 24 (June 1925): 304.

21. "Increasing Interest in Period Furnishings," *Good Furniture* 25 (July 1925): 3.

22. See Karen Halttunen, "From Parlor to Living Room: Domestic Space, Interior Decoration, and the Culture of Personality," in Simon J. Bronner, ed., *Consuming Visions. Accumulation and Display of Goods in America, 1880–1920* (New York: W. W. Norton, 1989), 182.

23. Helen Appleton Read, "Contemporary Decorative Art in America," *Vogue*, 1 August 1927, 66.

24. Richardson Wright, "The Modernist Taste," *House and Garden*, October 1925, 77.

25. Helen Appleton Read, "The Exposition in Paris," *International Studio* 82 (November 1925): 96.

26. Wright, "The Modernist Taste," 110.

27. Helen M. Daggett, "Gotham Likes Art Moderne, Buys It," *Furniture Record* 35 (May 1928): 62.

28. Quoted in Meikle, *Twentieth Century Limited*, 16.

29. Alastair Duncan, *American Art Deco* (New York: Harry N. Abrams, 1986), 23.

30. "A Complete 'Modern' Apartment Presents New Trend in Furniture," *Furniture Record* 56 (May 1928): 56.

31. "Editorial. Furniture Design Tendencies," *Good Furniture* 28 (June 1927): 277.

32. "Art Moderne—Shall We Take It Seriously?" *Furniture Record* 56 (March 1928): 56.

33. *A Completed Century*, 98.

34. "New Reed and Rattan," *Good Furniture* 24 (March 1925): 155.

35. "Woven Furniture: Its Distinguishing Characteristics and Latest Design," *Good Furniture* 28 (April 1927): 214.

36. Ibid., 216.

37. "Styles in Summer Furniture. What the Markets Are Offering for the Next Season," *Good Furniture* 30 (April 1928): 196.

38. Ibid., 197.

39. *Retailing* 1 (13 April 1929): 17.

40. Paul Frankl, *New Dimensions* (New York: Payson and Clarke, 1928), 56–57.

41. C. R. Richards, "Sane and Insane Modernism in Furniture," *Good Furniture* 32 (January 1929): 10.

42. "Decorated Interiors in Retail Stores. Exposition of Art in Trade," *Good Furniture* 28 (June 1927): 326.

43. "American Modernist Furniture Inspired by Sky-scraper Architecture," *Good Furniture* 29 (September 1927): 119.

44. Paul Frankl, *Form and Re-Form* (New York: Harper and Brothers, 1930), 31.

45. See Ypsilanti Reed Company advertisements, *Furniture Record* 60 (April 1930): 17; and (June 1930): 19.

46. Donald Deskey, "Style in Summer Furniture," *Good Furniture* 34 (April 1930): 201.

47. Juliet and Florence Clarke, "Porch, Terrace, Penthouse, and Sunroom Furniture," *Arts and Decoration* 35 (May 1931): 60.

48. Harriet Sisson Gillespie, "A Modern Sky Garden," *House Beautiful*, July 1930, 60, 88.

49. Howard P. Chudacott, "The Great Depression and the New Deal, 1919–1941," in *A People and a Nation. A History of the United States* (Boston: Houghton Mifflin, 1984), 368.

Wicker in the 1930s

On April 7, 1930, Levi H. Greenwood, the ailing chairman of the board of Heywood-Wakefield, died of a heart attack in Tucson, Arizona. He had been in failing health for a year and had been succeeded as president of the Gardner, Massachusetts, company in 1929 by his son, Richard N. Greenwood—great-grandson of founder Levi Heywood. Since 1927 the elder Greenwood had been working on plans to reorganize the firm's business operations in the face of declining profits and fast-changing market conditions. Since its inception in 1826, the Gardner firm had concentrated on the lucrative chair market, but in the late 1920s demand for Heywood-Wakefield's assorted wood chairs began to decrease. With smaller houses and apartment living increasingly the order of the day, far fewer pieces of furniture were needed to outfit a new home. Moreover, homeowners no longer found an eclectic mix of furniture aesthetically satisfying. As a result, a desire for small, coordinated suites of harmoniously styled chairs, tables, and case goods began to emerge. Except for its wicker porch and sun-room sets, Heywood-Wakefield

was unprepared to meet this rising demand. To compound the situation, the sudden onset of the depression had a devastating effect on already weak sales of new furniture. From December 1929 through November 1930 sales dropped seventeen percent and clearly threatened to decline even more the coming year. In order to survive economically, Heywood-Wakefield's president and board of directors were forced to act quickly and make some very difficult business decisions. Among the most wrenching was the determination, in 1930, to close the factory complex at Wakefield and relocate its rattan-splitting, mat-weaving, and furniture-making operations to the headquarters plant in Gardner, Massachusetts.[1] The impact was devastating. For several generations, the factory, established by Cyrus Wakefield in 1856, had been the town's largest employer. Moreover, for the first time in seventy-five years, *Calamus rotang,* the Far Eastern transplant, ceased to be an essential feature in the daily life of Wakefield, Massachusetts.

In 1930 Heywood-Wakefield not only economized by centralizing business and manufacturing oper-

ations, but more significantly for the future, awarded the well-known industrial designer Gilbert Rohde a lucrative contract to create entirely new lines of modern furniture suitable for smaller-sized houses and apartments. Richard Greenwood recognized that good design—not simply a cheap price—would be the single most important factor in remaining competitive in the coming years. With far less money to spend, homeowners already had signaled by their purchases that they wanted furnishings that were practical, well designed, and both made and styled to last. Gone were the days when the latest passing fad in period design or color scheme attracted customers. Heywood-Wakefield's determination to employ a free-lance design professional to update their mass-produced furniture was not original. Ficks-Reed already had turned to Paul Frankl to restyle its stick-wicker, and by 1930 Donald Deskey had totally redesigned Ypsilanti Reed's traditional woven furniture.

In an open letter headlined "A New Sales Outlook—Style . . . with a capital 'S'," printed in *Furniture Record's* December 1930 issue, Richard Greenwood announced

the company's innovative retailing approach: "Heywood-Wakefield will enter the new year with a completely reorganized merchandising and sales policy. . . . The depressed trade condition which has existed in the Industry during the past year has caused us to make an exhaustive analysis of furniture manufacturing and retailing, particularly as it relates to our own company. As a consequence . . . we have made a tremendous investment . . . in putting style into mass production." The new lines were not "ordinary, 'run-of-the-mill' furniture," but instead had a "custom touch, a distinctive beauty, a refinement of design, and finish which set it apart from the commonplace." Furniture dealers were urged by Greenwood to visit the Heywood-Wakefield displays at the midwinter commercial furni-

ture market in Chicago to see "the amazing progress made in one year by the oldest furniture manufacturer in America."[2] Accompanying the letter was a further declaration that must have aroused competitors' curiosity:

For 1931, Heywood-Wakefield announces complete new style lines of burnt rattan, stick reed, woven fibre and startlingly different sun room furniture. These lines have been designed and approved by Mr. Gilbert Rohde, nationally famous designer, in conjunction with Miss Isabel Croce, stylist and noted authority on fabric and color harmony. The sure, deft hand of Rohde and the unfailing good taste of Miss Croce have brought these new furniture lines to the highest possible style

Heywood-Wakefield Company, Stick-Wicker Set Designed by Gilbert Rohde, 1931. Photograph from Furniture Record *(April 1931), courtesy of the Library of Congress. In 1931 Heywood-Wakefield joined the modern design movement when president Richard N. Greenwood hired Gilbert Rohde to redesign the company's lines of wicker and wood furniture. Rohde created stylish, simplified furniture with frames composed of bundled reed rods.*

point. Piece by piece, and in every buying level, you will find comfort, beauty, simplicity of line, and color treatments which will please the discriminating public of 1931.[3]

The lines of wicker furniture Heywood-Wakefield introduced in 1931 were completely different than those the firm had offered the previous year. None of the models illustrated in the company's 1930 catalogue appear to have

Heywood-Wakefield Company, Modern Fiber Furniture Set Designed by Gilbert Rohde, *1931. Photograph from* Good Furniture *(April 1931), courtesy of the Library of Congress. Rohde restyled the machine-loomed furniture made at Heywood-Wakefield's Chicago plant. The inexpensive line was short-lived, because the Chicago factory was shut down in 1932.*

survived as production pieces. Gone were the dramatic "modernistic" shapes and jazzy colors of the late twenties. Instead, Rohde's designs and Croce's fabric coverings were far more subdued and tasteful: simple, flowing lines and understated textile patterns predominated. For the firm's lines of wood furniture, Rohde had pro-

duced coordinated "packages" including chairs, tables, sofas, sideboards, desks, dressers, and bookcases. These ensembles were available for every room in the house. Heywood-Wakefield was actually the first manufacturer to offer complete sets of mass-produced, contemporary-style furniture, and Rohde's stylish new designs immediately caught on with the "discriminating" consumer.[4] Between 1931 and 1939 the firm manufactured 250,000 copies of a vinyl-covered bentwood sidechair he designed as part of a living-dining room suite.[5] But in the early 1930s the company cleverly hedged its bets by creating two separate style lines—Heywood "Modern" and more traditional "Old Colony," also designed by Rohde. Incredibly, there was even a dark-stained "French Provincial" line of stick-wicker.[6] By 1935 "Old Colony" was more popularly termed "Heywood Maple," and during the late thirties the simplified honey-colored, early American line appears to have dominated sales— even for sun rooms.

After January 1931 Rohde's easy-to-manufacture modernist stick-reed, rattan, and fiber furniture designs were the only types of Heywood-Wakefield wicker advertised in the *Furniture Record*. Woven reed was discontinued altogether. In 1932 the Chicago plant, once the company's most active producer of traditional wicker, also fell victim to the depression and was closed forever. Only the Menominee factory of the subsidiary Lloyd Manufacturing Company continued with machine-made fiber furniture. Doubtless, economics played a prominent

Ypsilanti Reed Furniture Company, Tubular Steel and Rattan Patio Set Designed by Donald Deskey, *1931. Photograph from* House Beautiful *(June 1931), courtesy of the Library of Congress.*
Some of Deskey's contemporary-style patio furniture sets combined rattan and tubular steel. As the 1930s progressed, chrome-plated tubular and spring-steel chairs and tables finally replaced reed, rattan, and willow as America's favorite patio, garden, and sun-room furniture.

role in the elimination of hand-woven reed from the firm's product lines. Extremely labor intensive, handwoven reed was simply too costly to mass-produce. But contemporary design philosophy also assisted in the final demise of traditional basketweave furniture. The handmade look was out. The new aesthetic promoted simplified shapes and new industrial materials that suited machine production and more aptly symbolized the modern age.

The general public had its first in-depth exposure to modern design at the 1933 and 1934 Century of Progress Exhibition at Chicago. Planned well before the stock market crash when, in the words of one writer, "Santa Claus was the national patron saint and we believed there would be no end to our increasing prosperity," the Chicago world's fair celebrated revolutionary advances in technology since the city's founding.[7] It was very much an exposition for the machine age: the official slogan was "Science Finds—Industry Applies—Man Conforms." The machine was both its symbol and its reality: each of the major exhibit buildings, designed in a stark, modern style, was sponsored by a leading American industrial corporation. General Motors and Firestone both showed off their awesome assembly lines in vast, impressive edifices, while overhead the omnipresent Goodyear blimp further demonstrated the positive power of science and technology. The architecture of the vast fair also stressed the shapes and rhythms of the machine. Stretching for three miles along the lakefront, the various exhibit structures were fantastic forms designed by the very men who, in the late 1920s, had transformed the Manhattan skyline. The buildings, erected with the latest construction materials and techniques, were massive, cubist-inspired shapes painted brilliant colors—orange, deep violet, blue, and gold. The futuristic setting was completely dominated, however, by the 625-foot steel towers of the Sky Ride. Known locally as Amos and Andy, the towers supported an immense, Brooklyn Bridge–like structure on which aerial cars were suspended, shuttling visitors back and forth between the mainland and an island where part of the exhibition stood.

The Century of Progress Exhibition, staged during some of the darkest days of the depression, was oriented more toward the future than the past. The ahistorical, modern buildings were filled with technological wonders and represented a brave new world—the world of a machine-made tomorrow bursting with the promise of hope. The keys to this post-depression realm were production and consumption: the commercial exhibitors constantly urged fairgoers to lift the nation out of its economic slump by buying the latest in spotless, labor-saving devices. And one could always tell the newest and most efficient product by its sleek, up-to-date appearance. By 1933 modern design had become an important part of a political as well an artistic agenda. Since it looked toward the future, and not the past, it was intrinsically hopeful and progressive. As a result, it was allied with the optimism of President Franklin D. Roosevelt's recently introduced New Deal programs. Moreover, modernism was linked to an economic goal: manufacturers recognized that by restyling their products they increased sales and thus boosted the nation's economy. Industrial designers like Gilbert Rohde now played key roles in American life: the nation depended upon them to help lift the economy—and the country's mood—out of depression.

Rohde's modern furniture designs were prominently displayed in one of the popular model homes erected at the Century of Progress Exhibition. Previous world's fairs had included model homes—either glorifying the past or celebrating the future—but at Chicago they were far more numerous and played a much more vital and educational role. When the exposition opened in 1933 there were thirteen of them; by the start of the 1934 season their number had swelled to twenty. Among them were several historical re-creations—Abraham Lincoln's boyhood home and old Fort Dearborn—but most were demonstrations of the manner in which designers believed Americans ultimately would live. There was an all-glass house as well as an all-metal house, each filled with ultramodern furnishings. The simple, practical, and restrained designs of chairs, tables, and lamps in these display homes delighted average Americans and created, after the Chicago exhibition, a strong demand for mass-produced and affordable modern furniture. In 1939 one tastemaker declared:

Up to the time of the Chicago

exhibit, the consciousness of America's millions had not been appreciably dented by modern decoration. It had been little more than a phrase suggesting the arty ateliers of Paris and New York . . . beyond application to one's own normal scheme of living.

And it is for history now that they found modern decoration good. For the country-wide popularity of the new style dates from the time they came upon it accidentally in Chicago, admired its simplicity, its directness. its straight simple lines and chunky forms, and most of all, its patent liveableness.[8]

Rohde was responsible for furnishing the two-story, International Style "Design for Living" model house. It was decreed to be "symbolical of the average home of tomorrow" and thus "establish[ed] a pattern for the new era."[9] The name was actually taken from a current Broadway play and it proved one of the most outstanding exhibits in the fair's Home and Industrial Arts section. Rohde outfitted the various rooms with the minimalist furniture he had designed for Heywood-Wakefield, its subsidiary the Lloyd Manufacturing Company, and another of his progressive clients, the Herman Miller Furniture Company.[10] It was a popular exhibit. According to an advertisement Heywood-Wakefield placed in the August 1933 issue of *Furniture Record,* an average of six thousand visitors a day passed through the display, and as a direct result of their enthusiastic approval, leading stores were now placing "hun-

dreds" of orders for complete setups of the firm's "World's Fair Modern."[11] Inside the demonstration dwelling, Rohde had placed ensembles of wood and metal furniture, but outside on the back patio he had arranged a suite of boxy Heywood-Wakefield stick-wicker whose solid sides and backs were composed of vertical reed rods—reminiscent of the Wakefield Rattan Company's mid-1870s designs for ladies' work stands.[12] But the Design for Living House was not the only place where fairgoers could encounter Heywood-Wakefield stick-wicker. The firm had eagerly sought the exhibition's rolling chair concession—a business opportunity the directors of the Wakefield Rattan Company had rejected when it was offered at the time of the 1893 Chicago world's fair. Heywood-Wakefield shipped twenty-five boxcar loads of wheeled, Rohde-designed chairs to the site. For a fee, visitors could be pushed about the grounds in these sleek, streamlined vehicles by a corps of athletic young men dressed in snappy blue uniforms.[13] The fleets of Heywood-Wakefield's rolling chairs notwithstanding, the Century of Progress Exhibition marked the beginning of the end for the vogue for stick-wicker and even for rattan furniture. A new, more up-to-date material for modern furnishings had captured designers' attention and increasingly would catch the public's fancy—tubular steel.

Fully eighty-seven percent of the Chicago fair's displays contained chrome-plated, tubular steel tables and chairs.[14] With their springy, continuous S-curve frames, these modern-age wonders

soon replaced wicker furniture in the hearts and minds of Americans. Lacking back legs, the cantilevered chairs made sitters feel they were floating in mid-air. On porches, patios, terraces, and lawns across America, the era of rattan now gave way to the age of steel. In a 1933 article aptly entitled "Design Marches On," a writer for one of the major metal furniture manufacturers stated:

Every period of history has reflected in its furniture the customs of the people, their tastes and mode of living. Today we live in a swiftly moving age— an age of rapid transportation, worldwide communications, of airplanes, radio and skyscrapers. It is but natural, therefore, that the modern spirit should express itself in a striking and radically different kind of furniture—and that the furniture should be of steel. This is an era of steel and steel sounds the keynote of the practicality and energy and strength which dominates our modern life.

And so we have steel tubular furniture, truly expressive of modernity, as graceful as a soaring airplane, as virile as a skyscraper, as fresh and intriguing as a debutante.[15]

Tubular steel was described in much the same terms as had been rattan decades ago: its "remarkable flexibility" permitted the creation of "many unusual and artistic designs, designs which are impossible of attainment in . . . other kinds of materials."[16] It was also decreed to be comfortable, resilient, and even weather-proof.

Ypsilanti Reed had pioneered in the production of tubular steel chairs trademarked Flekrom. Designed by Donald Deskey in 1928, they had been modeled on nickel-plated production pieces created in 1927 by Mies van der Rohe. Paul Frankl, too, had been an early American adherent to metal piping. But in 1929 Mies's springy "MR" chair influenced the directors of the W. H. Howell Company, a Chicago manufacturer of cast- and wrought-iron novelties, to undertake the large-scale production of modern tubular steel furniture. Howell had already reintroduced a spring-steel garden chair based on a historical French design from 1865 which had found immediate favor in Manhattan sky gardens.[17] But by 1930 the Howell firm was retailing new chrome-plated, tubular frame chairs for inside use, and for outdoors, brightly enameled ones. Visitors to

the 1933 Chicago world's fair encountered the firm's comfortably upholstered "Chromsteel" furniture in several of the model houses and in many of the major exhibit buildings.[18] As a result, their sales soared. Another midwestern manufacturer who, after 1930, went into tubular steel furniture making in a big way was the Lloyd Manufacturing Company.[19] Marshall B. Lloyd had virtually invented the industrial process when, in 1913, he developed his revolutionary Lloyd Oxyacetylene Method to create continuous tubular steel pushers for his baby carriages. The company's chrome-plated furniture was displayed throughout the site of the Century of Progress Exhibition. It furnished the Hall of Science, the Electrical Building, the Travel and Transport Building, as well as numerous other exhibit areas—including the Design for Living

Heywood-Wakefield Company, Rattan Sun-Room Set, 1934. Photograph from Furniture Record (March 1934), courtesy of the Library of Congress. This sun-room set was one of Heywood-Wakefield's last rattan designs. By the mid-1930s, the company had ceased imports of rattan altogether, ending the first great age of American wicker.

house and, among other commercial displays, those of United Airlines and the General Electric Company. According to one of Lloyd's advertisements, millions saw it, admired it, and "WANT[ED] IT."[20] In 1934 the firm brought out an extremely up-to-date, streamlined set of tubular steel furniture created by California designer Kem Weber. The expressive forms were intended to appeal to a more upscale market than did their regular line of cantilevered tubular steel chairs—or their Lloyd Loom fiber furniture. By the end of the decade, tube-rolling machinery also had been installed in Heywood-Wakefield's Gardner, Massachusetts, factory. Ten years later, tubular steel truly had replaced rattan in many of the company's most profitable product lines. After World War II, it was used not only for indoor furniture, but for furniture used out-of-doors, baby and doll carriages, even railroad and bus seating. Just like the firm's old cane-cutting department, its tubing division even did a flourishing business supplying the needs of other furniture manufacturers—particularly in New England.[21]

Unlike woven reed, rattan furniture did not die out entirely during the depression. Although Heywood-Wakefield had ceased production of rattan goods by the late 1930s, the stiffer Malacca species remained popular with small-scale New York City manufacturers such as Grand Central Wicker and Sons-Cunningham, firms that made comfortable upholstered lounges and armchairs for the patios and sky gardens of the affluent. But, as the decade progressed, metal furniture—either in modern or traditional designs—dominated sales of summer garden furniture. A popular item in 1939 was an elegant pea-cock chair made of wrought-iron. It was based on an Oriental design in cane and rattan popular since the days of the China trade.[22] Things had come full circle. In the 1870s rattan and cane chairs made by the Wakefield Rattan Company and Heywood Brothers and Company had begun to eclipse cast-iron, spring steel, and twisted-wire garden chairs and benches. Now, five decades later, metal outdoor furniture had made a strong come-back; and in quantity, variety, and vitality of designs far surpassed patio and garden furniture made from *Calamus rotang*—previously a plant so entwined with the culture of America that it could almost be claimed as native to the soil.

Fashions in furnishings ebb and flow. In the early 1990s, furniture woven from cane and reed—and even willow—is once again in tremendous demand, both in America and Europe. Wicker has returned to the fore and is available now at a variety of quality and price levels and in a wide spectrum of styles—from historical to contemporary. Even the revolutionary Lloyd Looms, once silenced, have been whirling again for over a decade using a weather-resistant cellulose fiber. Antique wicker furniture made by the Wakefield Rattan Company, Heywood Brothers and Company, Heywood-Wakefield, and their various nineteenth- and early twentieth-century competitors is enthusiastically collected by a select group of individuals who appreciate its exceptional craftsmanship and its American industrial and design heritage. Museums and scholars increasingly are validating the previously little-appreciated contributions made by American wicker manufacturers to the history of the decorative arts. Leading contemporary furniture designers—on both sides of the Atlantic—once again are turning to the possibilities offered by time-honored materials and weaving techniques. In fact, so great is the worldwide demand for *Calamus rotang* and its by-products that its very survival is threatened in the wild.[23] Government agencies in the West are working closely with those in the Orient to create new plant-breeding techniques and conservation methods and thus ensure rattan furniture remains a part of daily life for decades to come.

NOTES

1. Wakefield, Massachusetts, Tercentenary Committee, *History of Wakefield Massachusetts* (Wakefield, Mass.: Tercentenary Committee, 1944), 83.

2. "A New Sales Outlook," *Furniture Record* 61 (December 1930): 24.

3. Ibid., 25.

4. Richard N. Greenwood, *The Five Heywood Brothers (1826–1951): A Brief History of the Heywood-Wakefield Company During 125 Years* (New York: Newcomen Society, 1951), 24.

5. Derek Ostergaard and David A. Hanks, "Gilbert Rohde and the Evolution of Modern Design, 1927–1941," *Arts Magazine* 56 (October 1981): 98.

6. Heywood-Wakefield Company, advertisement, *Furniture Record* 62 (March 1931): 3.

7. Eugene H. Klaber, "World's Fair Architecture," *American Magazine of Art* 26 (June 1933): 293.

8. Emily Genauer, *Modern Interiors Today and Tomorrow* (New York: Illustrated Editions Company, 1939), 11–12. Quoted in Sharon Darling, *Chicago Furniture. Art, Craft,and Industry, 1833–1983* (New York: Chicago Historical Society with W. W. Norton, 1984), 282.

9. "A Home of Modern Built to Live In," *Furniture Record* 67 (September 1933): 45.

10. "Design for Living House," *Furniture Record* 66 (May 1933): 36. Rohde was not the only contemporary designer employed by Heywood-Wakefield in the early 1930s. In 1934 the firm brought out a sixty-piece set of wood furniture designed by Russel Wright. The same year Kem Weber designed a series of tubular steel pieces for the Lloyd Manufacturing Company. See "Modern—With and Without Precedent," *Furniture Record* 69 (September 1934): 16–17; and "The Subtlety of Moving Curves Relieves Severity of Steel," *Furniture Record* 70 (March 1935): 13–15.

11. Heywood-Wakefield Company, advertisement, *Furniture Record* 67 (August 1933): 64.

12. "A Home of Modern Built to Live In," 44.

13. See illustration, *Furniture Record* 66 (May 1933): 56.

14. Sharon Darling, *Chicago Furniture*, 314.

15. D. W. Jones, "Design Marches On," *Furniture Record* 66 (May 1933): 49–50.

16. Ibid., 50.

17. See illustration, Harriet Sisson Gillespie, "A Modern Sky Garden," *House Beautiful* 68 (July 1930): 60.

18. "Sunshine and Steel for the Modern Home," *Furniture Record* 67 (September 1933): 76.

19. Lee J. Curtis, *Lloyd Loom Woven Fiber Furniture* (New York: Rizzoli, 1991), 81.

20. Lloyd Chromium Furniture, advertisement, *Furniture Record* 67 (September 1933): back cover.

21. Greenwood, *The Five Heywood Brothers*, 21.

22. Anne Moore, "Furniture for Outdoor Comfort," *Arts and Decoration* 50 (June 1939): 11.

23. "Endangered Furniture?," *International Wildlife* (January/February 1990), 26.

A Completed Century, 1826–1926. The Story of the Heywood-Wakefield Company. Boston: Printed for the Company, 1926.

Adamson, Jeremy Elwell. "The Wakefield Rattan Company." *Antiques* 142 (August 1992): 214–21.

Corbin, Patricia. *All About Wicker.* New York: E. P. Dutton, 1978.

Curtis, Lee J. *Lloyd Loom Woven Fiber Furniture.* New York: Rizzoli, 1991.

Deskey, Donald. "Style in Summer Furniture." *Good Furniture* 34 (April 1930): 201–06.

Gould, G. Glen. "Rattan, Willow, Grass, and Fiber Furniture. Part I." *Good Furniture* 24 (June 1925): 301–08; "Part II." *Good Furniture* 25 (July 1925): 30–36.

Greenwood, Richard N. *The Five Heywood Brothers (1826–1951). A Brief History of the Heywood-Wakefield Company During 125 Years.* New York: Newcomen Society, 1951.

Heywood Brothers and Wakefield Company. *Classic Wicker Furniture. The Complete 1898–1899 Illustrated Catalog.* Reprint. New York: Dover Publications, 1982. Introduction by Richard Saunders.

Iverson, Marion Day. "Wickerwork in the Seventeenth Century." *Antiques* 65 (March 1954): 206–07.

Kirkham, Pat. "Willow and Cane Furniture in Austria, Germany, and England, c. 1900–14." *Furniture History* 21 (1985): 127–31.

Menz, Katherine Boyd. "Wicker in the American Home." Master's thesis, University of Delaware, 1976.

———. "Wicker Furniture: Four Centuries of Flexible Furniture." *American Art and Antiques* 1 (September–October 1978): 84–91.

Ottillinger, Eva B. *Korb Moebel.* Salzburg and Vienna: Residenz Verlag, 1990.

Saunders, Richard. *Collecting and Restoring Wicker Furniture.* New York: Crown Publishers, 1976.

———. *A Collector's Guide to American Wicker Furniture.* New York: Hearst Books, 1983.

———. *Wicker Furniture. A Guide to Collecting and Restoring.* Rev. ed. New York: Crown Publishers, 1990.

Saunders, Richard, and Paula Olsson. *Living With Wicker.* New York: Crown Publishers, 1992.

Scott, Tim. *Fine Wicker Furniture, 1870–1930.* West Chester, Pa.: Schiffer Publishing, 1990.

Thomson-Johnson, Frances. *The Complete Wicker Book.* Des Moines: W H Books, 1978.

ABOUT THE AUTHOR

Jeremy Adamson, born in Toronto, Ontario, Canada, has degrees in art history from the University of Toronto and a doctorate in the history of art from the University of Michigan. He has taught at The Johns Hopkins University and at the University of Toronto. Associate Curator at the Renwick Gallery of the National Museum of American Art, Smithsonian Institution, Washington, D.C., he has held curatorial posts at the Art Gallery of Ontario, Toronto, the Glenbow Museum in Calgary, and the National Gallery of Canada. As an independent curator and writer, Adamson has organized exhibitions for the Corcoran Gallery of Art, the Library of Congress, the Renwick Gallery, and the Canadian Embassy in Washington, D.C., and is the author of a variety of studies in American and Canadian art.

THE NATIONAL MUSEUM OF AMERICAN ART

The National Museum of American Art, Smithsonian Institution, is dedicated to the preservation, exhibition, and study of the visual arts in America. Its publications program includes the scholarly journal *American Art*. The museum also has extensive research resources: the databases of the Inventories of American Painting and Sculpture, several image archives, and a variety of fellowships for scholars. The Renwick Gallery, one of the nation's premier craft museums, is part of the National Museum of American Art. For more information, or a catalogue of publications, write: Office of Publications, National Museum of American Art, Smithsonian Institution, Washington, D.C. 20560.